Map of the Dead

Also by Murray Bailey

Secrets of the Dead

Singapore 52
Singapore Girl
Singapore Boxer

I Dare You
Dare You Twice

Black Creek White Lies

Map of the Dead

Murray Bailey

Heritage Books

First published in Great Britain in 2016 by Heritage Books
This edition published 2018

3455431

copyright © Murray Bailey 2016

Set in Plantin Light 11/16pt and Tahoma 10pt

ISBN 978-0-9955108-4-5
e-book ISBN 978-0-9955108-3-8

Printed and bound by Clays Ltd, Elcograf S.p.A.

Heritage Books, Truro, Cornwall

For Nicole, Annabelle, Alexander and Harry.
For your love and laughter.

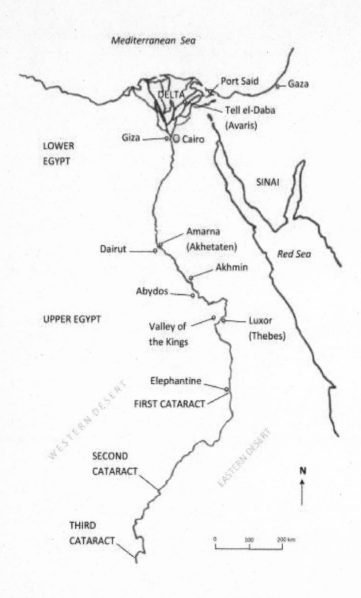

Mediterranean Sea

Port Said — Gaza

DELTA

Tell el-Daba
(Avaris)

Giza — O Cairo

LOWER
EGYPT

SINAI

Amarna
(Akhetaten)

Dairut —

Akhmin

Red Sea

Abydos —

UPPER EGYPT

Valley of — Luxor
the Kings (Thebes)

Elephantine

FIRST CATARACT

WESTERN DESERT

EASTERN DESERT

SECOND
CATARACT

N

THIRD
CATARACT

0   100   200 km

The First

ONE

Neither Alex nor her dad were happy with Ellen cycling to and from the exhibition. Especially not at night. Naturally, Alex had focused on probabilities. He'd said something like: You are eleven times more likely to be killed cycling than in a car—mile for mile. Although three-quarters of bike accidents are urban, half of fatalities are rural. So you are three times more likely to be killed cycling in the countryside.

What about cycling in the countryside at night? Winding roads, no street lights, speeding cars and no expectation of meeting a cyclist. There are no available statistics, but you are almost guaranteed to be hit by a car.

According to Ellen's dad anyway.

When she was a schoolkid, her dad's friend had been flattened by a truck. At least they guessed it was a truck from the extensive damage. He'd been cycling home in the dark, with lights. The truck driver hadn't stopped. No one was ever arrested for it. One day a loving father of two, the next day roadkill. No doubt that's when Ellen's dad formed his view.

A car came around the corner ahead, its lights dazzling Ellen. She instinctively swerved towards the verge. Mud

1

and gravel spun under her tyres but she managed to brake and stop. Her hands were trembling as she started again. Only a mile to go to the village and her rented bungalow. She'd text her dad as soon as she got in, to stop him worrying.

The whole journey from Highclere Castle to the village was less than two miles as the crow flies. A little further by winding road.

It hadn't been an issue until recently, until the British Museum had put on the Egyptian exhibition. Now she had to wait until the exhibition closed before she could continue with her research. And it was November, so the sun had set by late afternoon. After midnight in the Hampshire countryside, no moon in sight, it was pitch-black.

Eventually the lights of Old Bramsclere gave the oak trees ahead a ghostly orange outline. Almost home. She relaxed. Thoughts of the latest discoveries began to supplant her fear of cycling in the dark.

Working with the researcher from Berlin had been the major breakthrough, realizing that their investigations were linked. Serendipitous synergy, he'd called it. Showing off his use of English probably. But the sum of their combined research was definitely greater than the independent parts. She hadn't heard from him tonight, which was unusual. Lately he'd become more cautious about what he put in emails.

"It's too sensitive," he'd said. "We should both be careful." And then last week he'd been convinced that someone was following him. Was he just paranoid? Did their finding really have such dramatic implications? Maybe.

She'd followed his instruction at the weekend, storing all the sensitive stuff in a secure place. She'd planned to tell her best friend but at the last moment decided against it.

"We need all the proof before we publish," Marek had warned her. "The evidence of the murder isn't enough. This is huge and the only way to protect ourselves is to issue the full story all at once. That way, killing us won't stop the truth getting out." He was such a dramatist! Maybe their discovery wasn't that big. Maybe Marek was just believing his own hype.

Ellen propped her bike beside the rear door and put the key in the door. Odd, the door wasn't locked. Perhaps, in her haste, she'd forgotten to lock it. After all, she was exhausted. Late nights, lots of caffeine, and a thousand thoughts whizzing around your head weren't conducive to sleep. She put the key in the lock and double-checked it for security. She glanced at the kitchen clock. Almost 2am. She'd take a sleeping pill tonight. A good night's sleep and maybe, providing Marek was available, they could finish the translation and solve the final clue.

"Hide it," Marek had emailed.

"If anyone finds out, I'll be in trouble," Ellen had replied.

"You'll be in more trouble if we lose it. Let's not take any risks."

She pulled her notebook and laptop from her backpack and put them on the dining room table. She used that room as an office. It had once been a single-bed bungalow. Now there was a small bedroom in the loft. Her room. The downstairs bedroom was Pete's aunt's. He looked after the place while she was in the Canaries for her health. Apparently she planned to return but after six months had decided to rent out the little room.

Ellen texted her dad, popped two sleeping pills and was asleep within thirty minutes of climbing into bed.

Did something wake her? She looked at her phone: 9:45. Her mind was groggy from sleep or maybe the tablets. She turned over and closed her eyes again.

A noise downstairs made her sit up. Pete? What was he doing here? He usually came over at weekends, sometimes stayed over in his aunt's room.

She could hear him in the kitchen. He'd be making himself breakfast. Ellen's stomach rumbled. She'd been so engrossed that she'd not eaten a meal last night. The thought of bacon and eggs made her get up. She pulled on her dressing gown and started down the steep stairs. Hopefully the grogginess would go after food and some strong coffee, she thought as she steadied herself with the banister.

She turned in the hall and saw Pete silhouetted against the dining room window.

"Hello," she said. "I wasn't expecting you."

The figure straightened. Her back brain registered that he was taller than Pete, but it hadn't told her front brain yet. The man was standing by her laptop. Her papers were on the floor.

"Pete, what the hell?"

The man stepped forward. The front brain got the message: not Pete!

She breathed in, tried to sound confident.

"What the hell are you doing? Get out. Get out!"

He raised his hands. "Sorry. I didn't think anyone was in. I was just—"

"Get out!" She realized she sounded hysterical.

The back door was open.

She backed away, giving him a clear route to the exit.

She was about to say "I'll call the police!" when he stepped forward again and she saw intent in his eyes. Ellen spun. Within three strides she was up the stairs. Her heartbeat was pounding in her head. *Phone! Get the phone and call the police.*

She scrambled up, sensed him close behind. At the top she kicked wildly, made contact, heard him grunt and a thud. She dived but not for the phone. She had a cricket bat under the bed, a gift from her dad worried about her sleeping in a house on her own. Her slick fingers closed around the handle. It slid out and she jerked upright ready to use it.

4

The stranger grabbed her and was saying something. The tone was threatening but she couldn't hear. Her mind screamed panic.

Fight.

She twisted and turned, threw herself into him, pushed, scratched and then something hit her on the side of the head. The room blurred and darkened. She scrabbled more, lashing out as her legs seemed to give way. And then she was floating—a weird sensation after the fight. It lasted less than a second. Then something hit her again.

The man stood at the top of the steep staircase. *Crazy bitch.* The girl lay crumpled at the bottom. He picked up the cricket bat, descended and poked her. She didn't move. He waited a second and then whacked her on the thigh. Still no movement, except the judder from the force. He reached down and checked her neck for a pulse. Shit! No pulse, and her neck looked broken.

The man stepped over her and dialled on his phone.

"She's fucking dead."

"What?"

"The house wasn't empty. The girl was upstairs. Came down and went fucking nuts. Like that cartoon character. Spinning and spitting and lashing out. The fucking dusty devil, that's what she was like."

"Tasmanian Devil."

"Yeah that. Crazy cow. Anyway, she fell, broke her fucking neck. Stupid bitch."

"OK, we'll deal with that in a minute. You get the evidence?"

"I searched everywhere. I've got a pile of notes, a notebook and a laptop. Laptop's password protected, of course, but I don't think the notes help much."

"What about the girl. Did you get her to talk?"

"That's what I've been telling you. She just went ballistic. Totally nuts. I never got a chance to get her to say anything."

5

The line was quiet for a moment. The house was quiet except for a ticking: hot water in pipes, the heating maybe coming on.

Eventually the other guy spoke. "What's the risk?"

He looked around. The question was about evidence that he'd been there. The risk the police would know it'd been foul play. The risk he'd be traced through DNA.

"We fought. She scratched me. Yes, it's high risk. The boss is gonna do his nut."

"OK, bring the laptop, notes and stuff. Destroy the rest. And Lemmy…"

"Yes?"

"Don't fuck that up too."

TWO

Alex MacLure bounded down the steps outside the British Museum. It was mid-afternoon on a bright, feel-good day. He nodded to Eddie in the box by the gate.

The old guy waved back. "See you tomorrow?" he called through the glass.

Alex grinned. Before he'd started his new life he'd hated routine. Not now. The difference was that now he was in control. He could do his research at home some days—if he wanted—and yet here he was at the museum. Truth was, he didn't do nine to five; he varied his hours based on how he felt. He could arrive when the gates first opened, flash his ID card and be let in with the staff. And, on a good run, he might stay until closing, which was 8pm at this time of year. Yes, his new life as a researcher, out of the rat-race, was fantastic.

There was a large gaggle of Japanese teenagers by the railing. Mostly dressed in black, they seemed uncertain about whether the museum was open to the public. Or maybe they were just waiting for someone, a teacher or guide perhaps. A couple sat on a bench enjoying the sun. A man in a blue suit strolled in his direction on the opposite side of the street. Maybe he'd also finished early for the day. Or maybe he took a detour through Bloomsbury to avoid the rush-rush of city life.

Alex could relate to that. A short walk from Oxford Street and yet it was an oasis of calm. Regency and early Victorian buildings, five storeys tall, would have crowded any other street. Here they were majestic, simply majestic.

Alex could have jumped on the Central line tube at Tottenham Court Road but he didn't. He had all the time in the world. And why go in a sardine can through the Victorian sewers of London? Well, unless it was chucking it down. In the two months he'd been coming to the museum it'd only rained heavily twice. And on those days he'd timed his journeys to avoid the worst of the crush.

If you drew an east–west line on a map of London, starting at the museum, you'd be just south of Alex's house after one and a half miles. About thirty New York blocks. But London wasn't built like that. Most roads weren't straight and there was no direct route. By foot, the journey was closer to three miles. Less than an hour, if he wanted it to be that is.

He walked west, chose a road north for a hundred yards and then headed west again. For variety, each day's zigzag was different. Each day he'd find something different along the route.

With the sun in his face he found himself thinking about archery. A new hobby only two weeks in. It'd replaced Lindy Hop dancing, which hadn't been for him. Sally, the archery instructor, said he had a good eye and a strong arm. Maybe she'd been flirting a little. Maybe it was just an honest observation. He had scored the highest of all the students at both lessons so far. And he did go to the gym three times a week, so he was undoubtedly fit.

His route twisted and turned: west, north and then west again. He'd reached the edge of Marylebone Village and it was like stepping through a curtain. The air was cleaner, the sky even more blue.

Upmarket cafés and restaurants were everywhere. He found a trendy-looking place and was surprised by the reasonable price of the food. Not that he needed to worry about the price. Not really.

There was a cluster of tables on the pavement outside. Without thinking, he looked at his reflection in the window. Girls commented on his smile and nice blue eyes. He wasn't bad looking. Maybe just a bit shy. Which was pretty dumb for a thirty-five-year-old, he realized. Perhaps tonight he'd ask Sally for a coffee after archery. Nothing to lose, everything to gain. That was his new philosophy.

"What yuh 'avin?" a waiter said in a soft Jamaican accent. His name badge read: Sammie.

"The sumac grilled chicken, please. And a Sanpellegrino limonata."

Alex sat at a table outside and a moment later had a glass of sparking lemon.

He thought about his research, trying to obtain conclusive evidence of who the pre-dynastic pharaohs were. Kings of Egypt dead for five thousand years with little beside tantalizing clues.

"Penny fer 'em?" Sammie said as he put a plate of grilled chicken with pitta and dips on the table.

Alex began to explain. A few words in and Sammie held up a hand. He leaned in close and whispered.

"Man, yuh need fi get lay." You need to get laid.

Alex nodded. "You're probably right."

Sammie chuckled and patted Alex on the back. "Enjoy di food, man."

Parked five cars before the café was a white van. Behind the white van, a man in a blue suit was looking in a shop window. He watched the waiter deliver a plate of food to MacLure's table, laugh and retreat inside. The man in the blue suit used his phone.

"Fox," he said, using his call-sign. "The rabbit has stopped and ordered food. You have plenty of time. At least another half an hour."

Forty minutes later, Alex was outside his flat: a Georgian red-brick in a suburb called Maida Vale. Not a trendy street, not yet anyway, but give it another five years... perhaps. Although he'd thought that five years ago when he'd bought it. The house price wave had been moving west from the affluent area around Warwick Avenue. But it had petered out to a ripple.

Like most of the properties it had been split into four flats. There were six concrete steps to the communal front door. As he ascended he could hear his house phone ringing. It stopped.

He opened the door to his apartment. Topsy, his twelve-year-old cocker spaniel cross, would be excited to see him.

"Topsy?"

It was unusual for her not to be at the door as he entered. He headed for his bedroom in case she was asleep. No.

Back in the lounge, he heard a scrabbling at the back door.

"Topsy?"

More scrabbling.

The dog was in the garden. The dog flap was closed.

Locked.

Somehow, Topsy had knocked the latch and locked herself out. He flicked it aside and she pushed through and into his arms.

"Daft dog," he said, rubbing her head.

The latch hadn't failed before, but he guessed there was a first time for everything. He'd take a look at it later.

The TV was already on: a chat show. He left it on all day because Topsy liked it and seemed to think it was company.

Alex sat on the sofa, switching on the news. Topsy jumped onto his lap and looked at him with her liquid brown eyes. He shot the breeze with her for a few minutes, describing his day and asking about hers. She'd had a walk with Nadja, a young woman who cleaned his flat once a week as well as walking Topsy each day. They'd been to a park. She'd sniffed some familiar and some new places. At least, that's what he imagined she'd said.

The home phone jingled. He just managed to reach it.

"Hello?"

"Have you heard the news?" It was his mother. Her strong Scottish accent had an edge. She wasn't a sentimental woman but her tone said that something bad had happened.

He waited a beat. "I'm watching the news now."

"I don't mean on the TV."

"What news, Mum?"

"About Ellen? About the accident?"

"What accident?" He felt his throat constrict. Topsy looked at him with concern.

"Ellen's house. There's been an explosion."

Alex couldn't speak. He waited for his mother to continue.

"Ellen's dead, Alex. Your friend is dead."

11

THREE

Alex nursed a cup of coffee. It was his second but the hangover was still there. He assumed the fog in his head was the result of the bottle of red he'd knocked back last night. Maybe it wasn't a hangover. Maybe he just felt rotten.

The café overlooked the canal, a short walk from Paddington station.

London had over sixty miles of canals. They ran around North London like an inner ring road, coming south into Paddington and then round to Islington via Regent's Park. The Grand Union met Regents Canal at Little Venice, a pretty spot just a hundred yards away.

Alex sighed at his own reflection, as if the image was of someone who could sympathize. There was no beauty in this day.

Ellen was dead.

It had hardly begun to sink in. His friend—strike that— his best friend since university was dead.

On the towpath, a man was untying a barge. Alex could see a woman on board, laughing. Ellen used to laugh a lot. She could also be very serious, especially about her research, her fascination with Egyptology. Her enthusiasm had been so infectious that he'd finally caught the bug and changed career. She was explosively bright, like a neutron star, dazzling and chaotic. And yet at other times she could sink into a dark place.

Alex tracked a young man past the window. He entered the coffee shop. Wiry, haunted eyes, tousled dark hair. It was Pete.

Alex raised his hand. Pete nodded, pointed at the counter and mouthed something about a drink. Alex showed him he already had one. A few minutes later Pete pulled up a bar stool. He didn't speak, just stared out of the window. The barge Alex had watched being untied had now gone and another was manoeuvring into the space. Dark, oily water churned around the stern.

A long minute passed. Pete took a slug of his coffee.

"I've just got back from the house," he said, his voice edged with pain.

The house: the bungalow where Ellen had lived.

Alex turned to look at Pete. He didn't really know him. Ellen had introduced him once. He was her landlord while she was staying near Highclere Castle—the mansion where Lord Carnarvon, the 5th Earl, used to live.

Pete held his hand out in front of him. It shook. "I can't believe it," he said.

"I know."

"Sorry. Of course. You must be… devastated."

"Numb. Numb is the best way I can describe it."

Ellen hadn't just been Alex's friend. They'd had a brief fling after university. And even though they'd agreed to end it, the closeness had never gone. As far as he knew, she'd never been with anyone else, never shown any interest. Alex had a spare room. He could have rented it out but he didn't. He thought of it as Ellen's room. She could stay whenever she wanted to. She had some things there. What was he going to do with them?

Alex said, "So what was it like—the house?"

Pete stared outside. "Like matchsticks. Hardly anything left. It was flattened, wood strewn everywhere. It's hard to

13

believe it was a house." He paused and seemed to be on the verge of tears.

Alex said, "You can't blame yourself."

Pete put his fingers over his mouth and sighed. The bungalow had been destroyed by a huge gas explosion. It hadn't made the national news but Alex had seen the photo on the website of a local newspaper.

Pete said, "I was responsible for the house, responsible for the gas."

"Did you know there was a leak?"

"No."

"Did you have the boiler serviced?"

"My aunt had it checked before she went away. The certificate will have gone, but I'm trying to trace the plumber who did it. We'll need the proof for the insurance."

"And how's your aunt taking it?" It was her house. Pete just looked after it because she was abroad somewhere.

"Oh, definitely more upset about Ellen getting killed than worrying about the house. I wouldn't be surprised if she stays in the Canaries as a result. Nothing to come back for, not really."

Alex finished his drink and pushed away from his stool. "Well, good to see you, Pete. I guess I'll see you next at the funeral?"

Pete nodded and then said something Alex didn't expect. "Did she tell you about her research, Alex?"

"A little. Why'd you ask?"

"When I saw her last week, she was really excited about it. Seemed to be making real progress or had a breakthrough."

Alex smiled, recalling her face, her eyes bright with excitement. "That was Ellen. She could be so thrilled over little things. I'm good with numbers and numerical problems." Alex almost laughed at the memory. "I worked out that she was looking at a cuneiform number rather than a hieroglyph. It represented eight. I also realized a symbol

14

might be a surveyor's measuring rope. You'd think she'd solved *The Times* crossword puzzle, she was so happy."

"She mentioned treasure or gold. I think she was following clues to something hidden." Pete looked intense. "You don't think...?"

"What?" Alex hadn't really been listening.

Pete said, "Maybe Carter and Carnarvon hid something. I read that they were in trouble from the Egyptian authorities after finding King Tut's tomb."

Alex winced. Ellen hated Tutankhamen's nickname.

"So, do you think Ellen had found something?"

"I don't know."

"She didn't tell you?"

"No." Alex thought about the last time he'd seen her, at the weekend. Two days before the explosion. Two days before her death. She'd seemed a little agitated, stayed a night and was gone in the morning when he got up.

Pete gripped Alex's arm. "Maybe you should do it for her."

"Do what?"

"Finish the research. She must have been close to finishing, with the breakthrough and all."

It seemed like a reasonable idea. After all, his own research wasn't making much progress at the moment. He could complete her research and make sure Ellen got the recognition. But then he really didn't know much about it.

Pete broke into his thoughts. "Let me get you another coffee." He guided Alex back to the bar stool. "White? Sugar?"

"White, one sugar. Just a small one though."

Pete went off. When he returned with two cups, Alex said, "It'll be hopeless. We'd need her notes. My guess is they were destroyed in the explosion."

Pete rubbed his head, thinking. "But what if she didn't have all her notes with her?"

"Maybe, but I think it's unlikely. She wouldn't have left her laptop overnight at Highclere. She'd have taken it home. Do you know if it was found?"

"There was nothing left except large items. Even the fridge was in pieces."

"Maybe the police picked up something valuable? I don't know how these things work."

"Good idea." Pete nodded. "I'll get in touch with the Thames Valley cops, see if they found anything. Meanwhile, maybe you could check her stuff at your flat. She had stuff there, right?"

Alex was pretty sure Ellen hadn't left any research in his house. A few books and clothes, yes, but not her work. "Sure, I'll check."

They drank in silence for a few minutes. Alex found himself watching the activity on the canal again.

"I really cared about her, you know," Pete said quietly.

"Me too."

Pete swivelled, raised an eyebrow. He really looks like he hasn't slept, Alex thought.

Pete maintained the expression but said nothing.

"What? You were about to say more, I think."

"We might have become an item. You know, it was early days but there was something there."

Alex didn't comment straightaway. Was it likely that Ellen would fall for this guy? He didn't think so. Ellen would have told him, wouldn't she? Best friends talk about things like that. He'd been honest about the girls he'd dated. In fact he talked to Ellen a bit like a guy.

Was Pete Ellen's type? She appreciated intelligence. Pete didn't strike him as measuring up in that department. But then again, didn't women sometimes go for the opposite, for the excitement? He briefly imagined Ellen intimate with this other guy and shook the image away.

He tried not to sound dismissive. "We'll never know."

"Yeah, sorry, it was insensitive of me to mention it." Pete touched Alex's arm again. "Oh, I almost forgot. She

16

prepaid her rent. It's like two thousand pounds. I can't keep it. Can I transfer it to you and then you can pass it on to her folks?"

"Surely you can just send it to them."

"Ah, you see, I said Ellen and I might have become an item. Well, I met her parents and they didn't like me. Silly, I know, but I'd rather not be in touch. Please?"

Alex thought about it. What did it matter? "Fine," he said, and gave Pete his bank details.

Pete finished his drink. "I want to help," he said like an announcement. "She told me about getting close, about the treasure. Maybe she said something to me that didn't register. You know, because I'm not into the Egypt stuff."

"Sure."

"Oh my God! I've got an idea."

Alex leaned forward, intrigued.

Pete continued: "Highclere Castle."

"What of it? As I think I said, I'm sure she won't have left her work there."

"No." Pete was animated now. "We should go to Highclere. You and me. We should see if it triggers anything, any ideas and memories of what she said. And, you never know, maybe she did leave something out. You have a pass, don't you?"

While the British Museum exhibition was on at Highclere there was heightened security. Alex's British Museum pass would get him in. He'd used it a couple of times visiting with Ellen. "Sure," he said.

And so they made a plan. They'd go tonight. Pete had access to a car, so they could drive to the remote spot.

On the walk home, Alex realized he was feeling more positive. Doing something rather than moping about definitely helped. And who knew, maybe he *could* complete her research.

FOUR

Pete's plan was to arrive after closing so that they wouldn't be disturbed. The gatehouse was in darkness and the gates locked. They parked on the grass and climbed over fencing that bounded a field.

Highclere Castle was not really a castle. It was a manor house that had once been classically Georgian in appearance. Less than 150 years ago it had been transformed to look castle-like with a central tower and ramparts.

"I remember it from *Downton Abbey*," Pete said, and quickly added, "Though I never watched it. It looks smaller."

At night, the main entrance doors were locked, and Alex led the way around the side, through tall wooden gates into a courtyard.

"The servant's entrance," Pete said, and put on a baseball cap. He pulled it low over his brow. He handed one to Alex, who shook his head.

"Come on, man," Pete said with a laugh. "We're a team, aren't we? Put it on and play along."

Alex acquiesced and stuck it on his head. "The Egyptian exhibition was mothballed during the years of the TV series here," he said. "Now it's back and covers most of below-

18

stairs. It's bigger now too. Now that the British Museum has supported it." He took out his museum ID card. "There's extra security but, as I said before, my ID can get us in."

"What sort of security?"

"Oh, most of the exhibits from the museum are in locked and alarmed cabinets. And there's a security guard..."

Pete shook his head. "You didn't say anything about a guard!"

Alex knew the guy would be upstairs in the comfortable office. He'd mostly like be watching TV or asleep. And, anyway, what if he did see them on the monitors? Maybe it would seem odd being there so late, but Alex could argue he was doing research.

"He won't be a problem," Alex said as he swiped the card. The door lock clicked open.

"Pete?" The other guy had taken a few steps away. "Really, there won't be a problem. I've a right to be here."

"But I haven't."

"We'll blag it. Not a problem."

Pete took another step away. "You go in. I'll just do a quick recce outside."

Alex was about to respond but Pete had gone. He stepped into the hallway and hit the light switch. There was nothing in here, just a long corridor. Alex went to the end and through a door. A few minutes later Pete came in behind him, a little out of breath.

Pete said, "Are the lights a good idea? I thought we would use torches."

"Why? We're not being secretive." Alex studied Pete's face for a moment, suddenly concerned. "You better not be up to anything. This is about Ellen's research."

"Sure, I just thought... I just don't want us to be disturbed."

"We won't be. The guard can't see the basement lights from his room, plus the house is pretty hidden. Lights down here aren't going to attract anyone. And, on the off chance we get discovered, how bad would it look if we were snooping around with torches?"

"Fair point." Pete stepped past. They were at the bottom of some stairs. "Where are we?"

Alex walked on into a small room. "This is the start of the exhibition," he explained. "These are all genuine artefacts from Carnarvon's collection. They are all from tombs, so we have lots of these doll-like things called shabti, as well as personal items like combs and jewellery."

"Good, when you explain things, keep it simple for me. None of the fancy historical names. OK?"

"Not a problem."

Pete walked around slowly and asked a few questions about items that were displayed inside secure glass cabinets. Finally, he said, "Anything leap out at you?"

"No."

They descended a ramp and saw a large cabinet with a more modern display. It was about Lord Carnarvon. There were photographs and toys from his childhood but also diaries and photographs relating to his work with Howard Carter.

"Carter was really the Egyptologist," Alex said. "Carnarvon financed his digs, most of which weren't very successful."

"Have you read these diaries?"

"No, but I know Ellen did. She was interested in the man as well as the history."

Pete tried the cabinet. "Can you unlock it?"

"To get the diaries, you mean?"

"Sure."

"I don't have a key. I'd need to be here on official research. We'd have to come back... Hey!"

Pete had a penknife out and was trying to jimmy the lock. Alex grabbed his arm and pulled it away.

"Don't..." Pete's eyes flared with anger but it was only brief. "Sorry, you're right. Maybe we'll come back... officially."

Alex led them onwards into semi-darkness. The next display was a glimpse at what Carnarvon and Carter allegedly saw before they broke into Tutankhamen's tomb. Pete peered through a slit in blackened glass. "Wow! It must have been incredible."

"Yes, but it's of no interest to us. It's all fake."

They proceeded through a blackout screen and Alex hit the lights. A wall of gold dazzled them. "Wow!" Pete said again.

"The main exhibition," Alex said. "This used to be mostly replicas, but most of the artefacts in glass cabinets are real.

"What about this?" Pete touched the huge, ornately carved box-like object that had blinded them with reflected light.

"It's an outer casket. The sarcophagus was surrounded by a series of caskets like this. And no, it's not real gold."

"So Ellen wouldn't have been interested in it."

"Unlikely."

"And this is the famous death mask?" Pete was standing in front of a glass cabinet.

"Again a replica."

"Shame. So apart from Carnarvon the man, what else was she interested in?"

"At the moment her focus is... was on New Kingdom communication."

"Sounds exciting," Pete said with sarcasm.

"You see the hieroglyphs on everything?" He ran a hand over the carved symbols on the casket. "Well, it was really an ancient language mostly used by priests and the higher echelons of society. They believed it was the language of the gods. A more cursive form developed, but everyday writing was cuneiform. Cuneiform was widely used internationally in the region. It was literally a wedge-based alphabet that could be easily written in clay."

"Uh-huh." Pete studied a royal-blue and golden vase.

"Ellen was particularly interested in hidden and double meanings. I couldn't help very much because I'm a numbers guy rather than language. She showed me some symbols and it was part of a puzzle she was solving."

Now Pete looked interested. "See them anywhere—these symbols? What are they? What are we looking for?"

Alex was already checking out the hieroglyphs. "Lots, but in particular you could look for spirals, pillars and geese. Maybe anything that looks like cuneiform."

"The wedges."

"Right. Like an arrow with the head the wrong way round."

They both completed a circuit of the main exhibition. Alex shrugged. "I don't see any of them."

"Go round again. Maybe you missed them or maybe you'll spot something else she might have been interested in."

They spent almost an hour in the room, with Pete going back over items and showing frustration each time Alex drew a blank on Ellen's research.

There was one more exhibition room. The old kitchen had been converted, with glass display cabinets all around. Pete led the way.

Alex said, "This room used to just contain the Carnarvon family memorabilia. The items you now see are all mostly from the British Museum, minor Egyptian artefacts that weren't displayed in London. These are genuine, but any link to Carnarvon is tenuous at best."

Pete did a quick circuit. "So nothing else?"

"The research room."

"What? Where Ellen did her research?" Pete could barely contain his excitement.

Alex took him across the first corridor and into a small side room, probably once a boot room. "Well, more of a coffee room. I don't think…"

Pete was already opening cupboards and searching for clues. Alex looked in the bin. Empty.

He moved it aside to get at a cupboard door.

"What's that?" Pete said over Alex's shoulder. There was a ball of paper in the gap between the last cupboard and wall. Someone probably missed the bin and it just got wedged there.

Alex fished it out and smoothed open the small piece of paper. It looked like it had been torn from a notebook. Four lines were written on it:

~~The Carnarvon Tablet~~
Moses?
12, 8 and 40
Tutankhamen

"Ellen's writing," Alex said, handing it to Pete to look over.

"What's the Carnarvon Tablet?"

"It's about a stela—"

"Simple, remember," Pete interrupted. "What's a stela?"

"A stone marker known as a stela. Sometimes to mark a boundary. Sometimes like a plaque. The Carnarvon Tablet was taken from one of the temples. There had originally been two."

"What happened to the other one?"

"No one knows. Carnarvon's notes said there were two but these were later changed to one tablet. Anyway, she's crossed it out. I don't think—"

Pete wasn't listening. "So Ellen was trying to find out what was on the other tablet? That's the research. And maybe the other tablet was gold?"

Alex shrugged. He remembered Pete mentioning treasure when they were in the coffee bar. It didn't seem likely. "Could have been, but…" For some reason Alex held back. The number twelve; one of the symbols he'd interpreted for Ellen. To him it looked like a surveyor's measuring device. It was a line with twelve knots, two of which were bigger: the third and seventh. He'd told her it was much more than just a measure. Twelve knots could make up a triangle with sides of three, four and five. The ancient Egyptians thought of it as having magical powers. They called it the golden triangle.

"Well?" Pete had asked him about Moses and the numbers.

"I don't know what they're about."

"But why write *Moses*? He didn't have anything to do with... Oh wait, of course he did. He led the Jews out of Egypt, didn't he?"

Alex wasn't in the mood for history lessons. He said, "Tutankhamen is obvious. Most of this exhibition is about Carter and Carnarvon's discovery."

Pete said, "What else then? Maybe it was a message about some treasure. I keep thinking maybe Ellen was onto where more of King Tut's wealth was buried."

"Tutankhamen. Ellen hated the name King Tut."

"OK, Toot-an-car-mun then. What do you think? Could she have been onto something?"

Alex shrugged again. "Look, Pete, you've got to understand what it's like to be an archaeologist. It's not Indiana Jones. It's hardly ever about finding buried treasure. It's about piecing together the past. It's like solving part of a puzzle. Archaeologists get a kick out of discovering the tiniest thing."

Pete asked more questions but Alex's energy drained away. What had started out as a diversion, a distraction from Ellen's death, now seemed pointless. There was nothing here of interest. What he really needed was her laptop. That's where her research would have been. And that had been destroyed in the explosion. However, as they drove back to London in silence, Alex couldn't help but think he had missed something.

24

FIVE

Alex took out Topsy for a long walk in Regent's Park. He'd been tired after the late night and spent the previous day moping about and for the second day had no enthusiasm for work. He'd been through all the photographs he had of Ellen on his phone and laptop. He'd grazed on TV and he'd pulled a few books from the bookcase and browsed them. A well-thumbed paperback entitled *The Oxford History of Ancient Egypt* caught his attention. It was in the wrong section, with novels rather than the text books. He tried to recall the last time he'd picked it up. Ellen had given it to him when he'd first helped her. There was a scribbled *thanks* and a date, two years earlier, inside the front cover.

"Think you can memorize the King List?" she'd challenged as he opened the birthday present. The King List was the accepted chronology of the pharaohs. Accepted because there were alternative versions and disputes, but Alex gave it a go. He'd managed fifty-eight names from the Eighteenth Dynasty—which included Tutankhamen—to the start of the Twenty-first. He wrote down those he could remember now and managed half. He knew he was killing time but opened the book at the chronology section and tried again to learn them. After an hour he'd done pretty well but lost interest. That was when he decided to get out of the flat.

He was sitting on a bench watching kids play football when his mobile rang.

Nadja.

"You don't want me walk Topsy today, Mr MacLure?" She insisted on calling him by his surname even though he'd protested.

"Sorry, Nadja, I completely forgot the time."

"I walk her later. If you like?"

Alex looked at Topsy, whose eyes immediately brightened. "I think she'd like that. Thanks. What time suits you?"

"Five all right?"

"That'll be great." He was about to end the call when Nadja spoke again. Her voice was different.

"Mr MacLure?"

"Yes?"

"I've been cleaning ..." Of course she had. Was she going to ask for more money? Why mention it? She continued after a hesitation: "I found mobile phone. In your house, I mean."

"What? Where?" Alex tried to remember if he still had an old phone somewhere. Maybe an old Nokia.

"Spare room. It was behind bedside table." She sounded a little awkward. "I know you don't ask me to clean in there much, but it has been while... and... well I had time."

Alex's mind was spinning. Nadja didn't know Ellen was dead. She'd cleaned the spare room and found a phone. It must have been Ellen's. Who else could it belong to?

He was already standing and heading back. Topsy bounded beside him—as well as any twelve-year-old cocker spaniel can bound that is.

"OK, just leave it on the coffee table. And see you later."

"Five o'clock," she confirmed.

The phone was an Apple model, the one before last. It was white. Ellen used to have one of those, didn't she? It had to be hers. She'd been the only one to stay in the room for over a year. But then again it was an old model. Could it have been there longer?

It switched on. It was charged. How long did a battery last if unused? He had no idea, but surely not a long time. Not a year. It had to be Ellen's.

He tried some numbers that might be Ellen's passcode. Obvious ones: the month and year of her birth; the day and month; her age and house number; her age and number of the house where she was born. None worked.

He tried his birthday. Wrong.

That was five attempts. He stopped. A message had warned him that the phone would be locked for a minute. How many tries before it locked for good? There had been a case where the FBI had obtained a warrant to force Apple to unlock a phone. They could have cracked it themselves but too many attempts caused the phone to wipe its contents.

He googled it.

Ten.

Four numbers with ten alternatives each meant ten thousand alternative combinations. He put the phone down. He wouldn't try again until he was pretty sure he had the right number.

In his enthusiasm to check out the phone, he'd overlooked his answer machine. The display flashed three messages.

There was one from his mother "Just checking in" and two from Aysha Milwanee of *The Sunday Times*. Her first message asked him to call her. Her second explained that she would like an interview. *The Sunday Times*—there was part of him excited by the thought of being in such a prestigious paper but, at the same time, a gnawing in his stomach, a distrust of the press he couldn't explain. He googled Aysha Milwanee and saw that she was attractive, in a bookish sort of way, and an investigative journalist rather than a gossip merchant.

He dialled the number she had left.

"Aysha Milwanee." Her voice had a businesslike but approachable lilt.

"Alex MacLure, returning your call. You said you wanted to interview me. What about?"

She introduced herself before saying, "It's mostly about your friend Ellen Champion. I understand she was pretty exceptional. I thought I could write a human interest piece about her life."

"And the accident?"

"And the gas explosion, yes."

Alex thought for a moment.

Aysha added, "I can't guarantee it'll be worthy of publication, but I've spoken to her family and other people who worked at the museum. It won't take long, just a bit of depth from your perspective. Wouldn't you like to celebrate her life?"

He acquiesced. What harm could it do?

Milwanee said, "I'll be there in twenty minutes."

When Alex put the phone down he looked at the white phone on the coffee table. Should he tell Pete? He'd promised to report if he'd found anything of Ellen's. But then Pete had said he'd ask the police whether they'd found anything at the house.

He sent a text.

Hi, Pete. Did the police find anything?

After five minutes he stopped willing his phone to ping with a message and made himself a cup of coffee. It was another half an hour before the doorbell rang and the reporter was at his door. She was pretty, but not as good-looking as her photograph, and she smiled apologetically, her teeth brilliant white against her dark skin. When she leaned in to shake his hand, he smelled a delicious floral perfume.

For a moment they stood a little awkwardly, until she looked around and said, "Where shall we sit?"

He indicated the dining table and sat at an angle across from her. With deliberate movements, as though preparing herself, getting into the right frame of mind, she took a digital recorder from her handbag, placed it on the table and then took out a notebook and pen. She looked into his eyes.

After pleasantries she said, "Let's start with you deciding to change career. You were working as the financial controller at Shelley's Recruitment Agency and you just left."

"I gave up being an accountant to study archaeology full-time. I'm doing a PhD in Archaeology—ancient Egyptian studies."

"At...?"

"Macquarie University in Australia. My specific area of interest is before the First Dynasty." He began to give details, names and dates but she wasn't interested.

"Nice if you can afford it. Not many people can just give up work."

"I won the lottery."

She smiled and raised her eyebrows, not believing him.

He said, "No, really. I could pay off my mortgage and do what I wanted. I was always good with numbers, but that's not the same as accountancy. It was a means to an end. So when I could, I quit."

"Everyone's dream." She smiled disarmingly. "So, back to Egypt. You were particularly interested in Tutankhamen?"

"Not really." He shrugged but then felt a lump in his throat. "That was Ellen's area of research."

"OK, let's talk about Ellen. You were close, right?"

He tried to respond but couldn't for a moment. He blinked as his eyes prickled.

29

"Sorry, that was insensitive of me," Milwanee said. She pushed her hair back and smiled encouragingly. "Let's talk about you again for a bit." She opened a notebook. "You made the papers five years ago. A woman had her handbag snatched at Warwick tube station. You intervened, tackled the thief and got the lady her bag back. 'Have-a-go Warrior of Warwick Avenue'." She looked up from her notes. "That was you, wasn't it?"

"Yes. That's what *The Sun* called me."

"And you declined to give interviews. Why was that?"

"Personal reasons." He looked at her and saw that she knew. After a moment, he said, "Because of my father."

"You didn't want the press—us—raking up the dirt? Was that it?"

"Not really dirt... I guess the thought of all my personal life laid bare for all to see was too uncomfortable."

Milwanee said, "He'd just committed suicide."

"That's right. It was a difficult time."

"But now?"

"It's in the past. I'm over it. I just ask that you don't go into details, don't mention the investigation into his tax affairs and embezzlement."

Milwanee smiled sympathetically. "It's not the story. Your father was an accountant and you entered the accountancy profession. Would I be right in saying it's connected?"

"With the naivety of youth, I thought it would be an interesting career. It was also a nod to the old man—to his innocence, I guess."

"So, Egyptology. Is it all right if we go back to Ellen...?" She hesitated, as if to judge if it was all right before continuing. "Was it Ellen who got you interested?"

Alex nodded. Milwanee waited for him to speak.

He said, "She was really smart. There's an object in the ancient Egypt exhibition at the British Museum—a granite ball..." He made a fist. "A little smaller than this. It was found in a shaft in Khufu's pyramid. As soon as she saw it

30

she knew it was like a ball bearing. She worked out they used the granite balls to help move the huge blocks. You know there's over two million blocks of limestone and granite each weighing about two and a half tons in the Great Pyramid?"

Milwanee raised her eyebrows.

"So that was her theory of the granite ball," he said, "and it was published in *Nature*."

"Was she your girlfriend?"

Alex was taken aback by the question. He instinctively held up his hands as though warding off the question.

"OK. OK. I understand, but it's about Ellen and it's not using any of your comments. I need to understand your relationship." Milwanee's voice was soft and her eyes did show care.

After a pause, Alex said, "We were just friends. No, that's not fair. She was my best friend. She had her issues, but like I said, she was very smart. She had an eidetic memory."

"Photographic?"

"Not quite the same. She could recall things, especially images, after a few exposures, but..."

"Yes?" When Alex didn't immediately answer she leaned forward a fraction. He could smell her sweet perfume. "You were going to explain."

"It seemed to come at a cost. She was bipolar and could suffer deep depressions. She could also be irrationally paranoid. That's why..." He stopped but then breathed in the perfume again and thought, *What the hell?* "That's why we ended it... being a couple, I mean. It was a long time ago, just after we left uni. But, like I said, we remained best friends and I tried to help her."

He leaned back and wondered why he had just been quite so open with this stranger.

Milwanee must have noticed, and she also leaned back. "Cute dog," she said, as if spotting Topsy for the first time.

31

She was curled up on the rug by the radiator, half asleep, half watching the proceedings.

Alex's phone pinged. A text from Pete.

"Excuse me," he said, reading it.

Don't speak to anyone!

Alex replied:

Why?

Police. Reporters. Stay low.

"Everything OK?" Milwanee asked.

Alex texted:

Why?!

Ellen's death suspicious!

The room blurred for a moment. Alex looked at the reporter. She smiled attractively.

"What's this really been about?" he asked.

She leaned in. "About Ellen Champion."

He said, "I hope that helps your article."

She looked dumbfounded. "Is the interview over?"

"I'm sorry, something's come up." He became aware of his heart pulsing in his neck. Could she see it?

She produced a fake beatific smile and suddenly the alluring veneer was gone. "Was that text about Ellen's death?"

Alex stood and took a step towards the door. "I think it's time for you to go."

She smiled sweetly again, "One last question?"

He looked at her suspiciously but didn't say no.

She said, "Were you involved in Ellen's murder?"

SIX

It didn't take long for Alex to find news about Ellen. The BBC had a top story on their news app:

Gas explosion: Police treat woman's death as suspicious
Police are treating the death of Ellen Champion, whose body was found at a house near Newbury, as suspicious. Post-mortem tests to determine cause of death are due later.
Det. Supt Charles Wardby, of Thames Valley Police, said there were significant discrepancies with the initial belief that the death was caused by a gas explosion at the property where Miss Champion lived.
He urged anyone who had met with Miss Champion in the past few weeks for either personal or professional reasons, to get in contact.
Miss Champion, 34, worked for the British Museum but had been based at Highclere Castle where she was carrying out research.

He called Pete. The phone rang for a while before it was answered.

Alex said, "I can't believe it. The police think she was murdered, for God's sake!"

When Pete spoke, he sounded ill-tempered. "They're just suspicious. It doesn't mean—"

"Have the police contacted you?"

"Yes. Just a short interview." Alex heard Pete take a long breath. "I'm sorry, mate, I'm tired. I work nights. Did I tell you that? Anyway, sorry, I'm half awake—was working till 6:30 this morning."

Alex said, "No, I didn't know."

"It's OK." He sounded less grumpy now. "Anyway, I don't think we should mention we've been in touch. Cops can be funny about things like that. They find connections and they follow them. Before you know it you're a suspect."

"Jesus. Have you—"

"Yep, it's happened to me before. Bastards. They turn your life upside down, find you are totally innocent and leave. No apology. No compensation. And your house and rep are left damaged." You haven't talked to the press, have you?"

The sudden switch almost caught Alex unprepared. "No, why would I?" he lied.

"Don't. The cops'll pick up on it. The hacks twist what you say and the cops'll assume it's true."

Alex didn't say anything. It was too late to undo the interview with Milwanee. With a bit of luck it wouldn't be published. After all, they'd hardly scratched the surface.

Pete continued, "I've already been contacted. God knows how they found my phone number. Just be careful what you say and who you say it to."

Alex spent the rest of the afternoon checking on the news but learned nothing new about the gas explosion. Milwanee had said murder but the police weren't disclosing their suspicions. Maybe she had jumped to the wrong conclusion. He read other articles where the police had said similar things. In nearly every case, murder was confirmed within a few days. My God, Ellen hadn't just been paranoid. Maybe someone was really after her. Maybe Pete was right about treasure after all.

The doorbell buzz made him jump. It was Nadja.

"I didn't like to just let myself in. That's why I rang bell," she explained as she came in. "Mr MacLure—you look like you've seen ghost."

"I thought…" He waved it away and forced a smile. "I can't remember… What were you…?"

She pointed to Topsy, who was up and wagging her tail. "I said I walk her."

He grinned. Of course. With everything going on, his mind seemed like jelly.

The doorbell buzzed again, only this time it was accompanied by firm knocking. Nadja automatically picked up the intercom phone and then looked awkward. She handed it to Alex apologetically.

"Alex MacLure?" a man's voice said.

"Yes."

"Thames Valley Police. Can we come in?"

Moments later, a tall, thin and swarthy-skinned man stood in the doorway. Indian, was Alex's initial assessment. The man showed his ID. Detective Constable Dixit. A step behind him was a woman, five inches shorter, with dark hair tied back untidily. Her ID said Detective Sergeant Belmarsh.

"Interesting name," Alex said. "Belmarsh, like the prison."

She nodded slightly and looked past Alex at Nadja.

"Who are you?"

"A neighbour," Alex responded, "who is just about to take my dog for a walk."

DS Belmarsh said, "I'm sure she can speak for herself. Your name, Miss?"

"Nadja."

She took out a notebook. "Miss Nadja…?"

"Dabrowska." She spelled it out for her as the sergeant wrote it down.

Belmarsh looked from one to the other as if assessing the veracity of the statement, then shrugged slightly and took a step towards a chair. "Can we sit?"

"Can I go then," Nadja said, attaching Topsy's lead. "If that all right?"

Belmarsh looked at Alex. "You have Miss Dabrowska's contact details should I need to speak to her?"

"Yes."

"Then you are free to walk Mr MacLure's dog, Miss Dabrowska." The way she said it made Alex think she didn't believe them.

When the door closed behind her, Alex sat in the same place on the sofa as before. "How can I help you, Detectives?"

Dixit introduced himself formally and said they were making enquiries following Ellen's death.

"I've seen the news," Alex said. "You now think she was murdered."

"There is an enquiry due to suspicions." Dixit squinted, maybe thinking, maybe just for effect. Belmarsh sat silently. She had the unnerving way of looking above his eyeline. It made her look part superior, part dopey.

Dixit said, "You'll understand that we can't disclose any details. Now, if you don't mind, we have some questions."

Alex remembered what Pete had said about them finding his phone number. "Before we start," he said, "how did you know where I live?"

Dixit's mouth twitched a smile. "We have, of course, interviewed Miss Champion's family. So..." He let his voice trail off and watched for recognition on Alex's face.

"OK. Of course, they know my address. And phone number. You could have called."

"We prefer to do these things face-to-face," Belmarsh said, which Alex interpreted as *catch you unprepared*. Dixit continued: "Now, if you don't mind, could you tell me how you know Miss Champion."

Alex explained that he'd known her for almost fifteen years, that they had met at Oxford Brookes University and had been close friends.

"She was your girlfriend?"

"In the past, yes. But a long time ago. We were just friends more recently. Hopefully you know that from her parents?"

Belmarsh raised an eyebrow. "A friend-with-benefits, then?"

"Just friends." Alex felt his chest tighten with anger at the suggestion, especially under the circumstances, but the detectives seemed to have moved on.

Dixit asked, "And she often stayed here, in this flat?"

"Yes." Alex pointed to the spare room down the hall. "In that room." Then, with emphasis, he added: "Which is not my bedroom."

"OK, we'll take a look in a moment." Dixit seemed to check his notes, maybe biding time. "And you worked together."

"Not really."

"Oh? She worked for the British Museum. Didn't you also?"

"Kind of. They don't pay me. I'm a research fellow."

"And Miss Champion?"

"Also a researcher but employed at the same time."

Belmarsh said, "Splitting hairs, Mr MacLure?"

Alex stared hard at the detective. "God, you suspect me, don't you? That's what this is about."

Belmarsh returned his stare.

Alex said, "She was my best friend. No way would I hurt her. If you're looking for a killer then you are looking the wrong way. For God's sake, I didn't do it. You need to be out there looking for the person who did!"

"Person?" Belmarsh continued the stare.

"Just a figure of speech. If you mean, do I know if it was one person rather than two or more, I don't." Alex breathed in and out. He was riled and could see that Belmarsh was more interested now he was angry.

Dixit was looking at the bookshelf. "You have a lot of books."

"I like reading."

"Mathematics and history the main subjects? Unusual combination isn't it?"

Alex shrugged, "I like puzzles. History is interesting, generally, but Egyptology, specifically because there are a lot of mysteries—unanswered questions."

Belmarsh said, "Talk us through your employment history, please."

Alex found himself telling the same story about being an accountant and switching to Egyptology that he'd told Aysha Milwanee earlier. Dixit wrote it all down.

"When did you leave Shelley's Recruitment?"

"Six months ago."

Belmarsh snapped a question: "When was the last time you saw Miss Champion?"

"Last weekend. Just two days before the explosion."

"Before she died," Belmarsh clarified unnecessarily.

"That's right."

Dixit wrote in his notebook. "The weekend of the 7th and 8th? All weekend?"

"From the Saturday night until Sunday morning. She would normally stay longer. I think she went to her mum's for Sunday dinner."

"Did she?" Dixit said with something in his tone that said she didn't.

"That's what she said." Alex felt his face flush as though he were lying, as though the policeman had caught him out. Had she said that? He added, "I'm fairly sure she said she was, anyway."

"And how was she when you saw her?"

"She was a bit anxious, maybe depressed, although she always denied it. She was often that way. That's why she'd come and stay. I think being with me helped her. Presumably her parents told you she was on medication for it. Venlafaxine."

Dixit wrote it down.

"What did you do when she was here on Saturday 7th?"

"We watched a film and had an Indian takeaway." When asked, Alex named the takeaway restaurant and the film. It was a recent release that he'd illegally downloaded. If guilt showed on his face, the detectives didn't seem to notice.

Dixit said, "Presumably you could find a receipt or something?"

"For the takeaway?"

"Yes, of course the takeaway."

Alex thought for a moment. "It'll be on my card statement."

Dixit nodded after taking more notes. "What were you doing on the evening of Monday 9th?"

"I was home. I took Topsy—she's my dog. We went out for about forty minutes. After that I made something to eat, watched a couple of things on TV and went to bed."

"Alone?"

"Alone." Alex realized this meant no alibi.

"And what were you doing during the early hours of Tuesday morning?"

"I slept until six, maybe a bit after, but definitely got up before six thirty."

Dixit pursed his lips as he jotted it down. After a moment of silence he looked up sharply. "Who would want to kill Ellen?"

Alex blinked. "I... I don't know."

"Did she have any enemies? Anyone she had upset or who was upset with her?"

"No."

"Can you think of any reason, any reason at all, that someone would do this?"

"No."

Dixit was silent for a while as he paged through old notes. Alex watched him uncomfortably.

Finally, Dixit flicked his book closed.

Belmarsh stood. She said, "Can you give us a quick tour?"

There wasn't much to see. The kitchen and lounge were open-plan. Alex's bedroom was off the lounge. The bathroom and the small spare room were dog-legged off a hall.

Belmarsh followed him into the spare room. Dixit stood in the doorway.

She looked around. There was a three-quarter-sized bed, a bedside table, a chest of drawers and a free-standing wardrobe. There was a fist-sized ornament on the window ledge: silver and turquoise-blue with hieroglyphs running round the coloured rings. On the wall was a painting of Topsy when she was much younger: brighter eyes, glossier coat and no grey around the muzzle.

Belmarsh asked, "So you say this is where Miss Champion stayed on the weekend of the 7th and 8th?"

"Yes. Although she left early on Sunday."

"Are there any personal items of hers?"

Alex opened the wardrobe. A couple of blouses, a coat and dressing gown hung forlornly on one side. "There's also the odd thing in the drawers. Not much."

"Mind if I…?" she asked. Before Alex could answer, the policewoman stepped around him and checked the clothes in the wardrobe. She took a photograph using her smartphone. "Just to remind me rather than spend time taking notes now," she said by way of explanation.

Belmarsh fished in the pockets of the dressing gown and found nothing but tissues. Then she manoeuvred around Alex again and pulled open the drawers. In the top drawer there were underwear items plus an open box of tampons, deodorant and a scattering of make-up. In the middle drawer there was a jumper, a pair of jeans, a scarf and neatly folded T-shirts. A spare sheet for the bed was in the bottom one. Belmarsh took a photograph of each one.

The bedside table had a single drawer. It revealed pens, pencils, a spiral-bound notebook, an open packet of paracetamol, some herbal tablets and a pillow spray called *Deep Calm*.

As she took a photo, Belmarsh asked, "Did she have trouble sleeping?"

"Quite often. Yes. It was nothing new. She's always been a bad sleeper." He realised his mistake as soon as he said it. Ellen was dead.

Belmarsh just watched him and showed no concern that he'd lost his best friend. She said, "And she stayed often?"

"Every other week or so. Nothing scheduled. Depended on when she wanted to be at the museum or just wanted a break and a curry."

"Because you were her *best friend*?"

Alex breathed in and out, trying not to get riled. "Yes. And convenient for work in town."

The detective walked out and down the hall. For the first time Alex realized that the other detective was no longer standing in the hallway.

Belmarsh took a brief look in the bathroom. "Everywhere is very tidy for a single guy. The bathroom is spotless."

"That's because I have a cleaner. Nadja—I mean Miss Dabrowska."

"That's nice." The detective smiled. "And does she do anything else for you?"

"Just cleaning and dog walking." Alex said pointedly.

"Not another friend-with-benefits, then?"

Alex felt his chest tighten again but said nothing.

As they returned to the lounge, Dixit was standing in front of the bookcase. He turned and exchanged a nod with Belmarsh.

Dixit said, "You certainly have an eclectic mix of books, Mr MacLure."

Alex shrugged, waited for more, but the detective wasn't forthcoming.

Belmarsh said, "Thank you for your help, Mr MacLure. We'll be in touch if we need you further."

The two detectives moved to the door and turned. They took another long look around the open-plan space.

Alex said, "If Ellen was murdered, please find the person—or persons—who did this."

Dixit opened the door. "We'll do our best, sir."

For a moment, Alex watched them walk towards the communal front door. Then a thought struck him. "One minute. Can I ask if you found a laptop at the house—the one...?"

Dixit responded, "Where she was found? We can't tell you that, I'm afraid. Why?"

"Her research," Alex said. "I can't find her research. And maybe, if she was murdered, maybe it was about that."

Fox, the man who had been in the blue suit, knocked on the rear door of a white transit van. Without waiting for a response, he opened the door and climbed in. Another man, codename Bat, sat on a chair in front of a bank of electrical equipment. He wore headphones that were askew and covering only one ear.

Fox said, "Any news?"

Bat nodded. "They were detectives from Thames Valley Police. The woman got MacLure wound up, but apart from that it was just an exploratory interview."

"Do you think *the rabbit*"—he emphasized the name— "knows anything?"

"If he does, he's a good actor." Bat focused on the equipment, turned a dial and said, "But listen to this."

Fox heard Alex say: "I can't find her research. And maybe, if she was murdered, maybe it was about that."

"OK, so he's suspicious it's about her research." Fox pulled out a phone and dialled.

After it was answered, he listened and then said, "Nothing so far. It doesn't look like the rabbit knows anything."

The person at the other end asked a question. Fox said, "My opinion: if it wasn't an accident then someone has done us a favour."

He listened again and then ended the call. "We're to stick with it," he said to Bat. "Just in case."

SEVEN

DI Jackson looked up from the autopsy report on his desk and rubbed his eyes. His gut had been right. Murder. He knew the young detectives thought of him as the old timer and past it. Undoubtedly they knew he'd been passed over for promotion many times. Undoubtedly they knew his face didn't fit, that the Super didn't like him. Maybe they worried that their own careers would be limited under him. Maybe, but he didn't give a damn. They should respect his instincts. He smiled at the thought. He'd known the Champion death had looked wrong and he'd been right.

The three junior detectives, two sergeants—Limb and Belmarsh—and DC Dixit, looked at him expectantly. Dixit was a bright one. He reminded Jackson of himself, maybe twenty-five years ago, when he was ambitious, when he wasn't disillusioned with the police force.

"Time of death estimated as three hours before the explosion," he grunted.

DS Limb was perfectly groomed with a neat goatee. He wore smart grey suit trousers with a matching waistcoat and burgundy loafers. Mr Vanity, Jackson mentally labelled him. Which he knew was hypocritical since he could barely read the reports on his desk. His eyesight had deteriorated so much that he needed glasses. In the past two years he'd become longsighted but refused to wear reading glasses. Was that vanity or just a fight against ageing?

He tore his gaze from Limb's ridiculous footwear. They had little tassels, for God's sake! He looked at DS Belmarsh. "The trauma to the back of the head... an occipital fracture possibly from a blunt instrument. The majority of the contusions are post-mortem—likely caused by the explosion but perimortem marks suggest a struggle."

He opened the file at another page: the SOCO's report. "The forensic report confirms a gas explosion. No surprise there, eh? A gas explosion occurs when the gas and air mixture reaches a critical point. Any spark, flame or heat source can ignite the mixture. We get an explosion rather than just a fire because of the pressure build-up."

Limb chipped in, "And the explosion can stop the fire spreading."

"Exactly. In effect, it blows itself out as soon as it's created. So SOCO look for the point of the leak and ignition. In this case the leak was confirmed as the boiler." He paused. "The point of ignition was also the boiler. Probably when it fired up to warm the water."

Limb said, "Between three and three and a half hours after Miss Champion's death."

"Right." Jackson hoped his tone told the DS to shut up, stop stating the obvious. Glancing at Dixit, he continued, "But there was an inconsistency, wasn't there?"

Dixit took the cue. "There was evidence of a fire in the lounge."

Jackson nodded slowly. "A fire in the lounge. Not within close proximity of the boiler and not the cause of the explosion." He tapped the paper. "According to the report. So what the hell was it?"

Limb waited, whereas Belmarsh leaned forward, showing some engagement for once. She said, "The explosion was deliberate and the person who did it—who caused the gas leak—wanted to ensure it happened."

Dixit said, "Like an accelerant or primer."

"But it went out." Jackson nodded. "And I don't think he meant it to be an explosion. I think it was supposed to be a fire caused by a gas leak. We wouldn't have the discrepancy with the time of death if he'd just created a fire fuelled by the gas."

He spun the manila folder round. "So we have our confirmed murder investigation. Each of you read the file later. Meanwhile, how have your investigations gone so far?"

DS Limb reported his interview with Ellen Champion's parents. "Confirmed that Alex MacLure was her friend since university. They haven't seen him for a long time—years. No other notable acquaintances. She has a brother, eight years her senior. He's in Singapore working at some financial institution. Do you want me to speak to him, sir?"

Jackson said, "Not at the moment."

Limb continued: "Nothing from either neighbour." Limb provided the names and addresses. "They were both at home all night and during Tuesday morning. No one heard or saw anything unusual until the explosion."

"What about her landlady?" Jackson prompted.

"She's in Lanzarote. I finally spoke to her after leaving a couple of messages. She's been out there for four months and hasn't returned. Never met Miss Champion and was probably a bit shocked. She wasn't very talkative. Says she suffers from angina. On top of everything, the insurance claim seems to be stressing her out a bit."

"Give her a few days and try again. See if you can get more details out of her. Get to the bottom of what's worrying her. See if her story tallies each time. Probably nothing but you never know. Maybe there's a connection."

Belmarsh said, "You're wondering if Miss Champion was collateral damage?"

Jackson looked at the second DS. She looked tired. More tired than usual. She never discussed her private life. He understood she was a single mum and he respected her for the effort, though her animated arm movements could be annoying.

"Like I said, you never know. Until we get a firm lead, rule nothing out."

Belmarsh nodded and then reported that she'd spoken to the staff at Highclere, again with little in the way of discovery. "They all confirmed she worked long hours and didn't interact with the staff. I also spoke to her boss at the British Museum"—she looked at her notes—"Professor Beatrice Lloyd. "Miss Champion has been an employee and research fellow for over six years. Never any trouble. She recently turned down the chance to go on a dig in Egypt." She let her right arm flail for a moment, presumably as she was thinking. "Saqqara."

"Near Cairo," Limb said.

Belmarsh continued: "Champion wanted to help out at Highclere Castle instead, acting more like a guide. The prof gave me the impression she wasn't that impressed with Champion, though called her a nice girl a few times. Quiet but hardworking."

Jackson said, "Good. Why was she so keen to stay behind? As I understand it, most of these types can't wait to get out on a dig. And why Highclere?"

Belmarsh nodded.

Jackson said, "How was Alex MacLure?" He switched his gaze to Dixit.

"Alex MacLure confirmed he was the ex-boyfriend." He paused. They all knew the statistics. Roughly seventy per cent of women violently attacked or killed knew their attacker. Half of those were husbands, partners or ex-partners.

Dixit said, "There was no obvious sign that they were anything other than friends, although I find it odd that she left on Sunday morning. MacLure said she was going for lunch to her parents."

Limb chipped in, "The parents didn't see her on Sunday 8th. In fact, they hadn't seen her for about three weeks."

Dixit said, "Either he's lying or genuinely didn't know." He looked at Belmarsh. "Jo got under his skin."

She said, "He got quite agitated at one point. He didn't like any suggestion that there was anything other than a friendship between them. There was also an attractive Polish woman there when we arrived." She checked her notes. "Nadja Dabrowska. He said she walks his dog and cleans the house. I don't know, maybe she was more. Maybe Miss Champion found out about it. Secondly, the house was spotless. I think the room Ellen had stayed in had been cleaned. Could be innocent, but could also be hiding something. I tried to get to him, wind him up a bit."

"MacLure picked up on Belmarsh's name." Dixit grinned. "I didn't know it was so infamous. Jo has an interesting ancestor."

Belmarsh said, "Each time I mentioned there was something more between them, MacLure flushed. Friends-with-benefits, I kept saying. He didn't like that."

"Alibi?" Jackson asked.

Dixit said, "On his own Monday evening and claims to have been in bed all night."

Jackson waited.

"But most of all, I thought he was withholding something. He seemed very keen to know if we'd found her briefcase. Her research."

Jackson looked at DS Limb, who pulled out a sheaf of papers that listed all the items catalogued at the crime scene.

"One leather briefcase. Burgundy," he said.

"Anything else?"

Dixit said, "While Jo checked out the bedroom where Champion allegedly stayed, I checked out the rest of the apartment. Nothing of interest except the books."

"Eclectic!" Belmarsh coughed into her hand.

"Quite a mix," Dixit said with a sideways glance at her. "There must have been a hundred books, mostly non-fiction, and one in particular caught my attention: a handbook of karate."

"Karate?" Jackson said, thinking. The victim had died in a struggle. The cause of death was a broken neck, not the blunt instrument trauma. Could it be MacLure? "OK," he said, dismissing them. "Let's get a look at the briefcase. And Belmarsh—"

"Sir?"

"Talk to MacLure's neighbours. I want to know if they had an argument when she stayed over."

EIGHT

Alex struggled to sleep. Since the detective's visit he kept wondering who had murdered Ellen. Who had a motive?

When he did sleep, he had the same dream.

He was walking on the path from the gym towards the low-rise block that stood on its own. His footfall echoed dull and leaden on the flagstones. The air was bitingly cold, the sky a patchwork of pewter and tangerine, and he knew it would be snowing before the end of the day. That's how it had been. It was as though he was there again, back at school, fifteen, only now he knew he was dreaming. He also knew, no matter what, he couldn't change what was about to happen next.

From behind he heard an odd pitter-patter that grew louder and louder. And then thwack! A force almost knocked him from his feet. Something was on his back, arms wrapped around his neck, choking him.

Alex swung around, forcing the attacker to let go. It was a small boy in his rugby kit and fresh off the playing fields. Tommy East, the scrum half. Others of the team ran up and formed a circle. Before Alex knew what had hit him, Tommy threw a roundhouse to the jaw.

He stumbled and Tommy kicked his legs away, sweeping him to the floor. There was a stamp on his chest followed by a flurry of kicks. One glanced off his head and again there was severe pain above his right eye. And then it was over and, through the fog of near unconsciousness, he heard the boys laughing as they walked away.

The assembly hall looked just like it had back in the day, its block wood floor smelling of varnish and the stage with its Prussian blue velvet curtains. The form master was there and he told Alex the culprit was in the rugby team; he knew because of the stud marks on Alex's shirt. So there they were, the whole damn rugby team lined up, all staring ahead, all thinking cold menacing thoughts.

Alex walked along the line, looking but not looking. When he walked past the little scrum half, their eyes met but, just like then, he couldn't bring himself to point Tommy out. The form master said something, and as Alex turned, he saw the man's face change into that of Detective Dixit's.

The man said something.

"What?" Alex couldn't hear. He leaned in.

"Who did it?" he snarled. "Point out the murderer!"

"I don't know! I don't know!" Alex felt panic rise.

He jerked upright, awake and drenched with sweat.

In was 4am, Sunday morning, and he was now fully awake. He got up, made a cup of tea and Topsy jumped onto the sofa next to him. He changed the TV channel. The new headline was that Highclere Castle had been burgled.

At 8:30 his phone rang.

Dixit.

The detective asked, "Have you seen the news?"

"Yes."

"Stay home. Colleagues from the Met are on their way to pick you up. We'd like you to help with our enquiries." That easy expression laced with so much meaning.

* * *

51

Nineteen minutes after Dixit's call, Alex's mobile vibrated and then his doorbell rang. He ignored them and continued to read.

A neighbour must have opened the outside door because there were heavy footsteps in the hall and then a sharp rap on the door to his apartment.

"Police, Mr MacLure," a voice called.

Alex rubbed Topsy's head. "I won't be long," he said. "Don't worry."

In the hallway, three uniformed policemen waited impassively. He stepped out and shut the door behind him, walked down the hall, two policemen ahead and one at his side.

As they stepped outside, the lead men reached the gate and cleared a huddle of reporters and photographers away, providing a route to a silver Omega with twin orange Metropolitan Police lines running along its length. The policeman beside Alex looped his arm through Alex's and walked him briskly through the gap in the bodies.

The rugby maul of reporters and photographers surged forward. A boom microphone swung close and the policeman at his side swatted it away. Alex ducked his head into the car and sat on the rear seat. A camera flashed and suddenly a reporter was in his face.

The man shouted, "What have you got to say about the allegations?" before the policeman pushed him aside and slammed the car door. Immediately, the mayhem was replaced by the quiet sanctity of the police car.

Alex settled into the black leather seat and stared straight ahead. He didn't notice the paparazzi chase the car along the road, snapping photographs at the window. He didn't pay attention to the route they took or even the destination. His mind was trying to grasp what was going on.

The Met officers took Alex to a police station in Chiswick. He was kept waiting for almost an hour before being ushered into a room with DC Dixit and an older man with grey hair and weary eyes.

DI Jackson introduced himself.

Alex looked around the walls, cream-coloured and spotless. No pins, no ancient Blu-Tack marks, no two-way mirror and no sign of a camera. On the table was a digital recorder but it hadn't been switched on.

Alex sat with a straight back and hands relaxed on the table in front of him. Between the detectives, but closer to Dixit, was a manila file. Dixit had a cheap blue pen in his hand and flicked it again and again around his thumb. Jackson, sitting directly opposite Alex, kept his hands under the table like a card player in a Hollywood western, threatening to draw a pistol.

"So, I've not been arrested?" Alex asked.

"We'd just like you to help with our enquiries."

"Can I have a solicitor?"

"If you want one," Jackson said. "Do you need a solicitor?"

Alex shrugged. "I'm not guilty of anything, so no, I don't need a solicitor."

"Good," Jackson smiled.

Alex said, "So, is this about the burglary at Highclere last night?"

Dixit said, "We'll come to that. Firstly, just to be open and clear, were you involved in any way in Ellen Champion's death?"

"No."

"You suggested we look at Miss Champion's briefcase, correct?" Dixit waited for Alex to nod. "Why was that?"

"I wondered... if Ellen was murdered, maybe it had something to do with her research. Maybe it was in her briefcase. Did you find it?"

"Was her research about something at Highclere?"

"I think so, but I don't know the details. And you know what it's like to be a detective. She was following threads, trying to answer questions about the past. That's what she found so fascinating."

"And you?"

Alex regarded the Indian detective and wondered what his point was. "Yes, I find it interesting."

"But not always so. For many years you were an accountant."

"Yes."

"Latterly at Shelley's Recruitment."

"Yes."

Dixit leaned forward. "You like to think of yourself as a mathematician, right?"

"I like numbers. I like looking for patterns. Same thing again—like detective work, I mean."

"What are the odds of winning the national lottery?"

"Do you mean getting all six numbers correct?"

"That'll do. What are the odds?"

"The probability of pulling six balls out of forty-nine is one in forty-nine times one in forty-eight times—"

"What's the answer?"

"One chance in thirteen million, nine hundred and eighty-three thousand, eight hundred and sixteen."

"So about fourteen million to one." Dixit raised an eyebrow.

"Yes, if you want to be less accurate."

"You know that and yet you claim to have played and won."

"It was a whim and I like certain numbers."

Jackson said, "You don't strike me as someone who acts on whims." He put emphasis on *whims*, perhaps mocking.

"Well each number has an equal chance of being drawn, irrespective of past draws—the so-called law of averages is nonsense. And sequential numbers are just as likely as any random combination. However I play the lottery every now and then when *the whim* takes me, and the numbers I chose were 2, 5, 10, 17, 28 and 41." Alex smiled but could see they didn't get it. "They are the ascending sum of the first six prime numbers, so 2 plus 3 is 5. Then add 5, the next prime gives you 10 then add 7 then add 11."

Jackson again: "And you won?"

"Five of the numbers…"

Dixit leaned forward and smiled. "So you won millions?"

Alex shrugged ruefully. "The problem was that there was a bunch of people playing the same sequence. Probably all number freaks like me. I got a few pounds shy of seven hundred thousand. Did you know there's a one in fifteen chance that a London telephone number is prime?"

Dixit ignored the question. "What was the date of your win?"

Alex gave him a date almost six months ago.

Dixit said, "We'll check of course."

Jackson said, "Because otherwise you can see why we might be suspicious of you coming into a large amount of money."

Alex looked from Jackson to Dixit and back. "Is this what you wanted to speak to me so urgently about?"

Dixit said, "We spoke to your ex-colleagues. They said you just resigned. They knew nothing about you winning the lottery."

"I did win. I didn't tell them for obvious reasons. If you have money, other people get jealous and want it. The only people I told were Ellen and my mother."

After a beat, Jackson nodded as though to himself and said, "Let's talk about the matter exciting the press this morning, shall we?"

"The burglary at Highclere." Alex had read the reports, which were thin on information. The theft had been executed with surgical precision, it appeared. There was one witness to the arrival but no one saw them leave. The guard had been "rendered unconscious" according to most, although one referred to chloroform or something similar. He was in his room and saw a dark-coloured van come through the gates. The CCTV was black and white so he couldn't report the colour, though he guessed blue and thought it looked like a Ford Transit. He hadn't been alarmed. It drove to the rear yard and he thought it was maybe a delivery. He'd left the room and headed for the rear door. Before he got there, someone was already inside. He briefly thought he saw a movement, possibly someone big, but that was all. He was reported as not requiring medical attention.

Jackson asked, "Where were you last night between the hours of 2 and 4am?"

"At home in bed. Alone. No alibis."

"Did you go to Highclere?"

"No. I was at home in bed."

"With no alibi," Dixit repeated.

Alex said nothing and waited.

Dixit said, "How did they gain access?"

Alex looked from one to the other. "I have no idea. Break the lock?"

Silence.

"They used a pass card—a British Museum pass card," Jackson said, and paused. "Your pass card, Mr MacLure."

Alex breathed in. He breathed out. "I think I'll call my solicitor now."

NINE

They left Alex alone while he waited for his solicitor to arrive. He'd called his mother who said she had one she'd recommend. A family friend apparently. She called back a few minutes later to let him know it would be Tanya Wilson. She wasn't a criminal lawyer, but she was good and would help. "She hopes to be there within the hour. And Alex... be grateful, no matter what," his mother added. "It is Sunday and she's doing us a big favour."

Alex said he would.

While he waited he also called Pete.

"Sorry," Alex said as Pete answered groggily. "Working last night?"

"As ever. What's up?"

"Have you seen the news about Highclere?"

"No... wait." The line went dead for a minute and then Pete spoke. "Shit!"

"I know."

"Frickin' hell, we were only there a few nights before."

"The police have brought me in for questioning."

Again there was silence. Alex could hear him breathing.

"Pete?"

"You aren't... You weren't involved in some way, were you?"

"No, I'm not! I've got my pass card but the police say it was used to gain entrance."

"You've got your pass on you?"

"No."

"That's a shame but I suppose it could it have been cloned."

"I guess. I know credit cards get cloned so maybe my pass card was cloned somehow."

"All right. They said your card had been used in the burglary. Did they show you the evidence? You know they sometimes say things just to get a response. They hope they can get you to confess. A sure sign is whether they've cautioned you. If they've not done that—"

"No they haven't."

"I think you're fine then."

"But we were there, Pete."

Again, just the sound of breathing on the line before he spoke. "Look, Alex, I don't want you to bring me into this. I don't want you to mention I was there."

"I don't know—"

"Shit, I just remembered I sent Ellen's rent to you. Have you transferred it to her folks?"

"No."

"Don't you see? It looks suspicious."

Alex thought about Jackson's interest in the lottery money. Would a few grand from Pete look suspicious?

"Alex? Don't mention me being involved. It looks bad for both of us. Worse for you because of the money. OK?"

"Fine," Alex said. When he ended the call he had a sick feeling in his stomach.

Tanya Wilson arrived late and apologized, blaming the traffic. She was petite, in her sixties with glasses and a severe haircut. Her age was in her hands rather than her face, which was smooth and expressionless. Before Jackson and Dixit returned, she asked for an update. She already knew about Ellen's death and the break-in at Highclere.

She took notes about the questions concerning their interest in his lottery win and his departure to study Egyptology.

"You've not confessed to anything?" she asked when he finished.

He responded, "I'm not guilty of anything!"

"They've not cautioned you or charged you?"

"No, just said I'm helping with enquiries."

"OK," she said without giving anything away on her face, and Alex wondered whether she believed that he wasn't guilty. This woman would be a great poker player, he thought.

She knocked on the door to signal they were ready. Five minutes later, Jackson and Dixit stepped into the room and sat. Dixit was opposite Alex, the manila file placed deliberately in front of him, one hand on top. Jackson sat opposite the solicitor.

The inspector pointed to the recorder on the table. "Before we start, would you object if we recorded this?"

Wilson nodded agreement.

Dixit switched on the device and introduced everyone.

"Good," Wilson began, "because, for the record, my client is here on his own free will to help with your enquiries. You have not cautioned him and I understand he has already made a statement that he had nothing to do with either Miss Champion's death or the burglary at Highclere Castle."

Jackson said, "Accepted."

Dixit said, "Before we took the break"—he nodded towards the solicitor—"we were just talking about the access to the back entrance to the building." He paused as if hoping Alex would comment then opened the folder. There was a grainy black and white photograph on the top. Dixit slid it towards Alex.

"Do you recognize this person?"

The picture was from above. A man wearing a baseball cap.

Wilson leaned across and whispered to Alex, asking if it could be him. He nodded.

Wilson said, "That could be anyone."

"The picture was taken from the security camera inside Highclere Castle over the rear entrance. I believe it's you, Mr MacLure."

Alex said nothing.

"The picture was taken just before the cameras failed. Only this wasn't from last night. This was from Wednesday night. Early hours of Thursday the 12th—12:13am. Do you deny that this is you in the picture, Mr MacLure?"

Alex hadn't considered that the cameras recorded images, but then he had just shown Pete around. It stuck him then that he'd used his pass card. Dixit knew his card had been used.

"I think it's me," Alex said. "I was there."

Wilson jotted down a note. DC Dixit nodded. "You used your pass card to gain entrance to the rear of the building."

"I did. I was there to look for clues about Ellen's research."

"Why so clandestine? Why did you disable the cameras?"

"I went late because"—he almost said *we* before remembering Pete's warning—"I didn't want to be disturbed. I wanted the peace and quiet to think about her research."

"And to case the joint."

Wilson leaned in and whispered that the best strategy was to stay silent now.

Alex shook his head. "No. I did not burgle Highclere. And I didn't need to case the joint, as you put it. I know the exhibit. I've been there many times."

Dixit said, "You disabled the security cameras."

"No." Alex shook his head firmly. "You can see I didn't because you have a photo of me entering. It would be odd for me to go in and then worry about security, don't you think?"

"Let's talk about the timing of this." Jackson used a friendly tone. "Three days before. You must admit it looks suspicious."

"It's a coincidence. I'm innocent. As I've told you, Ellen was my friend. She's the last person I would want to hurt, and I'm interested in her research not the artefacts from the exhibition."

Dixit put the photo back in the folder. "Let's talk about that, shall we?"

"Talk about what?"

"Hurting Miss Champion."

Alex was about to protest when Dixit continued: "Let's go back to the evening of Saturday 7th."

Alex waited.

"You got a takeaway and watched a movie, yes?"

"That's right."

"And you had an argument."

He was taken aback. "No."

"We spoke to your neighbours. One of them said you had an argument."

Alex shook his head. "Well, we didn't. If you mean the busybody in number 4, then she's unreliable. She's a crackpot who will complain about anything and everything. I once left my bike in the communal hall for a short while. It was only there for a few minutes and she knocked on the door to complain and ask me to move it."

Dixit said, "You had an argument on Saturday night."

Alex thought back to the evening. Ellen had been agitated early on. She said someone had followed her. Later, while they were watching the film, she'd jumped up and shouted. She said he was outside, but it was dark, and when Alex looked he couldn't see anyone. She'd then been cross with him. Had she raised her voice again, maybe a bit? Alex had calmed her down by going outside and looking. Again he saw no one, and that was it.

He told them the story.

Dixit looked dubious. "So you didn't argue."

Wilson stepped in. "Detective, my client has answered. Miss Champion shouted at someone outside. Someone she thought had followed her."

Dixit looked hard at Alex. "And you didn't think to tell us this earlier? Don't you think we would have wanted to know about someone following her?"

"Not really," Alex said. "That was how she was. She always thought she was being followed or someone was looking at her suspiciously. She was paranoid. I told you, she was on medication. She didn't like taking it because she could think better when she wasn't medicated, and that's when she was more likely to be paranoid. She'd also get cross if I questioned whether she'd taken her medication."

Jackson tapped his fingers on the table. There was no other sound for a while, before he said, "Why do you think she was murdered?"

"Was she definitely murdered?"

"Let's assume she was for the purposes of this exercise," Jackson said. "And let's also assume that the burglary was connected. Do you agree that it's too much of a coincidence?"

Alex nodded thoughtfully. "It seems that way."

"You're a bright guy, so what's your theory? You must have one."

"All I can think is that if someone killed her and that same person... or people... broke into Highclere Castle, then it was to do with her research. That's why I asked whether her briefcase had been found."

"It was," Jackson confirmed.

"And?"

Dixit said, "It was damaged and open. We found no evidence of research."

"So it was taken."

Dixit gave an almost imperceptible shrug. "If it had been there it wasn't found."

"Shame."

"Any other theories?" Jackson asked casually.

Alex shook his head.

Dixit said, "You are a karate expert."

"No."

"You have a book on karate."

"I studied it for a few years a while back. I made it to second kyu."

"Black belt."

"Two down from black belt. I wasn't very good so I stopped going. To be honest I didn't like getting hit, and the closer I got to a black belt the more it seemed the higher grades tried to prove themselves better."

The detectives said nothing, waiting for Alex to say more. He didn't.

Wilson said, "Well, if that's it—"

Jackson held up a hand. "One minute."

Dixit pushed his chair back, stood and left the room. Jackson informed the recording and then introduced DS Belmarsh. She entered, took Dixit's seat and opened the file.

"Tell us about your relationship with the deceased." She then repeated her assertion that Alex was more than good friends with Ellen. From the file she removed a photograph of Nadja wearing very little.

Belmarsh said, "I'm showing Mr MacLure a photograph. Please could you tell us her name?"

"Nadja Dabrowska. She cleans for me once a week and walks my dog."

"She used to work at Jaimeson's." The detective paused for a long beat, although her right hand reached back and forth. "It's a lap dancing club."

"I've not heard of it. I didn't know. And it's irrelevant. She cleans and walks my dog. I don't care what she used to do for work." Alex looked at Jackson as he spoke, avoiding Belmarsh's dopey eyes and irritating arm movement.

Belmarsh said, "She's very attractive."

"So?"

"You were having a relationship with her."

"No," he said, looking at Jackson.

Belmarsh said, "Let's talk about the money in your bank account."

For a moment Alex wondered whether she was referring to the money transferred by Pete. Did the police have access to his account? Eventually he said, "I won the lottery. I told you that."

"You looked unsure for a moment. What's the truth?"

Wilson leaned in. "He's told you, he won the lottery."

Alex said, "If you've checked, you'll know it's true."

"So no one gave you money to gain access to Highclere Castle."

"Of course not."

Belmarsh took a letter from the file. "I'm showing Mr MacLure a letter from the museum confirming his appointment. It's addressed to you." She handed the letter to Alex. "For the record, Mr MacLure is nodding."

"Sure."

Belmarsh pulled another piece of paper from the file, spun it, and then with her pen she pointed to a signature at the bottom.

Jackson said, "DS Belmarsh has placed a second letter on the table. She has indicated a signature." He paused and, looking at Alex, said, "Mr MacLure, please confirm that this is your signature."

"It is."

"The document is a letter which accompanied an application for the position of researcher. In the application you say you have a MA in Egyptology and claim to be enrolled for a PhD in Archaeology at Macquarie University—that's in Australia—specializing in ancient Egypt and the Eighteenth and Nineteenth Dynasties."

Alex said nothing.

Belmarsh said, "We've spoken to Professor Lloyd at the British Museum. She said it was Miss Champion who was

64

interested in what she called the New Kingdom. She said that you were researching Pre-dynasties."

Alex exchanged glances with Wilson and continued to stay silent.

Jackson said, "Have you spoken to an investigative reporter from the *Daily Mail*, Mr MacLure?"

"No, I have not. I gave an interview to a reporter from *The Sunday Times*, but that was a mistake."

Jackson raised his eyebrows and waited for Alex to say more. When nothing was forthcoming he said, "Are you aware of the story about your qualifications?"

"I saw the news this morning."

"The allegation is that your so-called master's degree is in fact a diploma. Do you have a comment on that?"

"It is a master's equivalent."

"A correspondence course that took you a mere six months to complete."

"Still an accredited course." Alex smiled tightly. "And, I'm published—papers in the *Modern Journal of Ancient...*"

"That may be, Mr MacLure," Jackson said, raising his hand to interrupt, "but what about the PhD claim? Are you enrolled at Macquarie University?"

Alex swallowed, his mouth suddenly dry. Ellen had encouraged him to take this route as a fast track to getting involved in the research. OK, so he'd cut a corner.

Jackson said, "Since you seem to be having difficulty, I'll answer for you. You aren't officially enrolled because the offer of the position was contingent upon evidence of your qualification, and they don't recognize the diploma. Therefore, your application as a researcher at the British Museum was fraudulent."

Alex had seen Milwanee's article on the *Daily Mail* website: Have-a-go Hero is a Fraud.

Wilson shrugged, "It's hardly a criminal offence to slightly exaggerate on an application form. Over eighty per cent of applicants embellish their CVs to persuade a prospective employer they are right for a job. Fake and fraud are words easily used by the British media to dramatize the news. Although his CV may have been given a favourable spin, Mr MacLure himself cannot personally be considered a fake. And as for a fraudster... he would have needed to have acted in order to make a profit or gain some unfair advantage. In terms of the law, I hardly need to point out the ridiculousness of such a claim."

Jackson stared hard at Alex. "You see, Mr MacLure, I have a theory forming. Perhaps you needed to take something from the Highclere exhibition—or maybe just be involved in the burglary. To do this you decided to work for the British Museum, thereby gaining access. Maybe Ellen Champion found out and you argued. Maybe you went to see her on Monday night and argued again. Maybe you had a bit of a fight and she died." He paused.

Alex shook his head. Did it really look that way?

Jackson resumed: "Was it an accident, Alex?"

"None of that happened. I am innocent."

Belmarsh said, "Or was it an argument about the other girl? Was Ellen jealous of the Polish tart?"

"OK, that is enough!" Wilson snorted. She placed a hand under Alex's elbow and they both stood. "Thank you. The interview is at an end."

Belmarsh made a closing statement and stopped the recorder.

Before they left the room, Alex stopped at the door and looked back at Jackson. "You have got it wrong," he said. "I really want to help with the investigation in any way I can."

Jackson nodded slowly. "Just don't leave the country," he said.

TEN

As Dixit and Belmarsh walked along the corridor, he said, "You didn't get under his skin this time."

"I guess he fell for my charms after all. By the way," she added, referring to DS Limb, "Mike's here."

"Was he listening?"

"No, just arrived. The boss is with him now." She led the way through Chiswick Police Station into the car park. Jackson was there with Limb. Another man joined them. He held a tape recorder towards Jackson.

He looked like a reporter and was asking the boss question after question. Jackson shook his head.

Dixit read his lips: "No comment."

As they got closer they heard Jackson finally lose it. "You're on police property. DS Limb, escort this gentleman out of the car park."

Limb stepped in the way. At first the reporter stood his ground. Limb went to grab or push the guy's shoulder but the reporter slipped sideways.

The guy said, "One more question. Is there a connection between the death of the Champion girl and the burglary at Highclere?"

Jackson snapped: "Go away!"

Limb took another step towards the reporter but the guy was now back-pedalling fast. He scuttled across the yard and through the gates.

"Bloody hacks!" Limb muttered.

Jackson shook his head. "Right, what did you find out?"

"Nothing confirmed."

Belmarsh closed in. "Have I missed something?"

Limb shrugged. "There's a suspicion that someone else was looking after the bungalow. The old lady in the Canaries hasn't been back for four months, so how could she be managing the property?"

"But no idea who yet?" Jackson asked.

"No, and the old biddy isn't talking."

Jackson moved towards his silver Vauxhall Insignia.

Belmarsh said, "Sir."

Jackson looked at her and raised his eyebrows.

"I still think we should have arrested him—MacLure, I mean."

Dixit said, "We don't have anything. All we have is speculation. MacLure didn't need to be in there just now. His solicitor kept reminding him, but I'd say he's honestly keen to help."

Jackson said, "We need to find a genuine motive."

"The Polish girl," Belmarsh said. "If there's something between them, she could be using him. Maybe she's connected to Polish mafia. Follow that and maybe we find the link to the stolen goods."

Jackson shook his head. "That's a lot of maybes."

"We should watch him at least," Limb said.

Jackson placed a hand on the roof of the Vauxhall, thinking. "OK, we'll keep an eye on him. Limb…"

"Yes, Boss?"

"He hasn't seen you before, so you keep tabs on our guy. I want to know what he does, where he goes, who he sees. And Belmarsh…"

"Sir?"

"You chase down the Polish connection. See if you can find a link to a gang. And if any of you see that damn reporter again, give him a kick in the arse from me."

Fox, posing as the reporter, stood under the overhanging building by a pillar. He was out of sight but just close enough to pick up a signal. As he'd avoided the clutch of the sharply dressed detective, he'd stuck a bug on his jacket. The guy hadn't even felt it.

As he hurried away, Fox could hear everything they said. Eventually, Limb—the one in the sharp suit—said goodbye and three car doors slammed. Moments later, an unmarked silver Vauxhall pulled out of the car park and headed west on Chiswick High Road. The inspector was driving. The woman, Belmarsh, rode shotgun and the junior Indian guy was in the back.

The guy posing as a reporter pulled out his phone and dialled.

"They've not arrested the rabbit," Fox said without preamble. "In fact they are nowhere. They have a theory that the rabbit is involved but have no evidence. They've got less of an idea about who's doing this than we do. Their best guess is Polish mafia, but that seems unlikely to me."

"Because of the dog walker?" The voice was deep and coarse from years of smoking.

"Yes. They suspect there's more to it, though I don't think so."

There was silence for a moment. Fox could hear the rasp of the man's breathing.

"Owl? What do you want me to do?"

The smoker said, "Stay on him."

"There's a complication. The police have him under surveillance too."

"Anyone that's seen you?"

"Yes."

"All right, stay on it until you can make a switch with Dog. After that, check out this Polish thing, just in case."

69

As Fox ended the call, MacLure and a bookish-looking woman came out of the main entrance. Fox also spotted Limb on the street pretending to read a noticeboard.

MacLure shook the woman's hand and walked away from the station. He crossed the road and turned right. Limb waited a moment and followed. A few seconds later Fox picked up the trail.

ELEVEN

Alex climbed a fence into his back garden. As he'd approached his street he'd seen a large number of people milling around plus vans parked on the opposite pavement. One had a TV company logo on the side. He quickly turned away and took a large detour, approaching the house from the opposite direction on a road perpendicular to his street. He climbed a wall and then a fence to get into his rear garden. He unlocked the back door, crouched and slid inside. Topsy rushed up and licked his face as he crawled into the lounge. He sat on the floor, leaning against the sofa. They couldn't see him from outside, not unless they stood on their vans, and he'd seen no evidence of that. The temptation to take a peek was enormous, but he fought it. If they saw him inside, his life would become hell. Instantly.

He had to get out, get away. He had two calls to make. First he called Nadja.

"Can you take Topsy?"

"For walk? Sure."

"No, I mean until further notice."

Nadja didn't respond straight away.

Alex said, "Nadja, I need your help. I need to get away from this. The media are all over it. Hopefully it'll only be a few days."

"It's OK, Mr MacLure. Of course I do it. Take as long as you need to sort things out."

Alex thanked her profusely and rang off. Then he made the more difficult call.

Pete answered immediately. "How did it go?"

"Well they didn't arrest me, so I guess it went all right."

"You didn't mention me, did you?"

"That's why I'm calling."

"Fuck, what did you say?"

Alex let him sweat a moment before he said, "No, I didn't mention you were there. It was damned hard though. They were suspicious of the coincidence. And that damned baseball cap made me look guilty! You owe me for that."

"I don't owe you."

"Yes you do. If all I'm worried about is explaining a few thousand pounds in my bank account, I'd rather do that than face time in jail."

The line was quiet except for a slight static hiss. Finally Pete said, "What do you want?"

"I need somewhere to go. The press are all over me like a rash. I'm hiding in my own damned house!" Alex realized his voice was rising. Could they hear him? Did they have sensitive listening devices? He spoke quietly: "Where do you live?"

Pete started to make excuses.

"Where do you live, Pete? You're going to put me up for a couple of days while this blows over."

Minutes later, Alex was packing a gym bag. He kissed Topsy on the head and slipped out the back way.

Pete's apartment was on the edge of Hammersmith, just short of Fulham, and at the centre of a broad triangle between underground stations, a no man's land of red-brick Victorian mansion conversions. Alex left Hammersmith station and walked south along Fulham Palace Road. Exhaust fumes from the solid stream of traffic made the air so thick he could taste it. Despite the pollution, there were many people on the pavements, heading to and from the station. Walking: the unhealthy mode of transport on Fulham Palace Road.

Charing Cross Hospital looked like a classic 1960s' motel stuck on the front of a tenement block of glass and concrete. He'd briefly dated a nurse who worked there. They'd met at Lindy Hop and dated for about three weeks. Karen: the girl who smoked e-cigarettes like each one was her last. She said she smoked more now they were supposedly healthy.

Alex stopped at the railing and watched two orderlies chatting. One had an e-cigarette, the other a real one. Did Karen still work here? Was she even more addicted?

Out of the corner of his eye Alex noticed a man wearing sunglasses, a sports jacket and a stone-coloured baseball cap with the number 62 in black. Rule 62, it said. The guy had a beard and looked like he worked out; nobody special, just an ordinary guy walking along the road. Most people in London don't look at one another. But Alex had clocked the cap. He had first seen it going east on the Central line and then again at the Hammersmith tube station ticket barrier. The reason it attracted his attention was the number 62. The psychiatrist Sigmund Freud had a morbid fear of the number 62. Sigmund Freud was fascinating, not just for his contribution to psychology, but also for his theories on ancient Egypt.

At the station the man glanced at him and then headed for the opposite exit. And yet here he was on Fulham Palace Road. Was he a reporter?

Alex stayed at the railing, tense, ready to run if the guy challenged him. But the guy just walked past without a glance. Alex tracked him for thirty yards and watched him stop at the next junction. There, he seemed to be studying a book, possibly an *A to Z*. He looked back and their eyes met. It was for the briefest of moments, but enough to confirm Alex's suspicion: a tail, most likely a newspaper guy.

As the man looked away again, Alex reacted. He began to run in the opposite direction—back towards Hammersmith. His holdall banged on the railings and then his leg. In frustration, he slung it over a shoulder. A tall man in a grey suit grunted as it grazed him.

Alex didn't stop. He called out an apology and ran.

At the next road he turned and followed the boundary fence of the hospital. When he came to the next right he took it. Now he was going in the direction he wanted and was parallel to Fulham Palace Road, but instead of continuing, he darted through an iron gateway into a graveyard. Margravine Cemetery. A long path curved gently for a few hundred metres ahead. He knew this. He had cut through here on a couple of occasions to reach Barons Court underground station.

No way could he stay on the path, it was too exposed.

He darted right, through a phalanx of crooked tombstones and statues. There, he paused to check that no one was watching before scooting to hide behind an elm tree. As he peered around it, the man in the 62 cap appeared at the cemetery gate.

Alex held his breath. Sweat covered his arms and his shirt stuck to his pounding chest.

The man walked through the gate and placed a hand on it, breathing heavily. He began scanning the cemetery but didn't move from the entrance. Alex shrank back behind the tree, counted to ten and peeked out once more.

No one there.

Was the man searching or had he left?

Alex sat with his back to the tree and waited, listening intently. It was a good five minutes before his heart had stopped trying to burst through his ribcage and his breathing calmed. He took an apple from his bag and slowly munched on it, relaxing more with each bite. After another ten minutes and no sign of the pursuer, Alex stood and looked around, before running in a crouch to another tree. From there he ran to the statue of an angel, a mausoleum, and then another tree. Following a route he'd planned, and constantly checking for the pursuer, he made his way through the ancient stones to the south gate. When he reached the street, he checked it was clear and began to walk.

Alex climbed the eighth and final flight of stairs and found Pete standing on the landing above, a glower etched on his face.

"I hope you weren't followed," Pete grumbled.

"There was one, but I lost him in the cemetery."

"You're toxic right now, you know that?" Pete led him into his flat. The lounge was spartan. There was a large screen TV. It was free-standing with a DVD player and an Xbox games console. Discs were piled high and scattered beside it. There were two chairs, old and worn, with curved wooden arms. The only other furniture was a side table by the door. It had a tray for coins, a bunch of keys and a yellow lanyard with a fob on the end.

"Cosy," Alex said.

"Beggars can't be choosers. And I'm doing you a huge favour."

Alex said nothing but glanced towards the doors off the room.

Pete nodded. "OK, a quick tour of the place then I'm grabbing a few hours' kip before I have to go to work." He showed Alex the first room. It was next to the front door, with one wall that must have been at the top of the stairs, and the other side looked out at the rear. There were no curtains, just grubby nets. The view was of the rear of an identical tenement block. They had gardens between them, although most had been paved and all had sheds, some so large they took up half the space. There was no furniture in the room, just a small fitted wardrobe and a mattress.

Pete shrugged.

Alex said, "I know, beggars and choosers again."

"I'll get you a sheet, but I'm afraid I don't have a spare duvet."

Alex followed him into the kitchen and was shown what was in which cupboard: the usual stuff in the usual places. Pete said he would clear half of one so Alex could use it.

After the kitchen was a door to the right. "The bathroom," Pete said, pointing. "And that's my room at the end. Help yourself to tea or coffee, although when I'm asleep during the day you need to be a church mouse."

"Of course."

Pete walked back to the lounge and looked out of the window. Alex joined him and checked up and down for anyone suspicious. Four storeys down, it was quiet except for a car trying to parallel park in a space that looked too small.

"That's rule one." Pete held up a hand and counted off with his fingers as he spoke. "Two: you do not tell anyone where you are staying."

The car trying to park bumped into a BMW and then took off without checking for damage. Alex turned back to Pete. "That's fine by me."

"Three," Pete continued, "you can only stay for three nights to help you out. And four, if there's any trouble, if there's any sign of reporters or the cops, you leave immediately. That clear?"

Alex nodded. "No trouble."

DS Limb called Jackson. "I lost him in Hammersmith."

"What was MacLure doing in Hammersmith?"

"I don't know, but here's the thing: someone else was tailing him too."

"Start at the beginning," Jackson said.

"After leaving Chiswick, MacLure took the tube to Maida Vale. From there he walked home via a roundabout route. He was avoiding the reporters at the front of his house and it looked like he jumped a few walls to get in the rear. There's a sixth form college opposite and I managed to get high enough so I could see into his flat. He was squatting in the lounge for a while and then disappeared, I think, to his bedroom. Anyway, shortly afterwards he crawled to the back door and let himself out. I was just quick enough to see him heading down the road again. This time he walked to Paddington and caught the tube."

"To Hammersmith?"

"You'd think he'd have taken the Hammersmith and City line straight there, but he didn't. He headed east and kept changing tubes at different stations. All the time, he was looking around, checking for a tail. But he never made me. Finally, we got the District line west and got off at Hammersmith. He stopped outside the hospital on Fulham Palace Road."

"For what reason?"

"Not sure, sir. I slowed down, hoping I wouldn't overtake him. After a moment, MacLure gave a guy a good long stare. The guy walked past but then stopped and looked back, dodgy as hell. MacLure took flight—bumping into me as he spun round."

Limb hesitated, thinking Jackson would comment. When the boss didn't, Limb continued. "The guy started chasing MacLure. He ran past me so I got a good look."

"OK."

"They ran around the back and by the time I got there I was just in time to see the other guy go into the cemetery. MacLure got away. I've no idea where he went, but the other guy lost him too."

"And you questioned this other guy?"

"I lost him." Limb heard Jackson take a deep breath, imagined his face reddening.

"Bloody marvellous, Limb."

"Yes, sir."

"Get your arse back here and... No, wait. I want a full written description of this other guy and I want you to spend the rest of the day walking those bloody streets until you find either one of them. Now get off the phone and start searching."

The man codenamed Fox sat in a parked BMW and pressed speed dial on his phone.

Owl, the man on the other end of the line, spoke first: "Where is the rabbit now?"

"He's still got one of the trackers on him." The trackers had been placed on and inside items when they'd broken into Alex's flat—the day Alex had found Topsy locked outside. "He's in a residential building on a road between Hammersmith and Fulham. I'm close by."

Fox had been lucky to find a slot, although another driver seemed to think he could get his car in the gap behind the BMW.

"And the detective?" Owl asked.

"Dog was following him. Turned out there was another tail as well. Amateurs, both of them. Even the rabbit made them. There was a chase and the rabbit gave them the slip. The copper lost them both."

"And this other guy?"

"The other guy following the rabbit... Dog's on it. We don't know who he is or his connection, but if he's not with the rabbit..."

He didn't need to finish. They both knew this was their first big lead.

There was a crunching sound.

"What was that?" Owl asked.

Fox said, "I've just been pranged. Idiot thought he could get in a space." Fox watched the other driver take off as though nothing had happened. "I can't stay here."

"Not a problem," Owl said. "You help Dog. Since we can track the rabbit, I'll have Cat take over from here."

TWELVE

Alex was up and eating a bowl of Rice Krispies when Pete came home from work.

"Make us a cup of tea, would you?" Pete put a cup next to the kettle and flicked it on. "Sleep OK?"

"A bit cold. I think I'll invest in a sleeping bag today."

As Alex made them both tea, Pete went into his bedroom, re-emerged and headed for the lounge.

Alex followed with the steaming mugs.

"Knackered," Pete groaned, flopping into a chair. "I have to find a job that isn't nights. Though being up for most of yesterday didn't help." He switched on the TV and Xbox.

Alex leaned against the wall and sipped his tea. "I've been thinking…"

"Can be dangerous," Pete chortled. He selected *resume* on the game that came on the screen.

"You don't want the press to know where you live." Alex shrugged. "And quite frankly I'm pleased about that."

Pete paused the game and looked at Alex, puzzled. "That's why you're here."

"Yeah, but it also extends to the police."

Pete didn't comment.

Alex continued: "The other day you said you didn't want the police knowing where you are. That doesn't make sense."

"Not sure what you're getting at."

"You told me you'd spoken to the police, that they'd interviewed you."

"Right."

"But you also didn't want me to mention you were at Highclere with me last Wednesday night."

"For your benefit as much as mine. The money…"

"I don't think the police interviewed you, did they? They don't know where you live. Do they even know you were Ellen's landlord?"

Pete looked back at the TV and started to play the game.

Alex said, "I think you're avoiding the police. What's going on, Pete?"

The question hung in the air.

Alex stepped in front of the screen.

"Hey!"

"What's going on?"

"Sorry, what were you saying? What's going on about what? I'm so tired, I could sleep for a week."

"I asked why you're avoiding the police? Shit, Pete. Are you somehow involved?"

"What? No!" Pete shook his head vigorously and gripped Alex's arm. "Sit down, I have to explain."

They sat in the armchairs, not opposite each other but at about ninety degrees. Their knees almost touched. Pete leaned forward. "I work as a security guard for an investment management firm in Canary Wharf. They take security very seriously, of course, not just of the premises but in recruitment. Background checks—you know, CRB stuff to make sure there's no criminal record."

"OK." Alex wasn't sure where this was going.

"I have a record. It was a long time ago." Pete told Alex a story about being fired and getting so angry he wanted revenge. He broke into the firm's office and was arrested and charged with breaking and entry with the intent to do criminal damage. "I served eighteen months in juvie. It's enough to stop you working most places these days. The whole security thing has blown up big time. So it works both ways. I get paid a lot of money to be a night security guard."

Alex finished his tea, which was now cold. "I still don't get it."

"I changed my name. Change your name and they can't trace you. Can you believe it? All those checks and they are useless if someone changes their name and doesn't admit to it on the forms. The CRB doesn't cross reference deed poll data or credit data. It all relies on trust and stupidity. That's why I can't get involved with the police. If they start digging, like they are doing with you, then I'm stuffed. Up shit creek without a paddle."

They sat in silence for a while, neither meeting the other's gaze.

Finally, Alex said, "Two new rules. I'm not doing you a big favour, I'm doing you a massive favour. I don't mention you to the police and I can stay here as long as I want."

"OK. And the second one?"

"You buy a spare duvet."

By midday, Alex decided he needed air and lunch. He left the house wearing wraparound sunglasses and a gabardine coat of Pete's he found in the wardrobe. From his holdall he pulled a book he'd brought from home: *The Oxford History of Ancient Egypt*. He stuck it in a pocket, turned up the collar of the coat and headed out.

He walked south towards Putney Bridge, stopping at a corner shop to buy a chicken salad sandwich.

By the time he reached the bridge over the Thames, he was feeling overdressed. For November, it was a warm day, and the coat aided his disguise but had been a bad choice for the weather.

The road and bridge were clogged with traffic and pedestrians. On the far side of the bridge was a lane down to the water. Only a few people strolled or jogged here. He ambled along the embankment towards the ridged concrete slipway outside the main rowing clubs. Cars lined the edge with a few gaps for rowers to carry their boats from the boathouses to the water. The boathouses had open doors and he surmised that the rowers were out on the river.

He sat and leaned against a post. Lumpy concrete prompted him to remove his coat and sit on it. He soon settled. The Thames was sage-green-brown and the tide was midway and going out. A rower in a bright orange scull laboured against the current. A woman walked past him, down to the water's edge and began to feed the ducks. Alex pulled out his book and began flicking through, trying to decide what to read. He had already made many pencil notes and turned page corners.

A honk from the swan made him look up. The woman squealed and backed away as a swan pecked at her empty bag.

Alex reacted quickly, fished in his coat pocket, found the sandwich, broke off a piece of bread and tossed it close to one of the ducks. When it had gobbled down this morsel, he threw another piece into the water. It sped away on the tide with the swan giving chase.

"Thanks," the woman called. For a moment he thought she was going to come over and talk to him, but she turned and walked away.

Alex picked up his book and flicked to the contents page. After the list of contributors and before the introduction was a handwritten series of numbers.

259252356124071912

His initial reaction was annoyance that someone else had written in his book. He studied the pen strokes and decided it was probably Ellen's writing. Twenty numbers with no immediately obvious pattern or relevance. Why would she write in his book and what did they mean?

A movement behind made him jump.

"Hey!" Instinctively Alex started to stand and turn. Before he was halfway up, a hand pressed on his shoulder and kept him down.

The man growled, "Don't move a muscle." His accent was thick East London. *Dan't moov a massle.*

Alex froze.

The man said, "Time to talk, sonny."

Alex strained his neck, twisting to see the man gripping his shoulder. He expected to see the same guy from yesterday: the guy with the 62 on his baseball cap. It wasn't. This guy was clean-shaven, bigger, heavier set. He wore a leather jacket and blue-mirrored, aviator glasses.

"You're from the papers... a reporter, right?" Alex said, trying to sound calmer than he felt. "I've nothing to say."

Aviator snorted. "I'll gut you like a fish. Now cut the crap and start talking!"

Alex's sweatshirt was tugged and he stood. Something pricked his side. He glanced down and saw a blade.

"Er... you aren't with the press?" he stammered. "Who are you?"

"Don't mess around with me, MacLure. I think you know all about the research. All about what your little friend found. Perhaps you need a little reminder."

What was this guy saying? How did he know about Ellen's research? "Wait—what do you know?"

Aviator pushed the blade deeper and Alex flinched as the point met flesh.

"OK! OK," Alex said. "I'll tell you what you want to know."

"Where is it?"

Alex took a long breath. "Ah, you've heard the news about things being stolen from Highclere. You think I know where it is. Well..."

"Shut up! Where is *it*—the item?"

"What item?" Alex's mind was spinning. What was this guy talking about? He wasn't interested in all the stolen stuff, just a single item. He must know what's been taken and think something was missing. Was that it?

Aviator moved his hand from Alex's shoulder and placed it on the left side of his head. Before Alex could pull away, the man's other hand was on the other side of his head, the handle of the knife pressed against his temple. The guy squeezed.

A jolt of pain burst through Alex's skull and he yelled. Between ragged breaths he said, "I don't know anything."

"Bullshit!" Aviator squeezed again.

For a moment things went black. Alex lost all sensation and then Aviator pulled him backwards.

Blinking tears from his eyes, Alex tried to regain his senses, quell the ringing in his head. After a few staggering steps he was spun and thrust against a wall.

They were in the gap between two of the boathouses, like a wide alley, shaded and hidden from a view of the bridge—and help.

Aviator punched him in the ribs and Alex doubled over with a cough.

"I really don't…"

"Bullshit!" the guy tapped the side of Alex's head with the butt of his knife. Not a heavy blow, but enough to make the light blink out for a moment and hurt like hell.

"Where is it?" Aviator asked again.

Alex couldn't think with this guy pressed against him, threatening. The thug wanted information that he didn't have. How could he…? The man hit him again with the knife, harder this time, and Alex crumpled to the floor.

His vision honed in on a broken bottle—could he slash the guy and get away? It seemed the only option.

"Hey, what's going on here?" A woman's voice snapped Alex's attention away from the bottle. The duck-feeding woman was standing at the entrance to the gap between the boathouses.

"Shove off, bitch, and mind yer own business!" Aviator snarled.

"I'm calling the police." The woman held up her phone threatening to use it.

The thug had his back to Alex and brandished the knife at her. "Drop the phone and fuck off outta here, lady, before it's too late."

Alex snatched up the bottle. As he started to rise, he realized Aviator was also making a move.

"Run!" he shouted, but it was too late. He saw the phone fly out of her hand as Aviator bulldozed forward.

THIRTEEN

The man lurched sideways and staggered. He gripped his shoulder and Alex saw a dark patch appear beneath his fingers. Then the fingers turned red.

"Run!" Alex shouted as he realized he'd heard a gunshot.

The woman stood with wide eyes, her empty hand still in the air.

He grabbed her hand and tugged her down the alley, away from the river, away from where he guessed the gunman was. As they reached the bottom, where the sheds met a thirty-foot wall, he looked back. Aviator was on his feet and heading towards them.

Alex pulled the woman into the space behind the shed on their left. She also glanced back and seemed to get it. They had to get away, make the most of the chance they'd been given.

The space had scattered debris: bits of rope, a buoy, planks of wood and a broken oar. They reached the daylight at the far side and saw Aviator enter the space behind them.

"Keep going," Alex urged her as the woman slowed. "He's right behind."

They squeezed between the next two sheds and suddenly they were in the open. Alex looked past the woman. Aviator wasn't there. Where was he?

A ping against the wood beside him snapped his attention back. Someone was firing at them! Had the shooter been firing at him all along and hit Aviator by mistake?

Just as Alex ducked back into the shadowy space between the shed and wall, Aviator appeared just twenty yards away. He was still holding his shoulder but he was grinning. Alex hesitated: confront the injured guy or dodge the bullets? A moment later, the decision was made for him. The woman was running towards the ramp, ducking her head as she went. Alex sprinted after her, copying the style as though it reduced the target area.

They reached the road together and he breathed for the first time. Her face was pale and she was shaking. "We've got to get out of here," she said breathlessly, and crossed the road.

Alex saw Aviator halfway up the ramp and decided not to wait any longer.

"This way," the woman said on the opposite side. She led him into an alley that came out in a yard. He chased after her as she crossed the yard out onto another road. Fifty paces later she was between buildings again and then stopped as they met a brick wall. She stopped and put her hands on her knees, regaining her breath.

Alex looked back, fearing their pursuer would be at the entrance at any moment. "We're trapped," he said between gulps for air. "We've got to go back."

"No, this way," she said, and pushed an industrial refuse cart to the wall. She scrambled on top and disappeared over the wall before Alex could say a word. He followed and found they were in a backyard. She walked calmly to a green door, opened it and walked in. Inside, Alex saw it was a fire exit. She closed the door and jammed a bar in the opening handle.

Alex stared at her. "How did you…?"

"Not yet," she said, leading him to a staircase. "Let's make sure we're safe first."

On the first landing was a door leading to a toilet. Beside the room was a window. The view from the window was of the backyard and the alley beyond the wall. There was no one in the alley: no Aviator and no one with a gun.

"I'm Vanessa," she said. "What the hell was that about? Who was that guy? Why did he attack you?"

Alex wiped sweat from his forehead. "And who was shooting at us?"

"What?"

"Someone was firing at us… or him. Anyway, he was hit."

Vanessa had her mouth open in shock.

Alex touched her arm. "Are you OK?"

"Oh my God, I can't believe someone was shooting at us. I thought I heard something but dismissed it as a starter's pistol—you get them all the time for the rowers. So that's why that guy fell over. I thought he'd just slipped." She took long calming breaths as Alex kept his hand on her arm. "I'm OK. I'm OK," she said eventually.

They looked out of the window again to confirm no one was there. She smiled weakly. "Come on, let's go downstairs. I'll introduce you to Simon."

Simon turned out to be the owner of the café they were in. They came in through the back door, and after Vanessa quickly glanced around, they sat at a table. It was busy with people queued up at a sandwich bar placing orders and it had ten tables, mostly occupied.

"One minute," Alex heard someone with an accent say. A man in a blue pinafore appeared and Vanessa stood to give him a hug.

"Simon. My cousin," Vanessa said, by way of an introduction.

"Pleased to meet you," Simon said, shaking Alex's hand. "And you are?"

"Alex."

Simon looked at Vanessa and raised his eyebrows. She gave him a playful punch. "Away with you. You have customers to serve. And when you have a moment, we'll have... two teas with two sugars. Is that all right?"

Alex nodded. When she sat down again, he looked at her properly for the first time. Maybe mid-twenties, with brown hair and dark eyes. She was good-looking in a sort of Mediterranean or Middle Eastern way. "I'm Alex," he said, offering his hand with a smile.

She took it. "We've established that already." Then she looked serious. "But what you haven't told me is what the hell is actually going on, and shouldn't we be calling the police?"

"I don't know. I really don't know what's going on. It's complicated..." He saw she wasn't accepting that and added, "But you are right about the police."

Simon returned with two mugs of tea and Alex waited until he'd retreated before dialling DI Jackson's number.

The inspector was unavailable and he was put through to DC Dixit. After Alex had recounted what had happened on the Putney embankment, Dixit asked for a detailed description of the assailant. He also wanted to know the precise locations of the attack and the bullet hole in the shed.

"Now drink your tea. It'll help," Vanessa said when he rang off.

After a few sips, he felt his heart rate slowing. He still checked out everyone who came into the café, but he was starting to relax.

She was watching him, a slight smile on her lips. "Better?" she asked. "Maybe you should eat something as well."

Then he remembered the sandwich he'd brought for lunch. "Damn, my book!"

"Your book?"

"My coat is on the embankment... I have a sandwich in a pocket. But I'm more concerned about the book I had with me. I dropped it when I was grabbed." He thought for a moment. "It's got sentimental value but I can't face going down there. They may still be around. They're probably out there right now looking for me. We'd probably recognize the guy with the aviator glasses again, but there was the shooter. We have no idea what he looks like. And maybe there are more."

"I'm intrigued about the book. What is it?"

Alex told her and she got up. "Just a minute," she said, and went behind the sandwich bar. When she returned she said, "Simon will send one of his staff to try and find it for you."

After a second cup of tea Alex began to tell Vanessa about the past week. She laughed softly at one point and he stopped. "What's so funny?"

"I had a sense we'd met before," she said. "But we haven't, have we? I've seen your picture online. You were the Have-a-go Hero suspected of fraud. Is it true?"

"A hero? I don't think so. Anyway, you're a hero for stepping in earlier. My attacker had a weapon, whereas all I did was stop someone who snatched a woman's handbag. The press love to exaggerate."

"And the fraud bit?"

"It's rubbish. Pure conjecture. The reporter connected a problem with my previous employer to me leaving—and coming into money." She raised her eyebrows at that, so he explained: "I won a chunk on the lottery. Meant I could stop being an accountant and do something more interesting."

"Which is?"

"Archaeology—or more specifically ancient Egypt. And that's really what the story is about. That's why the police are interested in me. That and the recent burglary at Highclere you must have heard about.

She nodded thoughtfully. "So that guy... do you think he was one of the burglars?"

"Maybe. He seemed to think I knew something about an item."

"And do you?"

"I have no idea what he was talking about. If he was one of the Highclere burglars, why didn't he know...?" And then Alex realized something. The news reports hadn't mentioned what was taken, so if it was something specific, this guy was definitely involved. "You know," he said, "I think the aviator-guy was definitely one of the burglars and they were after something specific. It was something they didn't find."

"But you don't know what?"

Just then a young man came to their table. He held out a folded gabardine coat with a book perched on top. The man also handed him a broken pair of sunglasses. "If these are yours, I'm afraid you won't be wearing them again."

Alex took them with thanks, stuck the glasses in a pocket of the coat and placed the book on the table.

"You're smiling," she said.

He opened the book at the contents page. "I don't really know what's going on," he said. "I don't know what Aviator was looking for at the Highclere Castle exhibition. But I do know one thing." He pointed to the twenty numbers that Ellen had written in the book.

"I think my friend left me a clue."

FOURTEEN

DI Jackson answered a call from DS Limb.

"I'm at the scene, Boss," Limb said. "I'm standing on the slipway by Putney Bridge."

"Any sign... of anything?"

"No sign of either MacLure or the guy he described. The same one I saw chase him outside the hospital. But that's not all."

Jackson waited.

"There are sheds here, like he said: rowing clubs. I've been all round the outside and there's no trace of any blood. Not that I could see anyway."

"Could it have been washed away by the tide?"

"Doesn't come up that high. He said they were between two sheds. And the bullet hole... well there are lots of holes in the sheds. They're made of wood and pretty old. Maybe there's a bullet hole, but I couldn't find anything... and no casings."

"Witnesses?"

"No, and no one reported anything to the Met. If there were gunshots, surely—"

"So you think he's lying?"

"He's not lying about the guy after him, but something doesn't smell right. I think we should bring him back in."

"Not yet," Jackson said. His twenty-five years' experience said "wait". DS Belmarsh hadn't found anything incriminating about the dog walker/cleaner. Yes, she'd worked at a dodgy club. Yes, it was run by the Slimowicz's, who were suspected of organized crime links. But that's where it ended. He looked at their wallboard with its photos, connecting lines and questions. They were no closer to solving this. He sighed.

"OK, Sergeant, time to come back to base."

Vanessa's cousin Simon brought them sandwiches and took away the ones Alex had bought. The packet was squashed and damaged. While they ate, Vanessa asked more about Alex's recent experience with the police and being chased through the cemetery. He told her he was staying at Pete's although he didn't like the guy. She told him she enjoyed travelling to exotic places, now lived in the Putney area and was currently studying for a psychology degree. She asked a bit about his interest in ancient Egypt.

"Wait!" she exclaimed. "I've just realized the connection... that girl who was killed in the gas explosion. She was at that Highclere place too, wasn't she? Is she the friend?"

"Yes."

"Oh, poor you."

He shrugged, a little embarrassed, "So you see, I'm pretty jumpy about this whole thing now. I don't think I'll be up to leaving the café for quite a while. Do you think I can stay here until it's dark?"

She thought for a moment. "I've another idea," was all she said as she got up. After speaking in whispers with Simon, she returned with a big smile.

"There's a room upstairs," she explained. "It's a studio flat that my uncle rents out. He's the owner of the building. Anyway, it's empty at the moment. The last tenants moved out a few days ago and it needs redecorating, but... Anyway, come and take a look."

She led Alex through the rear door and up the stairs, past the toilets on the landing. At the top of the next flight was a door.

There was a smell like old cooking fat, but the room looked bright and clean.

"What do you think?" Vanessa asked.

"Nice, but I don't understand."

"You can stay here for a few days. As long as you want in theory... though my uncle will be decorating soon and want to let it out."

"How much?"

She shook her head. "No. No... unless you want to rent it after it's refurbished. Then you can work something out with my uncle. Now, if you'd like to stay, I'll show you where everything is."

The tour didn't take long. The kitchen was at the back of the lounge and she showed him the contents of the drawers and cupboards. There was a small toilet and shower room combined. A bedroom had a double bed that took up most of the space. Apart from that, there was just a sofa and coffee table.

"I'll get you some bedding. I have a spare set at home," she said.

They were standing by the window. The paint was chipped and the glass in severe need of a clean but it would do.

"It's very, very kind of you," he said.

"Great. What about your stuff from Pete's house?"

"To be honest, I don't have much stuff there." Alex shrugged. "Just some clothes... Everything else is at my place in Maida Vale. The main thing at Pete's is my laptop."

Vanessa said, "You're suggesting you go out on the street again—with that thug and a shooter out there? I don't want to be a mother hen but I'm not sure it's safe for you to get your laptop just yet. Maybe we can sort something out."

"What do you mean?"

"I'll go."

"But like you said there's a shooter out there."

"I'll be fine. I'm a bit nervous about it but I'll borrow Simon's coat to look different, even though I doubt anyone's looking for me."

He shook his head. "You make me feel foolish."

"Nonsense! I'll be fine. Make yourself at home and I'll be back in a jiffy with some bedding." She grinned and he wondered what she was planning.

Twenty minutes later she returned with two black bin liners. The first had a duvet and sheets. The second contained clothes. When she handed the bag over, she gave a wry smile that he tried to interpret.

"These were my ex-boyfriend's," she said. "I'm not sure how long you'll want to stay so you'll need something to wear. He was bigger than you, but not too much."

From the bag, Alex put on a blue football shirt. "A Chelsea supporter, I guess. Why are you laughing?"

"The size of the shirt. I guess my ex was bigger than I remember! There's also some hair dye in the bag. Just in case you want to change your image. You'd look very different with black hair." She left him again because she had a lecture to attend, and promised to return later with a takeaway.

Alex first called Nadja to check on Topsy. After being assured that his dog was well and happy, he dyed his hair. At first the colour seemed extreme so he washed it again and again until it resembled something almost natural. Finally, satisfied with the result, he settled on the sofa with his book.

He turned to the contents page and studied the numbers. What was Ellen trying to tell him? What did the code mean? He went through the rest of the book and read the notes he had scribbled in the margins. Nowhere else was there anything that looked like a code.

Taking a break, he stared out of the window and realized Pete would be getting up soon. Maybe he was already up and playing on his Xbox.

Alex sent a text message thanking Pete for the room and hoping he hadn't been inconvenienced. Pete immediately responded, asking if Alex had found somewhere and that he didn't want to know the address.

Staying at Vanessa's, Alex texted back.

Of course, Pete didn't know Vanessa, but the suggestion that he'd moved in with a woman felt like an achievement.

He liked Vanessa and her crooked smile. He'd enjoyed chatting with her even though he was still tense after the incident. He recalled what she'd said about herself and how little he'd really learned, whereas she'd asked him lots of questions and seemed really interested. Could this be some kind of con? He'd read about modern slavery, how it started by someone on their own becoming indebted and then being trapped by financial commitments. He shook the thought from his head. It seemed ridiculous. Vanessa had been through a traumatic event with him; she wanted to help. And she was fascinated by what he had to say. He decided to retain some scepticism and, next time they met, he would make sure she spoke about herself.

There was no TV but Alex used his phone and logged onto the café's Wi-Fi. He found himself reading articles on modern slavery before forcing himself to stop.

It was after eight in the evening when Vanessa returned. She had a white paper carrier bag.

"Chinese for two," she announced, putting it in the galley kitchen. "I hope you like Chinese. I have chicken with yellow bean and cashew nuts, Chinese mixed vegetable and sweet and sour king prawns."

"Sounds great! But after what you have done for me, I should be buying you dinner."

"Another time perhaps," she said with a brief flash of her cute one-sided smile.

"Earlier you told me about studying psychology... as a mature student..."

"I hate that expression. Makes you sound so old! But yes, I'm a mature student, the same as you I guess. When I was young my parents were killed in a car crash... not sure why I told you that, apart from it may explain why I did a lot of travelling as soon as I could." She laughed. "I should psychoanalyze myself!" After a pause she said, "The Chinese—we should start before it gets cold."

She fetched plates from the kitchen and they served up the food. When he sat down and tucked in, he realized she was studying him.

"What?"

She said, "You seemed uncomfortable when I mentioned my parents. It's all right. I've accepted it—my parents getting killed, that is. It happened a long time ago and time heals. Anyway"—that crooked smile again—"I wouldn't be who I am if it hadn't happened, and I am happy with myself and my life."

He nodded. Time did heal. "My dad died... almost twenty years ago now. It doesn't seem that long ago, but yeah, I get it." He ate some more then said, "So where's the best place you've been, since you've travelled so widely?"

"I've been to every continent, though my favourite is Asia. Most people are amazed when I say my second favourite place was Cambodia—it's the image of starvation and the Khmer Rouge that puts people off, but it's such an unspoiled country, with hundreds of amazing temples."

"You said second favourite. What's the first?"

"Thailand. I found a little place on the coast that felt like paradise, hardly any tourists, no pressure, beautiful scenery and lovely people. I could have stayed there for ever."

"But you didn't. You came back."

"It was a nice dream, but I had things to do. I hid away for over four months, but I've promised myself I'll retire there one day."

"And now you're a mature student. Where did you say you were studying your psychology degree?"

She looked serious for a moment. "You're full of questions all of a sudden."

"I…" He choked on a piece of green pepper.

"Alex," she said laughing, "I'm just winding you up. Actually, the degree is politics. Psychology is just a module I'm doing at the moment. I admit I'm a bit embarrassed about politics. Telling people that normally kills conversation dead. Truth is, I'm thinking of becoming a lobbyist for the environmental movement to try and do something, not just about global warming, but more fundamentally about the way we treat nature—to stop expanding at the cost of our rainforests and the quality of our air."

"Very commendable," he said.

They ate in silence for a while before she said, "Any luck with the code?"

"The one in my book that my friend wrote?"

"Yes."

He shrugged, "No. And it's odd because she wasn't really a numbers person. You know, some people are more crossword than sudoku."

"And what are you?"

"Definitely a sudoku guy."

She thought for a moment. "Maybe that's why it's numbers. She's written it precisely because you are that kind of guy." She finished what was on her plate and stood. "I'll leave you to it then."

The announcement was so abrupt that he feared there was something wrong. "Everything all right?" he asked, following her to the stairs.

She gave him her crooked smile. "No. No. It's just that I need to get going." Then she surprised him by affectionately touching his arm. "I have a class in the morning. I'll come over later on."

"That would be nice." Then he paused because of the expression on her face. "What's up?"

"Your hair—it looks fine, almost suits you, but when you spoke, your eyebrows just went up. You need to colour them too! I'll tell you what, I'll bring some mascara with me tomorrow. That'll do the trick. And why don't I pick up your things from your friend's house?"

"Would you?"

"Not a problem. Send me his details and let him know I'll be in touch."

"He works nights."

"Not a problem. Maybe I'll get chance to pick them up in the morning."

They exchanged numbers and he followed her down the stairs, her brown hair tied in a long ponytail swaying across her back.

"Tomorrow, tell me more about your research. When I nipped out earlier I googled your name and Egyptology. You've written a paper on the gods of ancient Egypt. Perhaps you can tell me about it tomorrow?"

"I've hardly made any progress with my own research," he said. "Ellen's research was much more successful, although…"

"Although what?"

He shrugged. "To be honest I'm trying to find out. I think she was onto something but I don't really know what she had discovered. It looks like she linked something between Tutankhamen and Moses."

"Really?"

"Just a possibility. That and some numbers—eight, twelve and forty—that seem to have special meaning."

She opened the door and checked the street before turning back. "Tomorrow," she said, raising a finger, "tell me about your paper, and be careful… be careful you aren't too critical because there's something I'll need to warn you about." Then she slipped out and closed the door behind her.

FIFTEEN

The thing Vanessa had said about crosswords and sudoku played on his mind during the night. If they were a message for him, then Ellen was using numbers to express words. By morning he had it. In a film they'd recently watched together, spies had sent coded messages to one another using a book.

Alex leapt out of bed and snatched up his book and checked the numbers.

259252356124071912

Only now, he saw there were slightly larger gaps between some numbers. Deliberate? He hoped so. The first number was 259, the second 25. Let's see. He turned to page 259 and counted 25 lines. The next number was 2. He circled the second word on the line.

Isis

"Bloody hell!" Alex said out loud. Ellen had a fascination with the goddess Isis and it couldn't be a coincidence. The code was a triumvirate of page, line and word numbers. He marked it up.

259-25-2/356-1-2/407-19-12

Alex turned to page 356 and read the second word: is
On page 407 the word was key.

"My God, she's telling me Isis is the key!"

He paced the room. What did that mean? And then a thought struck him: sudoku not crossword. He texted Vanessa:

When you manage to get my stuff from Pete's, please check there's a phone as well as my laptop.

A moment later she replied:

Already been and dropped off with Simon. See you later.

Alex dressed quickly and rushed down to the café. It was almost seven in the morning and already busy. The smell of sizzling sausages and bacon was intoxicating.

"Morning," Simon called. He scooted out from behind the counter and dropped Alex's bag on the floor. "Cooked breakfast for you?"

"And coffee, please," Alex said as he opened his bag. Everything was inside: clothes, laptop and Ellen's phone.

Not Isis.

Numbers not letters.

He keyed in 1515 as the code.

The phone unlocked.

Alex spent the morning going through Ellen's emails on the phone. He'd hoped there would be a special message for him, probably in the *Drafts* folder. But there was nothing. His second expectation was to find a critical message about her research in the emails. Some were personal and many related to her interest in Egyptology but nothing jumped out as important. After almost two hours of reading and re-reading, he gave up.

When Vanessa knocked on his door he was browsing research papers about Isis on the Internet. She had a large cafetiere full of steaming coffee and a couple of mugs.

"Thanks for the bag," he said. "I hope it wasn't any trouble."

"You're welcome, and no trouble at all." She gave him a wry smile. "I didn't see anyone suspicious, although I can't say I liked your friend."

"Not really a friend."

"Everything all right?" she asked. "You seem sad this morning, if you don't mind me saying."

He shrugged. "It's just... Well, I worked out the code. You were right that the numbers related to words." He fished out Ellen's phone. "The clue was Isis."

She looked concerned.

"Not the Islamic State!" He laughed. "The goddess Isis. I translated it to 1515 and it unlocked my friend's phone, but either I'm missing something or it wasn't the big clue I supposed."

They sat and she plunged the coffee.

"Tell me about your paper... the one on religion."

"Yesterday you warned me to be careful. What did you mean?"

She smiled. "I'm Jewish. I know, it's not obvious, but I'm not Orthodox, not practising. But I am interested. I know there's a connection between Judaism and ancient Egypt, so I'm interested to hear that side of it, if you know anything. Over and above the Exodus and Moses stories, that is. Whenever there's talk of ancient Egypt and religion, it's often used in an anti-Semitic way."

She poured the coffee and seemed to be watching for his response.

"Well, I can assure you I'm not anti-Semitic, though I understand. You do know that the name Hebrew probably comes from the Egyptian word *Ibiru*? It means people who have stepped outside the law."

"There are other explanations."

"I'm sure. My article wasn't anything particularly new, but it was about the pharaoh called Akhenaten. He was the one who supposedly believed in the-one-true-god and it's thought his followers were *Ibiru* because of his beliefs."

103

"Ark-en-ar-tun..." She shrugged. "Can't say I've heard of him before."

"Akhenaten was Tutankhamen's father. He is often referred to as the heretic pharaoh because of his belief in a single god. Sigmund Freud... of course you'll know he was Jewish... was the first to suggest that Akhenaten was the pharaoh linked to Moses and..."

She laughed. "You couldn't help yourself, could you? I said no mention of Exodus."

He held up his hand: guilty as charged.

They talked for a couple of hours, first about the similarity of Akhenaten's religion and the Bible and then more generally about gods. The Ten Commandments was like a negative version of the *Book of the Dead*—a set of spells to prove ones worth for the afterlife. *I have not killed* became *Thou shalt not kill*.

"Your article said the number of gods multiplied over time," Vanessa said, returning to the piece she had read.

"Initially nine, headed by Ra, god of the sun. By three thousand BCE there were forty-two gods. As I wrote, the later ones were mostly derivations of the originals. Religion was big business, so you can imagine the shock when Akhenaten said there was only one god. He called him the Aten. Aten was basically the sun disc just before sunset."

"So Aten was Ra."

"I believe so."

"You mentioned Isis earlier. Where does she fit in?"

"Isis was the goddess of many things, including love and fertility. She was symbolized by either a throne or a vulture—they were revered for the protection of their young." Alex continued to tell her about other goddesses Nekhbet and Hathor who appeared later for childbirth and motherhood but were both symbolized by vultures in some form. "Just derivations of Isis," he said.

After a break for lunch in the café, Vanessa said, "So who was Osiris?"

"He was Isis's husband and, according to some versions, he was the son of Ra. He was the first mummified pharaoh and became the god of the afterlife. By the New Kingdom, there was a god called Amun-Min, who had been a soldier. After losing a leg in battle he returned home. On the way he made love to every lonely woman he met and fathered hundreds of children."

"And that made him a god?"

"Of fertility," Alex said. "He was caught and killed by the husbands but, even in death, the one-legged soldier still had an erection. He is depicted as a mummy with a large penis.'

"Ridiculous." She laughed. He liked the way her eyes sparked with interest and crinkled at the edges. "And what's that got to do with Osiris?"

"Osiris was murdered by his enemy, who chopped him up. Isis found the parts—including his penis—mummified his body and made love to him. She got pregnant."

Vanessa pulled a face. "Only a god!"

Alex said, "The stories would have been re-enacted for the masses and been great titillation. Anyway, side on, the mummy of Osiris appears to have one leg..."

"Like the one-legged soldier."

"Exactly! It would also not be surprising that Osiris would be shown in profile with a penis. So I'm pretty sure that Amun-Min was a derivation of Osiris."

"Reasonable."

Alex told her some more of the ancient stories until she checked her watch and jumped up. "Oops! I've a lecture in half an hour."

"You'd better be going."

She started down the stairs. "See you later, but no more stories about sex!"

Alex picked up Ellen's phone and opened the email app. He re-read ones that didn't seem personal. Finding nothing of interest, he tried the *Trash* folder. There were lots of mailing list offers and what looked like spam, but a few emails attracted his attention. The first was an email sent to Professor Thompson at Oxford University requesting a meeting to discuss Lord Carnarvon's death and items taken from Tutankhamen's tomb.

Alex copied his email address and sent the professor a note asking him to get in touch.

The second email of interest was confirmation of registration on a website called EgyptConfidential. It provided a link to the login page and Ellen's username. Her password was in the next deleted email.

On his laptop Alex signed into the website, which had a forum. Her username was Senemut, and she had exchanged emails with three people from the site: Sinuhe, Khaemhet and Mutnodjemet. The emails discussed various theories, but nothing struck him as relevant. He went into the account settings and changed Ellen's email address to his own. Then he sent a message via the site to each of the three contacts asking how they were. Nothing to frighten them off. Just to get them to respond. He signed it using Ellen's Senemut identity. If anyone responded he would get an email as well as a message on the site.

Alex checked his email to confirm his sent message also appeared, and it did. As he deleted it, another email arrived: a response from The Griffith Institute, St Anthony's College. Oxford.

Professor Thompson no longer worked there.

The Second

SIXTEEN

Razor, the man Alex knew as Aviator, sat in *The Pie Crust* café in the East End district of London. Sitting in the café was where the gang did their best thinking, so that's where he'd gone—to do some thinking. He'd eaten an unhealthy all-day cooked breakfast, just the way he liked it; none of this fancy American franchise rubbish at American franchise prices. It was late afternoon and it was already dark outside.

The items from Highclere Castle were stashed in a warehouse. Razor's job had been to deal with their inside man, but he'd screwed up with the gas explosion. Lemmy's job had been to trace the missing item but the boss had assigned him to following MacLure. Gazza's job was to sort the good stuff from the fake and co-ordinate the next phase with the boss. Gazza was the fence. When they were ready he would offload the items—and with his skill he'd pass off some of the fakes as the real thing.

He tried Lemmy's mobile but it went straight to voicemail. Gazza wasn't available and you didn't ring the boss. He rang you.

Razor doodled on the back page of *The Sun* newspaper as he thought. Lemmy had followed MacLure through Hammersmith but hadn't called in for a couple of days.

Had something happened to him or had he simply fallen off the waggon? In Gazza's view, Lemmy was unreliable.

So the boss had put him on the case. They had known where MacLure was holed up and he had followed the target to Putney Bridge.

There hadn't been much time, but the guy didn't react like he knew anything. Maybe he didn't. Maybe there wasn't anything to know. Jeez! What if their source had been mistaken? What if he'd been lying?

It didn't make sense. There was no reason for the source to lie. He had wanted a share of the big payday. He was convinced the Champion girl knew where the treasure was. She had solved something. It was just a matter of following the clues.

And who the hell had shot him? He thought about the wound on his shoulder—just a graze. He'd had much worse.

Did MacLure have someone protecting him? Unlikely. The way he ran off, it looked like he was scared for his life.

Was there another gang after the treasure? Razor wrote *Gang* on the newspaper and circled it numerous times until the pen tore through the paper. Could the source have another gang involved? Let them do the dirty work and then take the glory?

They had her notes—he'd found them in her briefcase. The main thing was drawings of the item that looked like a box with marks and Egyptian writing. Gazza had called it an *artefact*. However, there was no indication of size. He imagined it to be like a shallow music box.

He finished his meal and looked at the scribble in case he received some divine inspiration. It was just scribble, with the words *Gang, Lemmy, the source* and *MacLure* most prominent. He would keep hoping Lemmy would get in touch, but the only action he could think of was to contact the source. The whole thing had been his idea so maybe he would know where MacLure had gone. Maybe he would know what to do next. Yes, that was the plan.

As he turned into Bridge Road, heading for West Ham, a car horn sounded. Some idiot had cut across the traffic. Bloody typical, it's a BMW, Razor thought as he saw the offending black car. He shook his head and turned back the way he was going. After ten paces, something in the corner of his eye made him swivel with alarm.

The car drove slowly by. Two men inside, and both seemed to glance his way.

What the fuck? Razor glared at the driver: an *A-rab* by the look of his skin. The car continued and, after it disappeared into another street, he wondered whether his imagination was playing tricks, whether he was just being jumpy. It was the police he needed to keep an eye out for.

"Excuse me, I'm lost."

Razor snapped out of his thoughts. The BMW was right there alongside him. The driver had his window down and was leaning out.

"Can you help us find the Olympic park?"

As he bent to give the guy some abuse, Razor realized the passenger seat was empty.

Too late.

He heard a sound behind him. As he spun, a cosh connected with the side of his face.

The next thing he knew, he was waking up with a pain in his shoulders as he dangled from a rope tied around his wrists. He glanced down at his naked body. A rivulet of blood ran down his left leg and ended at the rope around his feet. He smelled oil and judged the room to be an empty garage. The Arab from the BMW stood an arm's length away, a tyre-iron in his hand.

Razor looked into the man's cold eyes and knew then that this wasn't a matter of how he survived this, but how long he held out.

When Vanessa returned, she brought a pizza takeaway menu. After they ordered, she asked about his afternoon.

"Any closer to finding what Ellen's research at Highclere was?'

"I don't think so. I found a web forum she was on discussing mysteries and theories."

She seemed intrigued. "Like?"

"There's stuff about where Akhenaten's body is buried and what happened to his queen—Nefertiti."

"I've heard of her."

"Which is odd—that people have heard of his queen but not Akhenaten."

"She was supposed to be beautiful, wasn't she? What happened to her?"

"I don't know about beautiful. She disappeared from the records about two-thirds of the way through his reign. If she'd died she would have been about thirty. There's an unidentified mummy referred to as the Elder Lady who could be her. Some think she may have become co-regent and changed her name. There's a stone bust of her in the Berlin Museum and some people think she looks over fifty."

"That's fascinating. So she probably didn't die young after all. But why would she pretend to have died at thirty?"

"Maybe someone else wanted to erase her legacy after that?"

Vanessa nodded thoughtfully. "So did Nefertiti also believe in one god?"

"She has what's called a *gate* at the temple complex at Karnak in Luxor. Pharaohs had them built as statements of their religious worth. They look a bit like triumphal arches. Nefertiti's is unusual because she wasn't a pharaoh, and it was destroyed in antiquity. Anyway, the thing is it's now been rebuilt and there are reference on it to many of the gods. So it's unlikely she just believed in one—at least when the arch was built."

The pizzas arrived and they opened the boxes on the table and shared them.

Alex felt mischievous. He said, "God has many names. The sun god Ra also had many names. Just like the God of Judaism: Jehovah, Elohim, Yahweh—"

"You could also list Tzevaot, El, Elyon, Avinu, Adonai and Shaddai, although many of those so-called names are really just titles."

Alex continued: "When a pharaoh died, the priests chanted the *Litany of Ra*. This was calling upon the sun god in all his seventy-five names to look after the pharaoh in the afterlife. As I said, I think Aten was one of these. Akhenaten's father called Him Ra-Horakhty."

"And you said he believed in just one god?"

"Not necessarily. Even if Aten was an aspect of Ra it doesn't mean Akhenaten only worshipped one god." Alex paused while he ate a slice of pizza.

"There's evidence that he erased the name of the god Amun—the hidden one—from the temple at Thebes. But I think that was more political, or perhaps even a lack of faith. Maybe he was disillusioned. You see, Akhenaten was raised to be a priest of Amun. He was the second son and never expected to become pharaoh. Anyway, Akhenaten didn't erase the names of the other gods, and their temples continued to be supported during his reign. At Amarna, where he had his palace and Aten temple, archaeologists have found evidence of multiple gods. They also found plans for a cemetery for bulls. The bull and a rock called the Benben stone were representative of belief in the god Ptah. The stone was in the temple of the Aten. That seems like a contradiction, and it's certainly inconsistent for someone who allegedly only worshipped one god."

"So you don't think this pharaoh was the founder of monotheism and hence Judeo-Christianity."

"That was Sigmund Freud's theory. Effectively, that god was the sun god. But, as I said, there's lots of evidence that Akhenaten didn't believe in just one god."

"OK." She looked uncertain.

"Well, why is there so much about him believing in one god? It's almost as though there's a move to convince people that the idea of God originated from an Egyptian pharaoh."

Before she left him for the night she said, "Tomorrow I think we do two things: one, we get you outside. It's about time you saw the sky again. There's been no sign of the aviator-guy. It's just a matter of how you're feeling. Will you do it?"

"OK. What's the second thing?"

"You mentioned your friend's research linking Moses to numbers."

"Yes."

"Numbers are very important to Judaism. Maybe understanding them will help understand her research."

"Not a bad idea."

"Great," she said. "In that case I'll introduce you to my uncle."

SEVENTEEN

Jackson and Belmarsh showed their ID and a constable lifted the cordon for them. They were outside a warehouse in the East End of London. Everywhere looked grey in the early morning light.

"I don't get it," Belmarsh said with a yawn. "Who called this in?"

"Anonymous tipoff during the night," Jackson said. He spotted the Met's OIC and raised a hand.

The detective came over, a sour look on his face. "What the hell is this?"

Jackson introduced himself and his sergeant. "You've found the Highclere Castle stolen goods, I understand."

The OIC introduced himself as DI Spears. "This is much more than your stolen goods I'm afraid. We've got a triple murder investigation going on here." He paused for a moment and then said, "OK, we'll keep our distance and I'll show you."

The building had crates and forklift equipment, all clearly disused. Huge lights hung from the rafters along with chains and pulleys. Judging from the dust and rust, the place had been abandoned years ago. There was a partition midway, and beyond that the rear of the warehouse was in deep shade, although there was a glow from the far right.

"No power," Spears explained as he led them towards the darkness. There was a series of offices at the very back. The end one on the right was lit by portable lights, with SOCO officers visible in their blue plastic suits.

"The three bodies are in the office," Spears said. "The goods are over here." On the left, an officer stood by three piles of boxes.

She nodded to the OIC. "The items seem to be separated into what looks fake and what looks genuine." She shone a torch over the closest box and used a pen to lift the flaps. Inside was a six-inch stone figure. "Genuine," she said.

Belmarsh said, "Are you an expert?"

The officer grinned.

Spears said, "We have a list. The thieves typed up a list of the contents and split it into 'genuine', 'fake' and 'appears genuine'. We reckon this was to determine the potential market."

Jackson nodded. "We have our own list." He turned to Belmarsh. "Check this list off against ours." To Spears he said, "Tell me about the bodies."

They left Belmarsh with the Met officer, and Spears led the way to the end office. They stood at the grimy window. The spotlights showed three bodies. One had been shot execution-style, and blood pooled dark around his head. The other two were lying alongside. One had no marks and the other was naked with cuts and burns all over his skin.

"They were under the tarpaulin," Spears said. "Initial assessment is that we have one killed in situ. The naked one appears to have been tortured and dumped here. The middle one was shot once in the head, once in the torso. Classic double tap. No blood on site so, again, killed elsewhere and dumped with the others."

He looked at Jackson. "What can you tell me?"

"Nothing," Jackson said. "If these are the Highclere burglars—and everything points to it—then why are they all dead?"

"Unless there was a fourth and he killed the others."

"Possible, I suppose." Jackson looked at the bodies. "No. Someone wanted information. They caught the naked guy and tortured him to find the others and this warehouse. Maybe the executed one led them here. Whoever did this didn't want the stolen goods but they wanted us to find them." Jackson shook his head. This was a weird case.

"Sir..." Belmarsh came over with a sheaf of papers. She hesitated a heartbeat as she glanced at the grim sight inside the end office. "Jesus! Do you think they're the burglars?"

Jackson nodded.

"And responsible for Ellen Champion's death?"

"Possible. I'd even say highly probable." To Spears he said, "We should get the investigators linked up—could be some connection to the girl killed by a gas explosion near where the goods were stolen."

"About the goods," Belmarsh said. "Everything the Estate and museum confirmed missing ticks off against the records here. All except for one. It's described as a ceremonial funerary block."

"A what?" asked Spears.

"No idea," Belmarsh said. "But I can assure you we will be finding out."

Fox sat in a café and looked out of the window at the cordoned-off warehouse. The Met police had been on the scene within twenty minutes of his anonymous call. The scene of crimes van arrived another twenty minutes later with their power cables and lights. Jackson and his sergeant drove up in his silver Vauxhall after another hour. He guessed they had battled through rush hour to get across London.

Perfect.

He pressed the speed dial. "All gone according to plan," he reported.

Owl said, "Did they know?"

"Some, but not all. Not nearly enough."

116

The other man said nothing but Fox was sure he heard relief in the breathing. He added: "And I've got the girl's papers—the ones they must have taken from her briefcase. She had made drawings of the artefact and taken notes about the hieroglyphs."

"Enough for us to work from?" There was real excitement in his voice.

"I think so. Now that we know this is the map, it should just be a matter of time."

"That's good."

"Although one thing bothers me. We know about the communications, but there's nothing in her notes. In fact, I worry that most of the research is missing."

"Like you say, let's hope it's just a matter of us solving this and putting it to bed once and for all."

Fox found himself nodding at his own reflection. This thing had been hanging over them for almost a hundred years. It would be a great honour to be the one who removed the threat, finally.

Jackson and Belmarsh came out of the warehouse, ducked under the cordon and got into the Vauxhall.

"Fox?"

"Yes?"

"What about the rabbit?"

"He should be in the clear now. They'll get all the evidence they need to wrap this up."

The man on the other end didn't say anything for a while. His breathing rasped. Then he said, "Keep him in play. In case he can find the bird's research."

"I'll use the reporter again. Feed her information about links between the rabbit and the Polish mafia. She'll lap it up and it'll support their theories."

"Good."

"And if the rabbit doesn't find the research?"

"Either way, you eliminate him."

EIGHTEEN

In the morning, Alex received an email. Not an Oxford University email address, but it was from the professor.

Dear Mr MacLure

Please accept my apologies for not picking up your email straight away. I have retired from my post at The Griffith Institute, St Anthony's College, Oxford. The email address is still active but I have to log on to the computer to check for messages.

Regarding your query, it has been some considerable time since I reviewed the private papers collection and I am sure you appreciate that the suggestion of missing papyri from the tomb of Tutankhamen is nothing new. However, I found your enquiry intriguing.

I would greatly enjoy revisiting the old documents and have reviewed a communication with the curator at New York's Metropolitan Museum of Arts.

I would enjoy discussing my findings with you and will be able to arrange for you to view the collection as requested.

I look forward to hearing from you again.

Yours sincerely

Emeritus Professor Christopher L Thompson

There was a phone number at the bottom and Alex immediately called it.

"Professor Thompson," a strong voice answered after the eighth ring.

"Professor, it's Alex MacLure."

"Goodness gracious, I only sent you a message earlier this morning." There was a pause followed by a slight chuckle. "Ah. You must excuse an old man. You know, I can't get used to this Interweb thing. My daughter has taught me to use a computer and this electronic post, but perhaps I should just stick to good old pen and paper?"

"Professor, I would like to arrange that visit."

"Oh yes. The visit to see Howard Carter's original notes. They are very interesting, you know. And as I said in my message, I think there is possibly some truth in what you are suggesting. In fact, I obtained—"

"Could I come tomorrow?"

"Tomorrow?" Thompson said after a hesitation.

"I really would appreciate it, sir, if you could arrange for us to meet tomorrow."

"Goodness gracious, you young people are always in such a hurry. Well, let us see. Yes, all right, if you meet me at the institute at 11am I will arrange for access."

With renewed purpose, Alex read through computer notes and Internet documents on the discovery of Tutankhamen's tomb. In Ellen's original email to the professor, she had suggested inconsistencies in the records. There was something suspicious about the events following the discovery of Tutankhamen's tomb and the death of Lord Carnarvon.

NINETEEN

It was mid-morning when Vanessa came in.

"How are you feeling about going out? Still up for it?"

"Ready and willing."

"Great! Sorry I'm later than I planned. I had things to do." She pulled a small black tube from a purse. "Before we go," she said, and waved it at him, "I'm doing those eyebrows."

She made Alex sit so she could apply mascara to colour his eyebrows. When she'd finished, she said, "Perfect!"

He looked in the mirror and had to agree that the dark eyebrows looked better.

Stepping outside, he couldn't help glancing up and down the street.

Vanessa pointed to a little black and purple Smart car parked across the street. "I've brought my car."

He was quickly inside and immediately felt better. As she drove she said, "I had to finish an essay this morning. It took longer than I expected. But there's no one following, I'm sure."

"So we're going to see your uncle?"

"Yes, and then we're having a picnic in Richmond Park"

Vanessa focused on the road for a while and Alex found himself looking in the side mirror for a tail. When they were stopped in traffic, she told him to adjust it so he could see better.

By the time they reached their destination of Fitzroy Square, Alex was calm. There had been no sign of anyone following.

The square had a central garden with trees surrounded by upmarket Regency-style properties: a tranquil enclave that said *money*.

Vanessa led the way through a black door into an office and introduced herself to the receptionist. They were shown through to what the receptionist described as a meeting room. Alex expected a formal table and chairs and was surprised to find themselves in a lounge with comfortable leather armchairs and a low table laden with a coffee pot, cups and biscuits.

The receptionist hovered by the door. "Please help yourself to coffee. I'll let Mr Abrahams know you are here."

Vanessa poured the drinks and they sank back into the chairs and waited.

Alex checked his watch after twenty minutes. Vanessa shrugged.

"Sorry, he's a busy man."

Seconds later the door swung inwards and a large man entered with a beaming smile. "Vanessa, how nice of you to call on me." His voice was thick, possibly from years of smoke abuse, and he used a cane to walk but, although Alex guessed him to be in his sixties, he had a barrel chest and big presence.

"Uncle Seth." Vanessa jumped up as he came in and, after he'd taken three steps, she met him halfway. He gave her a bear hug and she kissed his cheek.

Abrahams studied Alex, who stood. "So this is the young man."

Alex introduced himself and Abrahams indicated they should all sit. He checked his watch. "I've not got long I'm afraid."

"I know, Uncle." She grinned. "Alex and I—well he's been telling me about ancient Egypt and gods and I thought you'd be interested to meet."

Abrahams's eyes smiled. "I'm always happy to be of service." He looked at Alex, more serious now. "So this PhD you are doing, what's the research about?"

"My current interest is in the pre-dynastic period, particularly the boats of Abydos, but this isn't about me."

"Oh?" Abrahams looked at Vanessa and then back.

"Sorry, sir, I should explain. It's about my friend's research."

"I don't understand. Why can't your friend do his own research?"

Vanessa stepped in, "It's a long story, Uncle—and complicated."

"All right. What is your friend researching?"

"Communication during the New Kingdom—especially hidden messages, it would seem—and some things have come up that may be relevant."

"Particularly about the significance of numbers to Jews," Vanessa said. "I know you may be able to help there."

"Ah." Abrahams sat a little more forward in his chair, waiting.

Alex said, "I understand that the Bible—sorry, the Torah—has hidden messages based on numerology."

"You're talking about gematria," Abrahams said, "the interpretation of words as numbers. Like Nero Caesar being 666, the number of the beast." The old man chuckled. "There are different methods and different interpretations, but the traditional view is that the codes should only apply to the Torah in an exact letter by letter sequence rather than looking for patterns. Of course, the Torah was the only text communicated directly from God through Moses. What numbers are you particularly interested in?"

"How about forty?"

"That's not gematria. Forty is a significant number in the Torah: Moses spent forty days on Mount Sinai. In Genesis it rains for forty days and forty nights. The Israelites wandered in the wilderness for forty years. Elijah fasted for forty days..."

"So would I be right in saying it's not meant as literal."

Abrahams inclined his head.

"What about the numbers three, four and five?"

"Three represents completeness and stability. Five represents stability. Of course, the Torah is also known as the five books of Moses. There are five divisions to the Psalms and other texts. Four is less interesting, although recurs a lot: the number of questions, matriarchs, and angels that surround the Throne of Glory, kingdoms of eschaton, sages who enter paradise. But you mentioned these together so I'll tell you about three and four. Seven is one of the most powerful numbers, representing creation and good fortune. In gematria, *Gad*—which means luck—is seven. *Mazal*—which also means luck—is seventy-seven."

"And twelve?"

"Of course, there were twelve tribes of Israel, and in gematria it's represented by totality. Any more?"

"Last number: eight."

"Last but not least," Abrahams said. "The number eight is *Shleimus*, which means completion, or perhaps wholeness would be a closer translation. Bris milah is the eighth day."

Vanessa whispered, "Circumcision."

"*Chanukah*—the festival of rededication—is eight days. The *Mishkan* was dedicated on the eighth day."

"Mishkan?"

Vanessa said, "The Tabernacle. The dwelling place created by Moses."

Abrahams added: "After Israel sinned with the golden calf they were forgiven. The Tabernacle was the sign of the renewed closeness between God and his people."

"Can I ask you about Moses?" When the older man nodded, Alex continued: "I'm intrigued about when he led the Israelites out of Egypt. The Bible refers to the pharaoh as Pharaoh. No specifics."

"The accepted wisdom says it was Ramses II."

That was later than Alex had expected. Ramses was from the dynasty after Akhenaten and Tutankhamen. "People often talk about the Jews working in slavery to build the pyramids. But Genesis refers to chariots, not once but three times. Egyptians didn't have chariots until the Eighteenth Dynasty. This means the earliest the Exodus could have happened is Sixteenth Century BCE. About two thousand years after the pyramids."

"Ramses is said to have built two cities. In the Passover Seder, we talk about the Jews building store cities called Pithom and Pi-Ramesses. Not pyramids, I'll grant you, but it could have been forced labour."

"What about Moses' name?"

"It was the Egyptian name he was given." Abrahams shook his head. "I'm unsure of your point."

"Well, let's take Ramses, as an example. The name was probably pronounced more like Ra-Moses. Moses means 'born of'. Ra-Moses—born of the god Ra. Thoth-Moses—born of the god Thoth. It's similar to the 'son' we use at the end of surnames today. So, like the name of the pharaoh of the Bible, the name Moses also tells us nothing."

There was a knock on the door, which opened, and a young man poked his head around. "Sir, I have Goldmans on the line. It's that urgent call you've been waiting for."

Abrahams stood, using the cane to push himself out of the soft leather. He held out his hand and gripped Alex's with surprising strength.

"Interesting to meet you," he said. "If I can help further—particularly if you have any more numbers you'd like interpreting—please let me know. However, I must take this call."

"A final question," Alex said, realizing something. "When was the first Hebrew text written?"

"About three thousand years ago, I believe. I'm sorry…" Abrahams bade farewell and entered a lift with the assistant.

Vanessa drove out of the city. Thirty minutes later she stopped in Richmond Park. Turning the engine off, she swivelled and studied his face. The closeness and intensity of her look sent an unexpected charge through his veins.

"Do you think my uncle helped?" She was still close and he breathed in her perfume.

"It's food for thought. I certainly understand gematria better now, although, if there's some secret code in the Bible, it seems it relates to a later period than Ellen was interested in. Nice that he offered to work out the meaning if I find something."

She turned, breaking the spell between them. When she got out of the car she retrieved a small hamper from the tiny luggage compartment. "Lunch. Come on, I know a nice spot to sit."

She refused his help, and as they walked she said, "I saw a documentary last night about a pharaoh queen."

"Cleopatra or Hatshepsut?"

"Hatshepsut. It was about identifying her mummy using a broken tooth."

"She wasn't a queen of course. All pharaohs were kings, whether male or female. She reigned over a hundred years before Akhenaten and was probably the stepmother of his great-great grandfather."

"I remember they said she tried to establish herself as the pharaoh. Oh, and she had a secret lover. He was the architect of her tomb and built his own nearby. It had a connecting tunnel so that they could be together in the afterlife." She saw Alex smiling. "What's funny?"

"He was called Senemut—it's the ancient Egyptian name that my friend gave herself on an academic forum."

He wondered if Vanessa was going to comment on Ellen using a man's identity. Instead, she said, "It's very romantic: being together for eternity." She paused then said, "The documentary was billed as the last great mystery."

When she paused, he thought she had flashed her dark eyes. But her manner was suddenly matter-of-fact again. He said, "Not really, there are lots of unanswered questions. I agree they think it's the first confirmed mummy since Tutankhamen's found almost eighty years ago. Most of the royal mummies are missing, either stolen or hidden from tomb robbers." He sat on a tartan rug she laid on the ground. "But there are lot's more mysteries—I know Ellen wondered what happened to Akhenaten and Nefertiti." He saw a spark of interest in her dark brown eyes.

"That's interesting. Something else you know about her research."

"I guess, though she never mentioned discovering anything."

"But would she have?" She held up a hand to stop him answering straight away. "If she was about to crack a great mystery, maybe she would keep it to herself?"

"Maybe."

"Any progress with her big clue: ISIS?"

"Well, you know 1515 unlocked the phone. And there was an interesting email."

Vanessa waited expectantly.

"Long story short: I've been in touch with a professor at Oxford. Ellen had been in touch with him about one of the mysteries surrounding the discovery of Tutankhamen's tomb. The professor has access to private papers of Carter, Carnarvon and others of the time."

"Carnarvon." She looked eager. "So that would explain why Ellen was so interested in working at Highclere, right?"

"More important than going on a dig, yes."

She leaned forward. "So...?"

"Probably just me, but talking of significant numbers, Lord Carnarvon died in 1923, April the fifth." He paused. "Think about that date: Two... three... four... five."

She grinned. "Yes, that's probably just you. I know he died because of the mummy's curse."

"And he had a mark on his cheek just like Tutankhamen's," Alex said dramatically. "Seriously though, even if you believe in curses, there were none. Tombs didn't have curses. It was all made up—media hype—and later milked by Carter and the others for financial gain."

"But why? Carter must have been a multimillionaire after finding all that treasure."

Alex smiled. "You'd be surprised. Carnarvon was the financier, Carter the employee. They spent thirteen years trying to find the tomb. Then in 1922 they ran out of money, but Carter carried on, agreeing a final year's effort. Luckily he found the tomb that November. Carnarvon returned from the UK and the following February they opened the doorway to Tutankhamen's burial chamber. The state immediately swooped, after changing the law, and claimed everything. All the treasure belonged to Egypt and the archaeologists got nothing for their troubles."

"So Carter didn't become rich?"

"Not immediately. But six weeks later Carnarvon was dead, allegedly from pneumonia and septicaemia from an infected mosquito bite."

From the hamper she removed a selection of ready-made sandwiches and cartons of fruit juice. She shrugged apologetically.

"It's great," he said, selecting a crayfish and rocket sandwich.

"Back to Carnarvon then," she prompted. "So the curse was made up?"

"I think that was all for the newspapers. They were going crazy with the excitement of the find, and the theory of Tutankhamen taking revenge was just something else to be lapped up. It also helped Carter, who made his fortune from selling his story and doing an international roadshow."

Alex's phone rang, but he ignored it.

He continued: "I'm hoping the trip to Oxford will prompt something. I'm going tomorrow."

Vanessa said, "Oh that's a shame. I'd come with you but I've got other plans."

Alex's phone rang again. He pulled it from a pocket. Number withheld. He answered.

A voice said, "You aren't at the address in Hammersmith."

"Detective Dixit, how nice of you to call."

Dixit ignored the sarcasm. "Where are you, Mr MacLure?"

"At this moment I'm having a picnic in Richmond Park... with a pretty girl." He winked at Vanessa, who responded with her cute crooked smile.

"Tell me your whereabouts exactly. I'll be there as soon as I can. You said you wanted to help. Well, we would like your help now."

Alex smiled. "Of course, but meet me where I'm staying." He gave Dixit the address of Simon's café and suggested they meet in an hour.

"Great," Dixit said. "Then we can talk. It's about the missing item."

TWENTY

DC Dixit looked like a defeated man as he entered Simon's café. He sat at Alex's table and ordered a white coffee.

"What's up?" Alex prompted.

"Why didn't you tell us you had moved?"

Alex studied the detective and wondered why he seemed so angry. It had only been a couple of days and it wasn't as though he was trying to hide from the police. "I just hadn't got round to it. It wasn't deliberate and I'm happy to help with your investigation. You called me. I answered. I'm here now."

Dixit grunted. "Have you seen the latest article by your pal Milwanee?" When Alex said he hadn't, the detective continued. "She's claiming to have evidence of links between you and the Polish mafia. Are there any?"

"Absolutely not!"

They sat in silence for a while as Alex read the article on his smartphone. Aysha Milwanee reported that Alex was suspected of aiding the break-in at Highclere and that the plan was to sell the items on to the Polish. It mentioned the crime scene in the East End and the discovery of all of the stolen items as well as three bodies. All executed.

"That triple murder in West Ham… is that linked?"

Dixit said, "It certainly looks like that's the gang who stole everything."

"I don't get it," Alex said eventually.

"Quite honestly, I don't care if you get it. More importantly, though, the case has been taken over by the NCA. They've got it because of organized crime and it's being considered as gang war."

Alex finished his own drink and let his annoyance die down. "So, Detective, you wanted to see me—it's about something else, isn't it?"

Dixit's eyes twitched and he straightened as though trying to hide his state of mind. He forced a smile. "First of all, I have an update for you. We believe we have identified the person responsible for Ellen Champion's death."

"Who?"

"One of the victims in West Ham. His DNA was found on Ellen's skin."

Alex tried to shake the image from his mind. The guy had touched her. What had he done? Alex desperately wanted details but at the same time he didn't. Eventually he just said, "That's good news."

"Yes."

Then it occurred to Alex that if the case was solved and the gang's murder was being investigated by the NCA, what was Dixit doing here? "There's something else."

Dixit's eyes twitched again.

Alex waited for a customer to pass the table out of earshot before he leaned forward and said, "Come on, man. Let's stop playing games. If you are no longer interested in the murder, what's this about?"

"Stolen goods."

Alex shook his head. "You don't still think I was involved in the burglary?"

Dixit hesitated then said, "No, I don't." Emphasis on the *I.* "Let me run this by you. The gang disabled the cameras and got in through the emergency exit. They took some stuff from the main exhibit, although they didn't take King Tut's bust or the golden woman statue."

"Isis. The statue is of the goddess Isis. But they're so obviously fake. There was no security alarm on the statue. If it had been solid gold, it'd have had a permanent guard, I suspect. So they left them because they weren't stupid."

"Yes, they appear to have had at least some knowledge of what was genuine." All of a sudden, Dixit looked serious. "There's a small room after the black curtains. A room with the small artefacts in display cabinets—all around one side and a couple of free-standing ones."

"That's actually the first exhibit." Now Alex returned the seriousness. "Detective, why don't you just tell me straight?"

Dixit thought for a moment. "All right. They took all the stuff in that small room. It seems that was their main target, although they showed their knowledge of artefacts elsewhere because they took all the genuine British Museum stuff."

"And?"

"The important thing is not what we've recovered but what we haven't. The British Museum have identified everything that's theirs. It's the Highclere Estate that report an item missing."

Suddenly it made sense. The thug with the aviator sunglasses had wanted to know where the other item was. Alex said, "Jesus! The gang didn't steal everything. There was something missing!"

"That's what it looks like."

"What is it?"

Dixit pulled out a notebook and checked it. "The Estate describe it as a ceremonial funerary block." He made the shape of something about a foot square and a hand's grip deep. I'm not sure what that means, but the Estate say it's genuine but not particularly valuable."

"I know which one you're talking about. It was for the embalming process, the preparation of the body prior to

131

mummification. A religious artefact. A block of stone with ruts and holes for collecting and separating bodily fluids."

Dixit pulled a face. "Sounds like the description."

Alex pictured the religious artefact in his mind. "Surely it was a mistake. Like you say, it's not especially valuable or interesting. Could the gang have taken it and it's just not been found?" As he said it, he knew it didn't make sense. "Or is the Estate mistaken?"

Dixit said, "We're pretty sure the gang never had it. They catalogued everything else. As for the Estate making a mistake, I don't know. Of course, there's another option."

"Which is?"

"That you took it when you snuck in a few days before the robbery."

Alex could tell the detective didn't believe it. His body language was all wrong. Alex said nothing.

Eventually Dixit spoke again. "By the way, the coroner has released the body of your friend. I don't know if you've been told but I understand the funeral is at 1pm on Monday." He gave the address of a cemetery near Southampton on the south coast. Ellen's parents lived in a village close by.

Dixit stood to go and said, "Good luck." Then he surprised Alex by holding out his hand.

TWENTY-ONE

After Dixit left, Alex rang Nadja. She was stressed by all the media attention.

"They are saying I'm prostitute," she said, her voice brittle, as though she were on the verge of tears. "And I don't know this Slimowicz man. They say he is criminal."

Alex said he was sorry for causing her all the trouble. After the call he rang his mother and arranged for her to pick up Topsy.

"How long are you going to stay in hiding?" his mum asked.

"As long as it takes to blow over."

"Will you go to Ellen's funeral?"

He wanted to, but if the press were still reporting this nonsense it would just be fuel to the fire.

On his laptop, Alex searched for images of the ceremonial block.

Alex didn't see Vanessa that evening, but exchanged texts and finally received a **Goodnight** with a kiss. In the morning he caught the underground at Putney East to Paddington. He wore a beanie and sunglasses and avoided eye contact. At Paddington station he bought a ticket and caught the 9:35 to Oxford.

The journey should have been an hour for the four-carriage commuter train, but at Didcot Parkway, overlooked by monolithic cooling towers, the passengers were asked to leave the train. Work on the signals meant the final stretch was by coach.

The coach arrived at Oxford station later than the scheduled train and Alex jogged the half-mile to the Griffiths Institute. He'd envisaged an old building, typical of Oxford colleges, or perhaps something extremely modern. He was therefore taken aback by the row of Georgian houses. A small brass plaque declared he was at the correct property and so he knocked on the white front door.

A young man in a navy blue sweater promptly opened the door and smiled.

"Alex MacLure to see Professor Thompson."

"Yes, yes, come in." The young man stepped aside and beckoned Alex into the hall. "Up two flights and you'll find the documents in the first room on the left." He closed the door and disappeared into a side room, leaving Alex alone in the hall.

The wooden floor had a long Persian-style rug that led to the stairs. As instructed, Alex walked to the stairs and ascended two flights. There was no sound except for an occasional creak like the timbers of a galleon on the high seas. He stopped at the door and his knock seemed loud and intrusive. After a moment without response, he opened the door to find a reading room with tables and chairs. On one table Alex counted six cardboard boxes. The first contained three lever arch files marked as *Howard Carter's Diaries (Photocopies)* and the excavation seasons. The other boxes were topped with a list of contents in chronological order, being the original notebooks with other documents, photographs, sketches and letters.

Alex waited for five minutes in case the professor was about to join him. When no one appeared, he sat down and opened the first folder and began to read.

The notes became sketchy after the initial exploration of Tutankhamen's tomb. They even lacked detail about the official opening of the burial chamber on 16th February. When Carnarvon became ill, the entry read:

Found Ld. C. very ill with an acute attack of erysipelas and blood poisoning.

When he died fifteen days later on 5th April, Carter simply wrote:

Poor Ld. C. died during the early hours of the morning.

Unusually for Carter, he'd made no entries in the preceding five days except for the numbers 973 750. Later in 1923 there were strange codes with monthly headings, such as Oct. 3 11 4 7 35. Alex stared at the codes for some time but no inspiration came as to their meaning.

There were short entries that tended to relate to cataloguing and packing items to be shipped to the Cairo Museum and longer entries related to politics and frustration with the Egyptian government and officials. Interspersed was another code that had people's initials and a name, which may have referred to a ship or may have been something else entirely.

Alex was disturbed from his reading by the creak of floorboards. Moments later, the door opened and a small man, possibly in his eighties, entered the room and smiled.

"Professor Thompson?" Alex stood.

The man used a walking stick in each hand and Alex met him halfway, waited for the sticks to be transferred before shaking hands. He noted Thompson smelled of burnt toast.

"How are you getting along?" the professor asked, his silver-grey eyes sparkling with life and enthusiasm that was a contrast to his frail body.

"I've just got to the end of 1925."

The professor nodded and indicated they should both sit.

"Good, good. So what do you think, young man?"

"I was hoping you would tell me what my friend Ellen Champion discovered."

"All in good time. First I would like to know what you have discovered today."

"I knew Lord Carnarvon took items for his collection at Highclere Castle, but based on the use of codes in his notes, I'd guess Carter was also smuggling antiquities out of Egypt."

"Of course he was! And directly under the noses of the authorities. They caught him at it you know. In February 1924, the Service des Antiquities, under orders of the Ministry of Public Works to inspect the tombs, found Fortnum and Mason packing cases in the tomb of Ramses XI—used as a storeroom by Carter. One, a red wine case, was found to contain a beautiful wooden statue: the boy Tutankhamen's head emerging from a lotus flower. It was packed in cotton wool and medical gauze and was clearly intended to be shipped back to England because there was no catalogue entry for it. It is well known that many of the items Carter later claimed were held back from being sent to the Cairo Museum for scientific purposes are now housed in New York's Metropolitan Museum of Art."

Alex nodded.

The professor said, "What else did you discover?"

"I think he entered the tomb before he was allowed."

"He was supposed to be accompanied by a government official, but it certainly looks like they went in and reclosed the entrance. They explained it as a robber's hole made in antiquity and repaired, but the repairs look too new and disguised."

The professor's eyes glistened and creased with a smile. "Anyway, that's not why you are here. You want to know what Ellen was investigating. Sometimes you should look for what is not there."

"What does that mean?"

"Have you eaten?"

Alex looked at his watch and was shocked to see it was almost five o'clock.

The professor said, "The institute will be closing soon. Why don't we get a bite to eat and talk about the missing papyri?"

TWENTY-TWO

They settled in a bijou café off Broad Street, which was busy with the noise of chattering and crockery. Looking like eager co-conspirators, the two men sat close just so they could hear one another speak.

The professor said, "What do you know about the missing letters?"

"Nothing."

"Lord Carnarvon wrote to a friend and later the British Museum and mentioned a box of papyri." Thompson nodded to himself. "And a few days later he gave an interview with *The Times* and said:

One of the boxes contains rolls of papyri which may shed much light on the history of the period.

Although at the same time Carter said nothing about them."

Alex sat up. Documents from the period would certainly be of interest to Ellen. "Were they in code?" he asked.

"We'll never know. Like I said, they are missing. But more than that, no one ever said what was written on the papyri."

"Oh, so Carnarvon was mistaken then?"

"In Carter's book, published at the end of 1923, he goes out of his way to stress there were no papyri but rather rolls of linen. He explained the discrepancy based on dim candlelight."

Alex said, "That's not true! They had power from the tomb above and set up electric lights. It's in his notes."

"Precisely. Such an exciting find would have been checked immediately." The professor nodded. "Lord Carnarvon would have known straight away."

"So do you think Carter or Carnarvon kept the papyri?"

"Something undoubtedly happened," Thompson said eventually. "Papyri were expected because of what we now call the *Book of the Dead*—the instructions for reaching the afterlife. The directions and spells were written on the walls and bindings of the mummy. Allegedly, no *Book of the Dead* was found."

Alex said, "What did Ellen think?"

"She agreed that there would have been something. There were documents and they're missing."

"What do you think happened?"

"I think they held sensitive information. Carter and Carnarvon were heard arguing shortly after the find. Carnarvon dies and Carter keeps schtum—until he loses his temper with how he's being treated. Remember, he was out of money and the Egyptian government were taking all the artefacts. He went to the British High Consulate in Cairo and threatened to expose the truth about the Exodus."

Exodus! Suddenly the dots were being connected. Missing papyri, secret codes, Moses and the Exodus. No wonder Ellen was excited.

The professor was still talking. "It was a sensitive time for Britain in Palestine. They saw the establishment of the Jewish National Home as guaranteeing stability in the Middle East." The professor shook his head. "Ironic really. Ellen found something else in Carter's diary."

Alex waited.

Thompson said, "There are a great many contradictions in the records and there's a huge political one. Carter says that the high commissioner in Cairo was *in perfect sympathy* with his case. There's no mention of the outburst. And then a few days later on 4th December 1924, Carter's diary has an entry: **letter to Rothschild**. Lord Carnarvon's father-in-law was Alfred de Rothschild. But *Rothschild* can't refer to him because he was already dead so we think *Rothschild* refers to the House of Rothschild itself."

Alex said, "The most famous and richest Jewish family in the world."

"And known as the British government's bankers of the day."

So, Alex thought, Carter and Lord Carnarvon discover something sensitive. Carnarvon can't keep it to himself but dies a few months later. Carter denies they found papyri, even going as far as to explain his embarrassment as rolls of undergarments rather than documents. When things became intolerable for him he threatens both the British government and possibly the House of Rothschild.

The professor said, "There's no direct evidence, but Howard Carter's financial concerns miraculously disappear. Officially receiving no spoils from the Tutankhamen find, he ends his days a wealthy man."

"Wow!" Alex sat back and wondered where Ellen had gone with this theory. Did she find evidence to prove it?

"There's more," Thompson said, his eyes wide. "Lord Carnarvon's death was suspicious."

Alex knew he died of septicaemia. He'd been bitten on the cheek by a mosquito while at the site of the tomb. It became infected after he cut it shaving.

"There are a number of issues with the official version of what happened. The most obvious being that there were no mosquitos in the Valley of the Kings at that time of year! He allegedly failed to disinfect the cut and was reported by others as using iodine. Private notes held by the Metropolitan Museum report that Lord Carnarvon had trouble with his teeth just before he died. They chipped and fell out. That is not the symptom of simple blood poisoning but could be arsenic or, more likely, due to rare-metal poisoning such as mercury. Would you like to hear my theory?"

"Yes."

"I suspect that Lord Carnarvon took the papyri. He travelled back and forth between England and Egypt more often than anyone else and he would be the logical choice as smuggler. If there were arsenic or mercury on the documents, it is conceivable that, with considerable handling, over time the poison would build up and Lord Carnarvon's health would deteriorate until he eventually passed away."

"But surely Carter and the translator—"

"He was called Breasted."

"Surely they would have also touched the papyri and been poisoned?"

"Possibly. Breasted is responsible for some of the conflicting statements. He was also the one who reported the argument between his bosses. So maybe he wasn't directly involved. Also, just a few weeks before his death, Carnarvon wrote in a letter to Carter:

I may have done many foolish things and I am sorry.

Interesting, don't you think?" The professor stopped and looked deadly serious for a moment. "My theory is that they found the papyri and the documents were so politically sensitive that Lord Carnarvon—a member of the British establishment, remember, and related to the Rothschilds—read them, took them and destroyed them."

"What did Ellen think?"

The professor leaned forward and dropped his voice, "Your friend thought Lord Carnarvon was murdered."

TWENTY-THREE

On the journey back, Alex thought about the professor's parting words. He told Alex to be careful. Not "Take care". "Be careful".

"Some things aren't worth pushing."

"What do you mean?"

"You will have noticed that I'm no longer employed by the institute. I pushed and someone didn't like it. Anti-Semitism is an easy label and difficult to defend. I asked certain questions and it was easier for the institute to let me go than recognize that I was asking for legitimate reasons."

Alex watched the countryside blur past the window of the train. Jesus! If Ellen hadn't been murdered by the gang from the East End, he'd have wondered whether it was linked to what Professor Thompson was saying. That it was linked to the missing papyri. Of course, an alternative explanation was that the professor was using it as an excuse for being fired. Maybe it was nothing to do with his research.

When he arrived back at the flat, Vanessa was waiting for him.

"What do you think," Alex asked, "is it anti-Semitic to suggest a link between the establishment of Israel and blackmail?"

Vanessa plopped down on the sofa. "Depends whether it's based on evidence or is malicious. Is that what you found out today?"

"To be honest I'm not sure what I found out. What I do know is Ellen thought she was on to something. There appears to be a link between things either missing from or stolen from Tutankhamen's tomb and Exodus."

"Really?"

"Howard Carter threatened to reveal the truth about Exodus. And it looks like he was paid off to keep him quiet."

"And going back to evidence, did he have any?"

Alex sat and stretched. "That's the frustrating bit. That's where we hit the speculation. It could have been a bluff but if there was evidence then it was either lost or destroyed. And Ellen appears to have believed that Lord Carnarvon was killed for what he knew. Carter refused to talk whereas Carnarvon seems to have been all too willing to tell."

"Wow! I wonder whether Ellen found something at Highclere Castle that confirmed it."

"I don't know, but after you dropped me off yesterday I had an interesting meeting with the detective. He told me that there was something missing from the exhibition, and based on what the aviator thug said, the East End gang knew it was missing. They wanted it."

Vanessa moved and sat on the coffee table, her legs close to his. "What was it? What was it?" She was like a child eager to receive a birthday gift.

Alex waited until she settled, milking the moment of expectation. "A ceremonial block used in the embalming process."

Vanessa looked disappointed. "A what?"

"I know. Not as sexy as missing papyri, but missing all the same. I think we're making progress."

Vanessa leaned forward and gave Alex a long hug. Her hair smelled clean and fresh.

She said, "This is so exciting."

He held on until she released and gently pulled away. He grinned. "If only I could understand the relevance of the block. I've tried searching the web for inspiration, but nothing. I'm sure Ellen put this all together. Maybe the numbers come from the block. Maybe she converted them into words using gematria or something else."

"She was smart, your friend?"

"In a way most people wouldn't get." He described her personality and saw Vanessa nodding. Of course, she was into psychology!

"Bipolar?"

"Amongst other things. Also diagnosed as high-functioning autistic."

"Did she have therapy?"

"Definitely as a teenager, but I'm not aware of her attending since."

Vanessa's eyes creased with concern. "Ever attempt suicide?"

"She took an overdose of medication at seventeen. Her parents found her before it was too late. A few years ago she also went camping alone in the Arctic—deliberately didn't take adequate equipment and expected to die of hypothermia."

"What happened?"

"Came to her senses." He laughed wryly. "She told me it was too damn cold!"

She smiled but her eyes were still serious and concerned. "Sad," she said. "Sounds like a very troubled genius. But then again aren't they all like that?"

He said nothing for a moment and then: "Now I need cheering up. Let's go out. I'd like to treat you to a nice dinner—I know a great place in Primrose Hill."

The threat of rain in the distance gave the dark sky a surreal glow that reflected in the window of the Thai restaurant Alex had chosen.

"How did you know Thai is my favourite?" she asked as he held the door open for her.

"Call me psychic." He laughed, pleased to have impressed her, although he had to confess. "Actually, it wasn't too difficult to guess. You told me your favourite place was in Thailand. I was pretty sure you wouldn't have stayed four months if you didn't like the food. And I'm sure you'll like this place. It's unpretentious and authentic."

They were shown to a table at the rear and were handed menus. Vanessa chuckled over his pronunciation of some of the dishes, but when they ordered he was disappointed she just gave the numbers.

"Languages aren't my thing, I'm afraid." She shrugged at the look on his face. "I survived in Thailand by pointing at what I wanted and using a handful of words. I had to eat rice and fruit the whole time." Her light laughter made him suspect she was joking, but then she suddenly looked serious. "Do you mind if I ask another question about Ellen?"

"OK," he said with some trepidation, disappointed that the tone had changed.

"What medication was she on?"

"Venlafaxine."

She waited as the food was served and then asked, "How did it make her feel? Do you know?"

"She hated it—said it was a feeling of restriction and confinement. On the meds, it wasn't the real her."

"And sometimes she didn't take it?"

"Her head was clearer when she was off the medication. She thought faster too—sometimes too fast and could seem all over the place and talking fast. I always knew when she wasn't taking it even when she said she was."

"And what about you?" She gave a coquettish smile. "If you don't mind me asking."

Alex was unsure what she meant.

She said. "You're pretty smart yourself—and that thing with the numbers. Tell me something interesting."

He laughed. "Nothing like putting a guy on the spot. Let's see... OK, take three consecutive numbers where the largest is a multiple of three. Say ten, eleven and twelve. Add them together. If the answer is a single digit, it'll be six. If it is more than two then add them again and again until you have a single number. And that number will be six. So ten plus eleven plus twelve equals thirty-three. Three plus three equals six."

"Any consecutive numbers?" He nodded and could see her mind processing. Then she said, "Six! What's the explanation for that?"

"The magic of numbers," he said.

"You know that it's a special skill to see numbers the way you do. Don't be offended, but it is also often an indication of autism."

They exchanged looks and he shrugged.

She said, "Have you ever been in therapy?"

He stopped eating. "Briefly, after my dad took his own life. Although it was more counselling than therapy as far as I remember. But no concerns over autism or my mental health. And, unlike Ellen, I'm certainly not a manic depressive."

He could see she wanted to probe further but felt unable. She said, "Another question: why did you go to stay with that odd guy Pete when you couldn't stay in your flat? Why not go home to your mum?"

"It's difficult. She's struggled a bit since Dad died. Mum never worked, and he left a lot of debts. I also have a brother who has Duchenne muscular dystrophy."

She looked awkward. "Oh, I didn't know."

"It's fine. Of course you didn't. Duchenne only affects boys and most only make it until their late teens. Andrew is doing well in his mid-twenties but is totally dependent on Mum." He shrugged. "I'm very lucky. I had a fifty per cent chance of having it. Anyway, the point is home would be difficult and there's no spare room." He paused. "Just so you know, I send money home every month. I try and help

146

as much as I can but I can't live there. Of course, there's also the fact that they live in Surrey and"—he grinned, trying to make light of the subject—"I'm a Londoner now. I'd feel lost out there."

"I know what you mean."

After a while, and a relaxing glass of red, she said, "When I was a little girl, I used to have a terrible phobia of spiders. Not just the usual. I used to see them in webs even when they weren't there—cobwebs with hundreds of little black babies crawling all over them. I used to be afraid that the web was closing in, that it would surround me, suffocate me."

"Sounds awful."

She looked pale recounting the story. "It became all-consuming. My whole life became a state of fear and panic. At any moment the cobwebs would get me." She took a slow drink of wine. "It was a type of anxiety disorder linked to a fear of separation. A fear of losing everyone."

Alex touched her hand. He could see this was difficult.

She smiled weakly. "My parents were killed in a car crash when I was three. I was raised by my aunt and uncle. I can't recall my parents. I don't remember the crash—"

"You were in the car at the time?"

"Yes, but like I say, I don't remember. I thought I was doing fine. Thought I was OK without my parents, but the point is I was dealing with it in an unhealthy way. I was seven by the time they realized I had a problem: not sleeping and showing signs of OCD. Anyway, therapy sorted me out. I'm fine now. Though I still hate spiders!"

She took another sip of wine and squeezed his hand.

"Tell me to mind my own business, but I think you're handling a lot of issues. When everything settles down, I think you should try a bit of counselling again."

"You think it'll help?"

She leaned over and gave him a peck on the cheek. "It might."

On the way back, he asked if they could go via his house in Maida Vale. "I'm going crazy with so little stuff in Simon's flat. I'll pick up some clothes and more reading material. I've some books that might help with solving what Ellen was doing."

Because he was concerned that the paparazzi might be around, Vanessa suggested she go in and Alex wait in the car. She was only gone a few minutes when his phone rang.

When she spoke, her voice didn't show the enthusiasm he anticipated. In its place was something very different—shock.

"Alex... Oh my God. You need to get here. You need to see this!"

TWENTY-FOUR

Alex took no chances and kept away from the front of his house, cutting through the backyards to the rear of his property. The first thing he noticed was his kitchen window. It was open.

He stepped on a garden pot, looked in and saw the chaos that had once been his flat.

Vanessa opened the back door, her face ashen. "Don't touch anything," she said as she led him to his front door and into his wrecked flat. "Looks like they came in through the kitchen window."

The curtains were closed and the lights were off so as not to attract the attention of anyone outside. However, there was enough light through the gaps in the curtains for him to see the mess. In the kitchen, every cupboard door was open, every drawer was upside down. Utensils, paper, cans of food, packets and a host of odds and ends covered the floor. Even Topsy's dry dog food had been emptied out. Nothing was left untouched, unturned or unemptied.

The fridge freezer doors were open and a large pool of water had gathered around the base.

"They look for fake tins," Vanessa said. "People often hide valuables and money in tins—like leaving a key in a fake stone by the front door."

"The fridge and freezer?"

"Same thing."

He tiptoed past the mess into the lounge. The sofa was criss-crossed with gashes sprouting white cotton wool stuffing. The cushions were slashed and strewn on the floor. The TV was on its side and the back prised open. The books looked like they had been methodically searched and flung into a corner. Alex's only plant, a twisted fig tree, had been pulled from its pot and the compost scooped out.

"I'm so sorry," she said, looking into his eyes. "This is awful for me so I can only guess how bad you must feel."

He shook his head, unable to speak for a moment. When he found his voice, he said, "The rest of the flat?"

"Just the same, only where you have floorboards they've been pulled up in places. Everything looks like it's been thoroughly searched."

"What were they looking for—valuables? They didn't take the TV." He wondered if his voice sounded as quiet and strained to her as it did to him.

"The TV was probably too big."

He walked through to the second bedroom—Ellen's room. It was a scene of devastation. Some floorboards were jammed at angles or broken. The bedside cabinet was on its side, the drawers were out. Everything from the drawers was on the floor. He picked up the Isis puzzle-ball he'd bought for Ellen and placed it back on its base on the window ledge.

Vanessa said, "Can you tell if there's anything missing?"

He shrugged.

They went back into the lounge

He said, "Surely it wasn't valuables they were looking for—" He pointed to a clump of stuffing hanging from the back of the sofa.

Vanessa said, "They were looking for something hidden."

"What did they think I had hidden, for Christ's sake?" He shook his head and then sank down onto the sofa. She

150

moved a couple of books, dusted the seat and sat beside him.

"Maybe it's all linked. Maybe it's about Ellen's research. Maybe someone else thinks it's important. Maybe they think the clue is here."

He rubbed his face and pressed his temples to ease a growing ache there.

He said, "Who else would know about her research?"

"Think." Her voice was soft and encouraging.

"I really have no idea." He rubbed his face again and left both hands over his eyes.

After a while he said, "The people who murdered the East End gang. Who were they?"

"I know you don't want to believe it, but what if it is linked to your dog walker—the Polish woman? What if she does have connections to organized crime?"

He shook his head. Surely it couldn't be Nadja. When he had spoken to her she had been genuinely distressed. Hadn't she?

Vanessa put her arm around him. "Should we call the police?"

"Do you think there's any point? All I can see coming from this is more media attention. There's no way the police will find anything—and if it is linked to the East End murders, then it'll just confirm for them that I was involved somehow."

They sat in silence for a while. Then she stood and said, "We should have a drink." As he started to rise, she put a hand on his arm. "Just rest a while. You've had a shock. My grandmother always made a sweet cup of tea at times like these. You stay here and I'll sort us out a cuppa."

He watched her in the kitchen, find the kettle, fill it and begin to sort through the mess on the floor. She replaced the drawers and put things away—not in the right places, but he was beyond caring.

They stopped tidying. At a quick glance, the flat looked presentable, but Alex could still sense the violation, as though the walls had memory. The latch on the window was broken, but it closed with the semblance of security.

He left the house by the back door and retraced his route through the backyards. Vanessa was already in the car when he arrived. She three-point turned to avoid driving past Alex's house and made her way back to Putney. Close to Hammersmith, she visibly tensed.

Alex asked. "What's up?"

"I think we're being followed."

He swung around and looked through the rear window. It was too dark to see anything except halogen headlights right behind them.

"It's a BMW," she said. "I don't know where we picked it up, but it's been the same distance behind for ages."

"But—"

"You know on the way to the restaurant, I went through a light on amber? He went through on red. He jumped the lights! I'm sure it's the same car. I slowed just now and there he is, keeping the same distance behind."

"How well do you know the back streets around here? Think we can lose him?"

"Let's try."

At the Hammersmith gyratory, Alex pointed down the King Street. She took it still driving as though nothing was up. Once around the corner of the first right turn, she pressed her foot to the floor. Alex watched as the BMW came into sight, now forty yards back.

He lurched forward as Vanessa slammed on the brakes and skidded right at a T-junction. She accelerated, braked and swung left into a quiet residential street. When the BMW rounded the corner, they were fifty yards ahead.

Vanessa switched left and right through the maze of streets, but gradually the BMW closed the gap.

Then, when Vanessa braked to take a corner, the little car lurched as the BMW bumped it.

Vanessa screamed.

As they entered the next street, Vanessa hesitated, her hands visibly shaking.

"Go!" Alex yelled. "Drive, don't think!"

She reacted, but the rear window was now ablaze with the BMW's full beam. They took three more corners and each time there was a jolt as the BMW rear-ended them.

"Tell you what," Alex said, "let's slow it down for a while, because we're not going to shake them like this. I know where we are, take the next left and slow to a stop just before the next road on the right. Keep the engine running."

Vanessa complied and the BMW pulled back. When she stopped, the BMW stopped. The headlights dipped. Alex leaned forward so he could watch through the side mirror. Vanessa stared at hers. Two men got out.

When she spoke, her voice trembled. "You know this isn't the press, don't you?"

Alex said nothing.

"Oh my God they've got guns!"

"Go!" Alex shouted. "Right then immediately left."

The Smart car's tyres squealed as she slammed her foot down. They slid through the first turn and then the second.

"Now right again." Alex pointed to a car park entrance. "In there."

Vanessa took it, bumping over a concrete strip separating the entrance lane from the exit. The lane curved into a dark well before opening up into the orange glow of a multi-storey. On Alex's instruction, she stopped and cut the engine.

They sat in silence, barely breathing, their eyes fixed on the entrance. Alex cracked open the window. Immediately they heard a car accelerate past.

In the dim light he saw her look over and he responded with a whisper: "Maybe."

After forty minutes, Vanessa started up the car and reversed to the road. A car approached fast, but the lights weren't halogens. It wasn't a BMW.

When she spoke, her voice was still tremulous. "I should avoid Hammersmith, shouldn't I?"

She took them west. It was a long detour to the next bridge over the Thames at Mortlake. Shortly after, she picked up the South Circular and passed close by to where they had picnicked in Richmond Park.

In Putney, she didn't park outside the flat. It seemed a sensible precaution.

Inside, she opened another bottle of red and gulped down a large glass. They sat in the semi-darkness, the room illuminated by a street light close by. Neither spoke for a long while.

Vanessa said, "Something just struck me. Your friend left you the clue. It seems she wanted you to know what her research was about."

"Yes, and I've learned it seems to be something to do with Exodus and maybe Lord Carnarvon."

"OK, but what's the biggest mystery here?"

He thought for a moment. Maybe the wine was fogging his thinking? Then he had it: "The ceremonial block."

"OK, go with this for a moment. What if she left you her research and Exodus and Carnarvon are just a minor part. What if she wants you to know about the block?" She rubbed her forehead as if thinking. "Yes! And what if this other gang know that. Maybe they were searching your flat for her research."

Alex shook his head. "Maybe, but that gets us no closer."

She grinned like a schoolgirl. "Or maybe it does. Maybe the clue wasn't about the phone. Or maybe it was part of it. Maybe there's another clue."

It seemed to make sense, although he couldn't begin to think where another clue might be. Again they sat in silence and he found his mind drifting until it was unfocused.

The wine bottle was empty. Vanessa stretched. "Oh boy, I've had too much to drive again tonight. I'll sleep on the sofa. Would that be OK?"

Alex said, "No. You take the bed and I'll sleep on the sofa."

She fetched a blanket from a cupboard and handed it to him. "You're sure?"

"Sure." With all the adrenaline gone and then more wine, he felt he could sleep anywhere.

While she was in the bathroom getting ready, he stripped down to his boxer shorts, moved cushions to create a pillow and settled down.

When she came back, she leaned over and kissed his cheek. "Sleep well then."

He watched her retreat to the bedroom. She didn't close the door and he heard her settle into the bed. Within minutes her breathing changed.

Images drifted though his mind. He was talking to Detective Dixit one moment and the next they were walking through Highclere Castle. Then it wasn't Dixit who was with him in his dream. It was Vanessa. He felt like he was giving her a guided tour. When he showed her Carnarvon's secret turret cupboard, she smiled her crooked, cute smile. She leaned in and whispered something he couldn't quite hear. He could smell her musk. And then, without warning, she was there. Really there. She was standing close to the sofa, framed by the street-lit window and had nothing on but one of his shirts. Only one button kept it together.

"Vanessa?" he said, half asleep.

She placed a finger on his lips.

He started to pull himself up, but she leaned down. Her mouth met his.

Her kisses were soft at first and then more hungry. Her perfume and the touch of her skin sent such a charge through his body that he shook. She tugged away the blanket and he pulled her down, fumbling and then finally ripping off the shirt.

TWENTY-FIVE

When he woke up, they were on the floor. During the night they must have improvised with the sofa cushions creating a makeshift bed.

It was early and his neck ached from being at an odd angle. Vanessa was still asleep so he carefully slipped from under her arm. A little groggy with tiredness and the after-effect of the wine, but still tingling with the excitement of a new relationship, he went into the bathroom, flicked the lock shut and turned on the shower. Vanessa had left her handbag on the table beside the bath. He moved it so that it wouldn't get splashed, pulled back the shower curtain and stepped over the edge of the bath.

He started with the shower on cold, like he always did, a jolt to stimulate the body and brain first thing in the morning. After the first shock, he turned up the temperature and enjoyed the hot torrent as it pummelled first his head and then his shoulders. He felt the fuzz of a hangover being washed away.

As he rubbed shampoo into his hair there was a knock on the bathroom door and he heard Vanessa call something.

He turned to say "One minute" and slipped, put his hand on the curtain before realizing it wouldn't take his weight and grabbed for the towel rail. The towel pulled off and knocked some things to the floor, including Vanessa's handbag.

She knocked again, urgent this time.

"One minute." He climbed out of the bath and bent down for Vanessa's handbag. A few things had tumbled out and he replaced her purse and a laminated card. Then he stopped. His veins froze.

She knocked again. "Alex?"

He held the card and studied it—an ID card with her photo. But the name was different. She'd told him her name was Vanessa Reece. The name on the card was Rebecca Vance.

He wrapped the towel around his waist and unlocked the door.

Vanessa glanced at Alex, the ID, the handbag open on the floor, and then looked back at him.

She snapped, "You've been through my bag!"

"Who is this?"

"How dare you go through my things?"

"Who are you?"

She quietened then and her anger melted. After a beat, she said, "My name really is Vanessa."

He waved the card at her like damning evidence. "So who is Rebecca? Why have this ID?"

"Alex, I…" Her eyes went from side to side as though searching for a script to provide the right words.

"So you've been lying to me, haven't you?"

Her eyes stopped their flicker and fixed on his. Her face became calmer. "It's not like that." She stepped back from the door. "Let's get dressed and have a cup of tea and I'll explain everything."

Ten minutes later they were sitting in the lounge facing one another. Vanessa held a mug in both hands almost as if praying with it.

Alex said, "So?"

She looked up from the mug. "Rebecca Vance is my pen name. I'm a writer—freelance. If I had told you what I did, you wouldn't have trusted me." She paused, took a sip and added, "I wanted to tell you. I just hadn't found the right moment."

"Tell me one thing. When I met you on the embankment, was that by chance?"

She said nothing.

Alex shook his head and started to rise.

"No, it wasn't," she said quietly. "I followed you there."

"And the incident with the thug—the fight—that was a set-up, right?"

"No!" She put down her mug and looked at him with earnest eyes. "That was for real. I have no idea who he was or what he wanted. I was as scared as you, remember? You have to believe me."

"Actually, I don't!" He sighed and looked out of the window. "In fact, I don't know why I'm sitting here giving you this chance."

"But you are and that says a lot. Alex, look at me."

He looked into her eyes. They seemed genuine.

She said, "Yes, I'm a writer and yes I was following you, but since I've got to know you I've realized there's a much better story. Probably two. One is the story of Ellen's research and what you've found. That doesn't deserve to be in some stuffy specialist magazine. With your celebrity, with the crime at Highclere, the whole King Tut thing, this is mainstream—certainly Sunday papers. Maybe even a book."

"And the second?"

"The human interest angle—about you—about Ellen. Wouldn't you like to set the record straight?"

"There's a lot you don't know." It was all he could think to say.

"I'd like to find out."

Alex stood and walked around the room. He could hear the sounds from the street. His own thoughts seemed less distinct.

She said, "Give me a chance."

Eventually, he said, "I need time."

"I'll give you time. Search for my work—under my pen name—see the sort of thing I write. I'll start writing something on you, but I won't publish it, because I want us to work on it together. I want you to be happy with it."

He said, "Maybe. I should find somewhere else to stay no matter what."

"That's really not—"

"Yes it is."

"Look. I'm going up to York to a hen party and then the wedding. Let's get together when I get back. OK?"

"Sure," he said with little conviction.

Alex opened the door for her to leave. There was a moment of awkwardness as she said goodbye and he closed the door with her still looking at him. He stared at the back of the door, a cascade of thoughts running through his mind. After a while he realized he was just staring at the paintwork that needed touching up.

He picked up his phone and rang Pete.

TWENTY-SIX

Alex said, "Pete, I need your help."

"Why am I not surprised? You've fallen out with that tart, I'm sure. What was it? Did she find out about the real you?"

"Yeah, something like that. Are you in? Can I come over?"

Thirty minutes later, Alex was standing on his doorstep.

Pete looked at him with suspicion and then past him down the stairwell. "I hope no one followed you here!"

"The guys who followed me before, and the one who attacked me by the river. They're all dead. I'm not scared of them anymore. It's a bunch of other guys I'm worried about now. They're probably the ones who killed the first guys." Alex removed his beanie to show his dyed hair. "And I've got a disguise."

"What about the press?"

Alex nodded. "It's OK, no one has followed me."

"You look weird. The hair I mean."

"No change there then. Can I come in?"

Pete moved inside and Alex followed, dropping his bag on the floor.

Pete said, "So what's happened now?"

They stood in the lounge and Alex told him about Vanessa, about how she was actually a reporter. Freelance or not, she was still a reporter. She earned her living as a writer and he was her subject.

"Oh great," Pete moaned. "Shit, she met me. At least she doesn't know where I live." He looked inquisitively at Alex.

"I haven't told her. Anyway, why are you so paranoid? She won't connect you to your old conviction. Your job's safe."

Pete visibly relaxed. "So what progress have you made with Ellen's research?"

Alex told him about going to Oxford and the mystery about missing documents from Tutankhamen's tomb, how it was connected to Exodus and the uncertainty surrounding Lord Carnarvon's death.

"Shit! It's big then." Pete went through to the kitchen. "Cup of tea?" he asked, and then, as the kettle boiled, shouted, "So where do you go from here?"

Alex said, "I have no idea."

Pete returned with two steaming mugs of tea. "But where's Ellen's research if it wasn't in her briefcase?"

Alex shrugged and then pulled out his book. "The only clue was in here. These numbers." He opened the book and showed his friend.

"Any idea what they mean?"

"Yes. Isis is the key. I converted Isis into 1515— numbers not letters—and it was the code for Ellen's phone. What I didn't finish telling you before was Ellen wasn't just interested in Lord Carnarvon's death but also missing artefacts from when he and Carter found Tutankhamen's tomb."

Pete looked excited. "Missing artefacts? Like the missing one from Highclere Castle?"

"What? How did you know about that?" Alex glared. Suddenly his head throbbed from too much wine the night before.

Pete held up his hands. "Hey, steady. Now who's getting paranoid? It's in the papers. That's how I know. They found the stolen stuff with the guys who were murdered in West Ham. A funny block was missing. I think they called it the mummy stone."

Alex shook his head and explained what the ceremonial block was.

"There you go then," Pete said. "Missing artefacts."

Alex sank into an armchair and nursed the mug. He thought about what Vanessa had said: *Maybe the clue wasn't about the phone.*

"Scary about that other gang then," Pete said.

"What?"

"The people responsible for the triple murder. Executions, for Christ's sake. They're saying serious organized crime."

"Yeah, I suspect it was them who chased us last night."

Pete looked shocked. "What?"

"Last night we had a car chase like something out of the movies. Only it wasn't good. The guys had some sort of sub-machine guns."

"Shit man!"

Pete was talking but Alex's mind was back in his home, seeing the devastation. The way everything seemed turned upside down and inside out. He pictured the spare room and how he'd picked up the puzzle that he'd bought for Ellen. A wave of sadness washed over him. The room had almost been like a shrine to his friend. All he had was the book she'd given him and the phone he'd found. The only other thing to remind him of her was the puzzle. At least he still had that.

"What?" Pete said. "What are you thinking about? You've been miles away, haven't heard a thing I've said."

"Oh my God!" Alex said. He stood but suddenly felt lightheaded. The room spun. "Oh my God!" he said again.

"What, for Christ's sake?"

"Isis is the key."

Pete looked expectant, said nothing.

"My God, Isis is the key!"

"I get that, but what does that mean?"

Alex was laughing. "It's a puzzle."

"Yeah, I know that, but—"

"No, not a mystery. I mean literally a puzzle. Isis is the name of a puzzle. It's in my spare bedroom. I have a puzzle called Isis in my house." He clapped his hands. "I need to go home." Then he stopped. He thought about last night and being chased by the BMW through Hammersmith, about the men with guns who had probably been in his home.

Pete said, "What?"

"I need another favour." Alex smiled. "I need you to get it for me."

Owl rang Fox. "Cat has lost the rabbit."

"He's back at the Hammersmith flat." Fox let that message sink in, milking the news. He could hear Owl's rattling breath.

Fox filled the silence: "I've got him. He's going nowhere without me knowing."

Now Owl spoke. "You made a mess of his apartment and found nothing."

"I had to know for sure that the item wasn't there."

"You spooked him."

Fox knew there was no point in arguing. It had been the plan. Owl's tar-filled breathing sounded like the man was building up to something. Fox said, "Give me time. We have some of the bird's papers but it's only part of them. She must have done something with her research. It's out there somewhere, and if we don't get it, we run the risk of someone finding it."

"All right," Owl said. "The longer this goes on, the bigger the risk that the police pick up on us. We'll give the rabbit a few more days."

"And if he makes no progress, I end it."

"No," Owl said, surprising him.

"No?"

"Change of plan." Then, unexpectedly, he added an explanation: "I've promised Cat. You won't kill him."

The call ended and Fox shook his head. The old man was going senile. If he could no longer make the hard decisions then it was time for someone else to do it for him.

TWENTY-SEVEN

"Shit, your place… it's…"

Pete's words on the phone stung Alex. It was like he was there, seeing the mess again.

They'd waited until dark so that any reporter hanging around wouldn't spot him, but he'd failed to mention the break-in, the devastation—although it was nothing like as bad as it had been.

"Yeah, I know." He hadn't mentioned it in case Pete didn't want to go.

"You had a break-in and you didn't think I needed to know? You arsehole. If I'd known—"

Alex said, "You're looking for a metal ball the size of your fist. Silver with turquoise-blue rings. It's in the spare bedroom on the window ledge."

A few minutes later Pete called back. "I can't find it."

"It's sitting in its open box—a wood-effect cube. By the window. It should be obvious."

Pete snapped back, "It would be obvious if I saw it. But I haven't!"

"You're in the smaller bedroom at the back? On the window ledge."

"It's not here."

Alex ended the call and threw himself on the single mattress in Pete's spare room. So the burglars must have been back and had taken his Isis puzzle. Did that make sense? Why had they turned over the whole house and left the puzzle and then returned to get it? How did they know?

He heard Pete come back but didn't get up. The guy was annoyed and there was nothing to say. A short time later he heard Pete go out again and guessed he was off for the night shift.

Alex kept his clothes on to keep warm but sleep wouldn't come. He fired up Ellen's old phone and went through everything, checking all the apps in case there were any more notes or clues. When the first strains of morning lightened the night sky, Alex got up and headed for the kitchen and caffeine.

As he waited for the steaming mug to cool, he sat at the kitchen table with the phone and looked at the email again. Then he realized something. It hadn't updated for a couple of weeks—the last email in the *Trash* folder was dated the Sunday she'd left his house early. He went into *Settings* and *Mail, Contacts, Calendars*, and touched the email account. It was off.

Alex swiped it on.

A moment later the phone pinged with incoming mail. Alex checked it. Thirty emails, all junk, it looked like. He selected each one in turn, just to be sure before deleting them. And then he saw it: an email from someone with the Cairo Museum as the domain. Intriguing.

Not heard from you. Is everything all right?
Yours – Marek

Alex sorted his emails but found no others from Marek at the Cairo Museum. He went back to the new one and stared at it, wondering whether to reply. Wondering what to reply. He could pretend to be Ellen but that didn't seem right. If he said Ellen was dead that might frighten this guy away before Alex had managed to make proper contact.

But then how could he say he was replying on Ellen's phone?

While he was thinking, an event came up. Ellen's mum's birthday. Alex stared at the calendar reminder. Why hadn't he seen that before? OK, so it was her birthday today, but he should have seen it in the calendar as a scheduled event. Shouldn't he? Were there any other events he hadn't seen? The birthday event was in *Tasks*. Alex went into *Organizer* then *Tools* and then selected *Tasks*. There were two. The birthday reminder and one other.

A message. It had a reminder date of the day before she had died.

A dead chill ran though Alex's bones. There was no mistaking the meaning of the note. It was a message to him, like a warning from the grave.

Do not trust Pete.

Pete had been very strange when Alex had first turned up after the meeting with the police. He'd said he'd been interviewed by the police but they never mentioned him. And Pete didn't want them to know where he lived. He also virtually blackmailed Alex with the rent into his bank account. What had he said? *Don't mention me being involved. It looks bad for both of us. Worse for you because of the money.*

So they had never interviewed him. They didn't know he existed. Pete said he was concerned about his history, about losing his job. But was he really? What did he have to hide? Was he somehow involved? Ellen didn't trust him and she was warning Alex not to trust him.

Damn, he should have known there was something wrong. Pete had hinted at something between him and Ellen. Alex should have known it wasn't true.

And then there was the research. It had been Pete's idea to find out what Ellen had been doing. He kept mentioning treasure. God! It was so clear now. The guy thought Ellen had discovered something valuable and wanted it for himself.

Alex went into the lounge, located Pete's laptop and switched it on.

Password required.

Pete was probably one of those people who used the same password for everything. Alex had seen his lazy swipe of the keyboard: qwerty. He hit the keys and was in. Internet Explorer was open. Alex looked at the history. For the past few days, Pete had mainly searched for information about the ceremonial block. Then last night he had been on the Isis puzzle website and had checked forums for hints about how to unlock the puzzle.

There was only one conclusion: Pete had the Isis puzzle.

Alex began to search the apartment, starting with Pete's bedroom. After two hours of looking, first randomly and then methodically checking every possible site, he sank down at the kitchen table again.

Where would Pete hide it? He thought over and over. He got up again and prowled around the flat. In Pete's bedroom he found a loose skirting board, but there was just the wall behind it. In the bathroom he unscrewed the side panel. Here there was nothing but cobwebs and dust debris from when the bathroom had been constructed.

Where would I hide it? If it's here, it'll be inside something. No new inspiration came and he found himself thinking: What had Vanessa said? *People hide valuables in tins in the cupboards. Like food. In the fridge or freezer.*

The kitchen had a single unit fridge with a freezer compartment. The fridge wasn't well stocked—the usual minimalist guy-things, including a four-pack of beer bottles. He opened the freezer compartment door.

Embedded in excessive frost was a box of fish, and frozen mixed vegetables. He pulled them out. Behind were some burgers that looked like they'd been there since the last ice age and, next to them, a packet of peas. Only, the packet was more of a large lump than Alex would have expected. He pulled it out. Heavy.

Inside, surrounded by peas, was the Isis puzzle.

TWENTY-EIGHT

Alex was waiting for Pete when he returned home. He sat in the lounge, glared at the guy and held the Isis puzzle as though he was about to draw back his arm and throw it.

"You bastard!"

Pete glanced at the puzzle and then took a step back towards the door. Alex stood and leapt forward. He placed his hand on the door just as Pete grabbed the handle. Then he stepped between Pete and the door and pushed him into the room.

"You're going nowhere, pal," Alex snarled. "Not until you've told me what's going on."

Pete said, "I didn't wreck your flat!"

"You were looking for the Isis."

"Yes, but, honestly, it was in the spare bedroom. It was where you said it'd be. I was in and out quickly."

Alex stepped forward until Pete backed into the chair and sat down. Alex glared down at him. "So you took the puzzle. Did you open it?"

Pete shook his head. "I couldn't work it out." He then tried to look encouraging. "How about you? Can you open it?"

"Of course."

With the puzzle in his hands, Alex turned his back so that his friend couldn't see what he was doing. After a couple of minutes he turned back and held out his hands, a semi-sphere in each one. In the centre, like a bisected fruit missing a large stone, was a hollow space.

Alex said, "There's nothing inside."

Pete blinked rapidly. "You're joking?"

"What was in it, Pete?"

"I don't know. I honestly didn't know how to get it open!"

Alex glared again. "I don't believe you!"

"It's the God's honest truth!"

Alex snatched up the Isis puzzle and reassembled it in one smooth motion. He continued to glare. "You really didn't find anything, did you?'

"No."

"Damn! All that effort and there's nothing in the bloody thing. Mustn't be the clue I thought it was."

Alex spun around and marched away, picked up his bag from the spare room and headed for the door. As he left he said, "Pete, I never, ever want to see you again. Is that understood?"

TWENTY-NINE

Two hours earlier in Pete's flat, Alex had waited for the Isis to warm-up enough to handle comfortably. He'd solved the puzzle and opened it up. Inside had been a slip of paper like something out of a fortune cookie, only pink. On it was written: PAD140Δ

He was sure Pete didn't know how to open the ball. He was certain Pete hadn't seen the note. It was clear that Pete wasn't to be trusted, however, and so the strategy formed in Alex's mind: He would make Pete believe there was no clue—that the trail had ended.

While he waited, Alex went through his emails again looking for Marek while waiting for Pete to return home. This time he searched for the name rather than the email address.

He got one hit: Marek Borevsek. This time the domain was the Berlin University and had been sent just before Ellen had applied for work at Highclere Castle. It said:

Switching to the webmail and deleting emails

It was signed *Sinuhe*—one of the names from the EgyptConfidential forum.

Alex had been searching through the browser history on Ellen's phone for a sign of a webmail address when an email arrived on his phone from Vanessa.

The subject was *an apology*.

Alex—I'm so sorry about what happened yesterday. It was wrong of me to lie to you. If you'll never see me again, my only consolation will be that I would not have discovered the real you otherwise. If I'd told you upfront that I write for a living, you wouldn't have let me help you, you wouldn't have opened up to me. Alex, I've attached a working draft of an article about you. The problems of your past make you more human and add a dimension to the story that will endear the readers to you. Especially when they understand you've been working on Ellen's research. Nothing could be more exciting and intriguing than a secret about Tutankhamen. Anyway, read it and let me know what you think. If you don't want me to, I won't publish.

Take care

Vanessa

Alex read the article. It was the kind of thing that he'd expected the other reporter to write. It was positive and interesting without the scandal. She'd woven in the information they'd discovered about Ellen's research. The piece was clearly unfinished. She ended with a note about adding a conclusion and wrapping back to the start.

Could he give her another chance? He could not stay with Pete. Where else could he go? And she was rather nice and good company.

Yes, he could give her another chance, though this time he'd have his eyes open.

He typed a reply: **Cracked it!**

Moments later she was on the phone, breathless and without preamble: "Isis is the key?"

He explained that Isis was the puzzle from his spare bedroom. The one he'd given to Ellen. He also told her about Pete going to the flat and pretending he hadn't found it.

"I thought he was untrustworthy," Vanessa said.

Alex coughed.

She said, "Fair point."

"I opened it and there was a slip of paper inside with six characters: P-A-D-1-4-0 and then a triangle or the Greek letter delta."

She was quiet for a second. "Could this be a page reference again? Or is there a pad as in pad of paper? Perhaps it's line or page 140? Or pad as in apartment. Maybe it's an address?"

"I don't think it's a page reference, and if it's an address... well, there's not enough information."

"And what about the delta?"

"Well, it's often used as a mathematical symbol to mean difference."

"And what does that mean?"

He heard someone coming up the stairs. "Gotta go!" he said, and ended the call.

Alex prepared himself. Now to get Pete off the trail and out of the picture. A key turned in the lock and Pete entered the flat.

THIRTY

After pretending to storm out of Pete's flat, Alex checked that the street looked clear and then headed for Fulham underground station. He reversed the convoluted tube journey he'd taken to get to Pete's the day before. On the way, he typed a message to Vanessa apologizing for cutting her off and said it was about Pete and that he'd explain later. Then he said he was going back to the flat over Simon's café and hoped that was all right.

The message didn't go immediately due to the lack of signal, and he was in Putney by the time a reply from Vanessa arrived. She said she was pleased.

During the afternoon and evening he searched the Internet for something that would explain *PAD140*. He also tried again to find a webmail service that Ellen might have used, and although he made no progress he felt charged and his mind agile.

He wanted to send a text to Vanessa wishing her a nice evening. After trying a few alternatives, he opted for the simple line: looking 4ward 2 cing u sunday

Later he received the reply: I get into KGX at 15:44 will come straight over x

* * *

When he awoke his mind felt clearer than it had been since he'd learned of Ellen's death. He picked up his phone and looked again at Vanessa's text. He liked that she was putting a kiss at the end of her messages again.

She'd gone to York by train and she was arriving back at King's Cross station. KGX was a three letter acronym for the station. The realization made him spring out of bed. PAD wasn't the reference to a pad of paper or apartment. But it was a place. KGX was short for King's Cross station. PAD was the abbreviation for Paddington station. It was so obvious now he thought about it, especially since Paddington was the closest main line station to his home in Maida Vale.

Alex checked his watch—a little after 5:30, too early to call Vanessa. He sent her a text: PAD140 refers to Paddington station. Perhaps 140 is a locker number x

Within an hour he was at the station. He'd anticipated it would be deserted so early on a Sunday, but the main station was buzzing with people in yellow charity T-shirts. A few had placards, and a giant banner referred to a mass fundraising event.

On the main concourse he looked around, spotted a man behind an information desk and wended his way towards him. Arriving, Alex asked, "Are there lockers at the station?"

The man looked up from his papers. "Sorry, sir?"

"Lockers? Is there somewhere at the station to store something?"

"Not lockers." The man shook his head. "But if you have luggage you want to leave, there's the Excess Baggage Company. You can leave it there." He swivelled and pointed. "It's at the end of platform twelve."

Alex thanked him and made his way to the end of the concourse. He could see what looked like a shop front—a glass frontage with a blue sign above, but it was beyond the ticket barriers. A member of the railway company stood by the barriers and Alex approached him with a shrug.

"I need to go to the left luggage place," he said, "but I don't have a train ticket."

"Not open yet." The man checked his watch. "You've got twenty minutes, mate. Come back after seven and I'll let you through."

At the end of the barriers a coffee bar caught Alex's eye. The long counter ran on both sides of the barriers. He ordered a double espresso and a Danish pastry and made a comment to the attractive barista about the ridiculousness of the barrier, cutting off the café and Excess Baggage place. He guessed she hadn't understood because the young woman said something unconnected in a strong eastern European accent. He gave up the idea of making small talk, found a free seat and ate his breakfast.

At a minute to 7am he returned to the ticket barrier and the staff member opened the panels for him. "Mind you don't get on a train," the man said in all seriousness. "There are big penalties for getting on without a ticket these days."

"Just going to the Excess Baggage Company place—really. Thanks."

Alex slipped through and round the end of the platform, passing close to the coffee bar. Outside the left luggage place, he stood impatiently. The door was closed, but he could see staff inside. A knock on the door didn't attract their attention. After four minutes, a spotty youth finally came over and opened the door.

"You're supposed to open at seven," Alex said, but immediately regretted it when the shop assistant gave him a strange look. He thought back to his attempted conversation with the barista and had to remind himself that these people saw a million people a day, most of whom were in a hurry. There was no time to talk and interact, just do your job and get paid.

Alex took a breath and smiled. "Sorry, I'm just a bit... agitated today."

"A bit!" the youth snapped back. Then he mellowed as though his training was just kicking in. "Hey, it's OK. What can I do you for?" He lifted the counter and went to the far side.

"I've come to collect something."

"OK. Give me your ticket and we'll get it right to you."

Alex handed over the pink piece of paper.

"If that's a ticket, it's not from here."

Alex decided to bluff it. "Ah. I mean this is the reference but I've lost the actual ticket."

"Not a problem. There's a £15 charge for a lost ticket. All we need is your ID and a description."

"Ah. You see... I'm not really sure."

The youth eyed him suspiciously and then rolled his eyes. "Someone left your luggage for you?"

"Right."

"What's your name and address?"

Alex wondered whether it would be in his name or Ellen's. Since he didn't have ID for Ellen he provided his own name. Then he gulped as he realized the shop assistant might connect him with the recent publicity. The youth showed no recognition and casually pulled a form from under the counter.

"Address here." He pointed to the form. Then again at the bottom. "Sign here and show me some form of ID please."

"A credit card do?"

"Nicely."

Alex signed an indemnity, paid £15 in cash and the assistant took a photocopy of his card and checked the signature.

"All righty," the youth said. "Now, what am I looking for?"

"A package, I guess."

Again an odd look, but the young man disappeared for a while. Alex saw him return and place something under the counter.

"I see now. It wasn't left here, but sent for collection. You need to give me a three-digit code…"

"OK, 140?"

"Cool." The youth pulled a black leather briefcase from under the counter and slid it over.

As he swung the briefcase to his side, Alex was suddenly aware of another man in the shop. Their eyes met, but then the man produced a ticket and handed it to the assistant. False alarm.

Clutching the handles tightly, Alex walked onto the platform into a stream of passengers heading for the barriers. He had to wait for the station employee to be unoccupied and he held up the bag.

"Collected this from the luggage place—you let me through."

The man opened the barrier with the most fleeting of acknowledgements and Alex followed the crowd towards the entrance to the tube station.

Something grazed his arm. No, not a graze. Someone gripped his arm. "Hey!" Alex tried to pull away and looked into the face of a stern man wearing a brown suit.

"Alex MacLure," the man said in a monotone, "you are under arrest."

THIRTY-ONE

His head spun and he instinctively gripped the briefcase tighter.

"You are believed to be in possession or have been in possession of stolen goods," the man in the brown suit said, his voice low and controlled like he was trying to mask an accent. He flashed a warrant card, open then closed. "Police."

Alex looked around and said nothing.

The policeman was talking again. "What's in the bag, sir?"

Alex's head cleared a little. He said, "Did Jackson send you?"

"Yes."

There had been a hesitation and something in the man's eyes.

"OK, take me to him," Alex said, and hoped he didn't sound challenging.

The policeman didn't respond to the tone and continued to hold Alex's arm just above the elbow.

Alex nodded and stepped towards the escalator that descended into the tube station. After a brief tug he felt the policeman pull alongside and steer him down the steps rather than the narrow escalator.

To the right was a small retail outlet selling papers, books and snacks. To the left were ticket machines. A queue of yellow shirts spilled across the foyer and groups clustered in the centre—the fundraisers.

Alex, with the policeman jammed against his side, manoeuvred between the bodies. A board with the map of the underground split the crowd in two. Alex headed to the right, close to the map. At the last moment he jerked to the left, causing the man's arm to strike the board's metal post.

The grip was broken. Within four quick paces Alex was at the ticket barriers and waved his Oyster travel card. As he darted through, he glanced right and saw the policeman heading after him but with no sign of a pass or ticket. No way could he jump over the barriers, but as Alex glanced again he saw the man force someone out of the way and charge through.

Alex ran down the first escalator. At the bottom he turned to go onto the platform for the Circle line. A short distance along the platform was another exit. He took this and followed signs to the Bakerloo line. Before reaching it, he passed the exit route and ran along this to the escalators. These took him to the other side of the station with three exit options. At the top of the final escalator he looked behind. No sign of the pursuer. He passed through the barrier, turned right and emerged on the Paddington station concourse close to the platform twelve coffee bar. Without stopping, he scooted around to the left and up the ramp, through a wall of cigarette smoke, to the street.

A red bus was moving through the crossroads. He jumped on and sat down, panting. Close to the smoke-enshrouded entrance he saw the brown-suited man emerge, look around and disappear again.

Alex paid the conductor and stepped off at Edgware Road. He knew this area had a Costa Coffee with a quiet basement. He ordered a double espresso and went downstairs. There were seats for thirty or so customers but only two were occupied and neither person looked up as he found a chair opposite a TV screen that showed the view of the upstairs bar and entrance.

He placed the briefcase on the table in front of him and ran his hands over the surface and then along the edge as though sensing what was inside. It was fastened with combination locks, one on each side, three dials on each.

First things first. He took out his phone and called DI Jackson.

"Did you send someone to arrest me?" Alex asked without preamble.

"It's Sunday morning, Mr MacLure—"

"You picked me up last week on a Sunday."

"Fair point, but Highclere Castle had been burgled overnight. We were working. I am not working this morning."

"Did you send someone to arrest me?"

"No." There was hesitancy in Jackson's response. "What makes you ask that?"

"The latest rubbish from that reporter, saying I was definitely responsible for the break-in at Highclere Castle and was working with a Polish gang. It is nonsense. You know that, don't you?"

Jackson didn't respond immediately but when he did he said, "Yes."

Who the hell was the guy in the brown suit? If not Jackson's man then maybe another force. "Could it be someone from the Met?"

"Could who be? Are you saying a policeman is there to arrest you?"

So if not the Met police, who? There was only one conclusion: the other gang. The guys from the car chase with the guns. The guys who had trashed his flat. The guys responsible for the triple murder of the other gang.

"Mr MacLure?"

"Oh, yes. Sorry to have disturbed you this morning, Inspector. It must have been a reporter, someone trying it on. Just wanted to check it wasn't a policeman that I gave the slip."

"You sound a little strange. Is there anything you need to tell me?"

"Just the adrenaline and out of breath."

"Are you in trouble?"

Alex thought for a moment. Would it help to tell Jackson about the other gang? Maybe, but that might lead to the briefcase. He ran his hand over it. Too small to hold the missing ceremonial block. No, this contained Ellen's research.

"Sorry," Alex said again and ended the call.

He knocked back the coffee and stared at the combination lock. Two sets of three numbers. He tried 140 on each, even though he knew it was too obvious. Anyone collecting the case would know the reference number and would try 140.

What would Ellen choose? No! What would Ellen think Alex would choose? It would be a significant number.

She had known he'd won the lottery. Would she remember the numbers he'd chosen: 2, 5, 10, 17, 28 and 41? Six numbers but ten digits. He tried 251 and 017 but even as it failed to unlock he knew it wasn't right.

What were the numbers she'd written in his book? She'd used Isis twice. Why not use those numbers for multiple purposes? He tried to recall the sequence. He was pretty sure the first page number had been 256. Quite an interesting number. The lowest number that is the product of eight prime numbers. Four to the power of four. Relevant in computing as two to the power of eight. So maybe...

256 didn't unlock either combination.

Alex steepled his hands in front of his mouth and stared at the locks hoping for inspiration. *Come on, Ellen, what would you choose for me?*

After trying a few wild guesses and getting more frustrated, Alex decided to get more coffee. He checked upstairs before going back to the counter, ordering a long black this time.

As he paid, he saw the pink slip of paper in his wallet. He'd put it there with the credit card he'd used as ID at the baggage place.

He pulled it out.

"Sir?" The barista asked again for payment.

"Oh my God!" Alex whispered. "Oh my God! Ellen, you are a wicked genius."

In his haste to get downstairs to try the numbers that had just struck him, Alex forgot his coffee and had to be called back.

The number on the paper was 140. He'd already tried that, but 140 was special. Not only that but it was a pyramid number. That's why there was the symbol. It was an extra clue. Not a delta but a pyramid!

Start with a square base of balls and build them up. Not counting one ball on its own, the first pyramid was formed of a base of four balls with one on top. The second was a base of nine balls followed by four and then one. That made fourteen balls for the second pyramid number. The sixth pyramid number was 140. And the number of balls in a pyramid with a base of 140 by 140 balls was a six digit number: 924,490.

With fingers trembling with anticipation, Alex tried 924 on the first combination lock.

Click.

He dialled 490 on the second lock.

Click.

He lifted the lid.

THIRTY-TWO

Alex looked around the café. There were now four people downstairs but they paid him no heed. He studied the TV monitor half expecting someone to appear—maybe the fake policeman. After a minute of nothing suspicious, he tore his eyes away.

Inside the briefcase was a sheaf of papers in a red folder, bound by string.

Like a child will hold a Jack-in-the-box, with a mixture of anticipation and nerves, he lifted the bundle from the briefcase and worked the string free. The first few pages were emails from Marek.

We've cracked it! You were right about the code in the cuneiform messages.

Alex flicked through a few pages and saw images of clay tablets looking like a dog biscuit but with arrows and lines. This was cuneiform script, cramped and barely legible. Then there seemed to be a translation followed by a shorter passage with crossings out and suggested alternatives. He recognized the translation as an *Amarna Letter*, a record found at Tell el-Amarna, the site of Pharaoh Akhenaten's city. It was a strange message formally translated as:

To Napkhuria, King of Egypt, my brother, my son-in-law, who loves me and whom I love, thus speaks Tushratta, King of

Mitanni, your father-in-law who loves you, your brother. I am well. May you be well too. Your houses, Tiye your mother, Lady of Egypt, Tadu-Heba, my daughter, your wife, your other wives, your sons, your noblemen, your chariots, your horses, your soldiers, your country and everything belonging to you, may they all enjoy excellent health.

Marek had translated this as:

The pharaoh, through his brother, declared war with chariots, horses and soldiers to destroy the house.

Under this he wrote:

I think this is the record of the destruction of the city of Akhetaten or the palace. There's a name, transliteration of which is srq. It could be someone called something like Serq or it could mean the city was overrun with scorpions.

The next tablet translation was also obscure:

The sheep have been rounded-up (by the scorpion or blood?). Something about the way to afterlife being blocked perhaps?

Alex paged through many similar texts and then read through more printed emails from Marek. One said: Carter wrote of papyri not clay tablets. Maybe this is something else.

Marek's final email, dated just over a week before Ellen had been murdered:

I'm becoming worried. How close are you to getting it? We need to be extra careful and cover our tracks. I think you are right that they have killed—maybe even Lord C—and will not hesitate to kill to stop this information going public. Let's not communicate until you have the information.

The rest of the papers were Ellen's own notes and diagrams: her research. As he read, it became very clear what had happened, what she'd been doing at Highclere Castle and why she had taken the ceremonial block. He also knew now that he had to destroy the notes.

And then he saw the last page. Only, if he'd opened the bundle the other way around it would have been the first. It was a handwritten letter from Ellen.

Alex, if you are reading this then I know my worst fears have happened. Please take care. This discovery is huge but it is also very dangerous. We are convinced there are people who do not want this information to come to light.

The letter went on to tell him to find Professor Thompson at the Oxford institute, if he hadn't already done so. He would help understand the importance of what Carter and Lord Carnarvon discovered and Carnarvon died for.

There are two parts to this, Ellen went on to write. The first is the ceremonial block. The second is the hidden message. You'll find Marek's details in the bundle. He's done the translations and he's really the one behind understanding the story. He'll help you with the main part. The ceremonial block is a map. You'll understand when you read the story. I think the missing papyri included information too, maybe all of it. Maybe the map has already been worked out and there's nothing at the end. But I am absolutely convinced that whatever it is, or was, has immense consequences. Solve it, Alex. Solve it for me and, if it really is as huge as I think, find the truth that someone wants buried.

There were secure URLs and passwords listed. She wanted Alex to destroy the hard copies once he'd been through them and not print anything else.

I'm not sure what you'll find, but in the wrong hands, maybe this could be used in a damaging way. I don't know. Or perhaps the map was solved decades ago and we'll never know what lay at the end. But I know for sure that if it hasn't then this information could lead the wrong people to the solution.

She repeated herself a few times and he found himself imagining her state of mind. He figured she'd written this in the early hours of Sunday, bundling up the papers and leaving his house. She'd almost told him on Saturday night. He was sure of it. Maybe the fear that someone was watching stopped her. But he reckoned she'd left the phone and put the code in the Isis puzzle before leaving. She'd have bought the briefcase, possibly from one of the stores down from the café he was now in. She'd left him the research at the baggage reclaim and then gone back home. And two days later she was dead.

Alex felt a tear on his cheek and brushed it away, but her final words made him choke.

Thank you for being my friend.

If there is an afterlife, a Field of Reeds, our hearts are not heavy. The gods will welcome us and I will see you again.

Until then, I remain your—Ellen

It was almost lunchtime when he stopped reading and studying the pictures. Alex stuffed the papers into the briefcase and locked it. First checking the CCTV, he went upstairs and left the coffee shop. He crossed Edgware Road and headed back towards Paddington station. A spur of the canal ended close by and he reached the shops and plaza within a few minutes. From a convenience store he bought a cigarette lighter.

He walked across the deserted plaza to blue boarding behind which he knew a building had been demolished to make way for new offices. He followed the boards until he located a panel used as a door. After a quick check that no one was looking, he front-kicked the panel. It flew open and Alex stepped through.

Shielded in a corner of the hoarding, he opened the briefcase and took out the papers. He then began to scrunch them up until he had a pile of paper balls sitting on the open briefcase. Ironically, he realized that he'd created a paper pyramid, but he didn't smile. He didn't feel like smiling. It felt like he had lost his friend all over again.

He found a couple of wooden batons on the ground, snapped each in two and placed them almost pyramid-like over the paper to keep it in place. Then he lit the bottom of the pile. A tower of flame rapidly developed and then a host of floating ashes. When he was certain the papers were substantially destroyed, he scooped most of the remains into the briefcase and flung it into the ground works.

He walked back to Edgware Road and headed for the Circle line station. On the tube, he looked at his hands. Grey from the ash, he sniffed them absently and thought about Ellen's and Marek's work. Developed over months, destroyed in seconds.

The Third

THIRTY-THREE

On the secure site, the story that Ellen had called the first part had been written in sequence. There were gaps in the history that Alex didn't fully understand until much later. The clay tablets that were known as the Amarna Letters were from a library that had been the pride of the great ancient city built by the pharaoh Akhenaten. The sensitive sections had been coded and written by a different person who told the story of a boy who became a man of great significance. But his legacy had lain hidden for over three thousand years.

Although there was dispute amongst academics about exact dates of events, according to Marek, the story began about three thousand three hundred and fifty years ago.

1336 BCE, thirty miles south of Luxor

The boy heard the laughter before he saw the boat. A royal barge, he guessed. Certainly not a merchant—there was never jollity amongst the many cargo boats that passed silently along their poor stretch of the Nile. Yanhamu remained hidden on the bank as the majestic craft slid towards his position, its golden prow flashing in the morning sun. A giant blue pennant, almost as long as the barge itself, fluttered in the wind like a hunter's arrow, pointing the way downstream.

When she was close, Yanhamu counted fifteen oars on his side that dipped in and out of the water with slow, casual grace. And yet the noise from above deck rose and fell with shouts and screams and a melodic noise made by men with instruments. To Yanhamu's peasant ears it was like music, but without the banging and clacking. The laughter came mostly from girls, who he could now see dancing in clean white skirts, their breasts jiggling between necklaces of gold, emerald, turquoise and lapis.

Never in his nine years had Yanhamu seen anything so rich; it was a life of music and happiness that was alien to his own world in the village. Perhaps this was a glimpse of the afterworld where his mother now lived. He smiled at the thought of her dancing with the other women and wondered whether she was able to laugh now. She surely knew he was well and strong and that his elder sister, Laret, cared for him since their father had left two seasons ago. He'd gone with the other men to find work, as all men did when the floods were due. There could be no farming during flood season and so he had gone. When he didn't return, their aunt said he was working in the great city to the north. When he had made his fortune, he would come back and get them and they would never be hungry or want for anything again.

At the time, Yanhamu hadn't understood, and Laret said he was too young, but now he knew. What he wanted more than anything was for them to be a family again, to hear the beautiful music and laughter.

Yesterday, Laret had seen another royal barge. She had chattered all night about it, saying that something big was happening. She wondered whether it explained why the soldiers had been in their village. It was the wrong time of year for taxes, and a scribe with them took note of everyone's name, age and patron god.

"Who is my god?" Yanhamu had asked his sister.

"Anhuris," she had said, smiling. "You are strong and good and above all you are a protector."

"But I am so small and it is you who looks after me."

Again she smiled and held him close under their blanket. "One day, my Yani, one day you will be my protector."

When the barge had gone, the river became still once more. The duck he had spied at sunrise returned to the reed bed Yanhamu had been watching. He waited another fifteen minutes, barely breathing, watching the reeds and picturing the duck as it found its nest and settled. He felt the sweat prickling the exposed back of his neck. A black insect crawled up a stem close to his nose, but he didn't move. Then he saw it, the twitch of a reed that told him the duck was settling. Still careful, in case he was mistaken, he eased himself into position and pulled two sticks from his belt. With the smooth motion his father had taught him, he parted the reeds. "Imagine you are the breeze, Yanhamu," his father had said, and he heard his voice now. He breathed to calm his beating heart and pressed on. And there she was, a golden duck squatting low over her nest, unaware she had been found.

The need for stealth over, Yanhamu thrashed at the reeds. With a jump, the bird scurried into the undergrowth and seconds later burst through the far side, skittered across the water and into the air.

Yanhamu stepped into the silt and waded to her nest. Seven eggs. He knew the rule of *ma-at*: always leave three eggs behind so that Het would not be angry. He reached through the thicket and picked up the first, warm with life. He looked at it, studied its perfect form before placing it carefully into the satchel slung by his side. He did the same with the next and the next. When he placed the fourth in the bag, he found himself reaching for the fifth, the sixth and then the seventh. He held the final three, cupped in his hands.

His stomach growled. It had been a long time since he had eaten anything other than bread and onions. Surely the goddess would understand. He wondered whether She made the rule to protect the bird. If all eggs were taken, birds wouldn't reproduce and so there would be no future birds to give them eggs. It made sense although he knew other animals took the eggs and sometimes the duck produced another batch.

He said a prayer then to Het asking her to understand his family's need and to grant the bird great fertility and many offspring. Satisfied, he stood, scraped the Nile dirt from his legs and hastened back to the village.

"Laret, Laret," he called as he neared the outskirts. Then he pulled up and stared. There was a soldier standing at the main hut. He was talking to the matriarch and Laret was by his side. As Yanhamu neared, he spotted a tether around Laret's wrist.

And then the soldier handed something to the matriarch and walked away, Laret a step behind, her shorter legs hurrying compared to the big man's stride.

"Laret!" Yanhamu choked back the fear and began to run. Laret had been arrested! It must be a mistake. What could his beautiful, caring sister have done wrong?

By the time he reached the gate, his sister was over sixty paces away, heading for the river. Yanhamu caught hold of a cousin's tunic. "What has happened? What did she do? Where is he taking my Laret?"

The boy, older than Yanhamu by three harvests, tried to shrug off his grip and pull away, but Yanhamu's grip was desperate.

The boy grunted, "She's going to be trained."

"Trained?"

"As a palace dancer."

"But, she would never... I need her!"

The boy finally jerked out of Yanhamu's grip and laughed. "You simpleton, Hamu. She will be much better off... and the family is better off too." He nodded towards his mother, the matriarch still standing in the doorway.

194

Yanhamu guessed that she weighed a purse in her hands.

The boy said, "Since your mother died and your father left, you should think yourself lucky." He laughed again. "I myself would have sold you both as meat to the butcher."

Yanhamu barely heard this last remark. He was already running, his desperate feet kicking up dust like a sand viper.

He pulled alongside her. "Laret, don't leave me!"

She looked at her brother with tearful eyes but didn't stop. "I have no choice." She forced a smile. "But, my clever brother, I will be happy. There is a big festival and I am to be a dancer! I will dance like a princess at a palace."

Yanhamu continued to half walk, half jog beside the path. As they neared the river, he saw a boat with more soldiers and a gaggle of young girls on board. Desperate now, he rushed ahead and stood directly in the soldier's path. The man stopped and glowered.

Swallowing, Yanhamu looked into the big man's eyes. He wanted to tell the man to let his sister go, that she wanted to stay with him, that it was only the silver he had paid to the family that had persuaded her, but the words wouldn't come.

The man's face was like chiselled granite, his eyes almost as cold. He spat, "Stand aside you insolent pup or feel the lash of my staff across your peasant face." He raised his stick so suddenly that Yanhamu flinched in expectation of a blow, but he stood his ground.

The soldier snarled and then lunged, snatched Yanhamu around the waist and flung him out of the way.

"No!" Laret jerked her leash from the soldier's grasp, dived to her brother's side and helped him to his feet. She brushed dirt from his face and kissed his forehead. "Take care, little brother."

"Laret!" Tears sprang from his eyes and stung his cheeks then.

"Promise me you will think of me and pray for me. One day perhaps you will see me dance." She kissed him again and rushed along the path.

Yanhamu gaped in shocked silence as his sister stepped onto the gangplank and onto the boat. Immediately the granite-faced soldier barked an order and the boat was pushed from the bank. Forty oars were lowered into the water and, with the precision of a many-legged creature, the boat pulled smoothly away. Yanhamu noticed symbols on the side and he knew this represented the boat's name. He memorized them so that he could recall them later.

He began to run along the bank, following the boat, but his heart and legs were not strong enough to keep up and he was soon forced to walk. Gasping for air, the fear of never seeing his sister again pulled tight around his heaving chest. And then the oarsmen did something unexpected. In unison, they stopped and raised their oars to the sky. A low chanting began that raised in pitch and volume. At the front a man in a flowing white gown raised his arms. Yanhamu looked up and saw that the edge of the moon had turned a dusty orange. As he watched in horror the moon began to shrink as though a cloud of locusts swept across its surface, devouring all life. Then, when the whole surface was covered, the moon was dark mud-red.

Instinctively he felt for the satchel hanging at his side. He had broken the rule. Het was angry with him and had destroyed the moon. He knew then that his sister had been taken away from him as a punishment by the gods. He had defied them and there would be no Field of Reeds in the afterlife for him. On Judgement Day, before the great god Osiris, his heart would fail the test and be tossed to Ammut—to be eaten by the Devourer.

He clenched his teeth. A strength coursed through his muscles as the realization struck him: without Laret his earthly life meant nothing either. Breathing in deeply, Yanhamu tensed his young muscles and forced himself to walk again, and then, as fortitude returned, he began to run.

The redness of the moon faded, to be replaced by orange once more—the swarm of locusts seemed to be moving away. A noise from the river bank made him look. A small merchant vessel had been moored and the two men on board began to move, dropping their raised arms, ending their supplication to the moon.

Without considering dangers, Yanhamu made a decision and rushed into the water, to the boat's side. He called up to the man at the tiller. "Passage, my good man."

The sailor looked over the side, surprised, and then waved the boy away. He called to the man at the front who poled the bow away from the bank.

Yanhamu jumped and held onto the side, pulled himself up, but not onto the boat. "I can pay you!"

The first man looked thoughtful as he steered into the river. From the corner of his eye, he watched Yanhamu clinging to the side. "You can't hold on for long, and when you are finally weak you will drop and be food for the crocodiles."

"I'm strong. I won't let go," Yanhamu replied.

The man nodded. "So how much can you pay me, urchin?"

"I have seven large duck eggs."

The man waved him to climb on board. Yanhamu opened his satchel and stared with horror at the mess. Only two eggs remained unbroken. He handed them over and showed the snotty residue of the rest.

The man shook his head and took the two eggs. "If you are strong, can you also work?"

"I work very hard. By Horus, I am the hardest worker for my size!"

"Good, because you may have passage as long as you work. Stop working and you are over the side and may Sobek protect you."

Yanhamu began work at once by scrubbing down the timbers. After two hours in the sweltering sun, the sailor handed him a gourd of water and told him to go below and check the fruit, polishing and removing any which were rotten.

"Mind that you don't eat any, urchin. It is all counted and even the rotten fruit must be accounted for."

"I would rather work in the sun."

The sailor frowned. "Has the heat made you lose your senses?"

"I need to follow the soldiers' boat, the one with the forty oars. My sister is on board."

The sailor waved towards the hold. "I know the boat. It is called *The Heliopolis Black Bull*. Go below and I will watch for it. Don't worry, I won't pass without telling you."

Yanhamu read the man's face and knew he was honest. He nodded his thanks and scurried out of the cruel sun.

When he was eventually called to the deck, the sun had set and its parting still touched the encroaching night with a gentle light like a mosquito bite on pale flesh. Nedjem—for that was the sailor's name—had steered to the bank and told Yanhamu to jump ashore and tie them up. When he had finished, Nedjem patted him on the shoulder like a man. "*The Heliopolis Black Bull* is two hundred paces that way, after the merchants' quay."

"Where are we?"

"The City of a Thousand Gates."

Yanhamu shook his head. The name meant nothing, but then he knew very little of the places outside his village. Then he bowed his thanks, first touching his knees and then reaching out.

This made the sailor laugh. "Good luck, urchin, and Horus protect you."

Yanhamu ran along the public quay. People were tying up boats for the night and closing up warehouses. The first section smelled of beer and then there was a cattle enclosure followed by a timber yard and pottery

198

warehouse. The final section was a storage area for wheat and barley. Men looked at him suspiciously as he hurried past and a few called lewdly with the tones of drinking men.

Beyond the public wharf there was a grove of bushes and then a long quarried-stone quay. Five boats were moored, and in the rapidly fading light he realized three of them looked like the one his sister had been taken on. Just as he recognized the symbols on the side of *The Heliopolis Black Bull*, a man called out. He swivelled and saw a watchman with a fearsome beast on a chain rushing towards him. Yanhamu backed away but then stood his ground.

"Clear off, urchin!" the guard shouted as he stopped a couple of paces away with his animal straining at the leash. "Run now or my baboon will bite off your manhood." The creature showed its wicked yellow teeth as though it understood its master's warning.

"I don't have a manhood," Yanhamu said, straightening his back. "I'm only a child."

The watchman's face mellowed and he jerked the baboon back so that it sat obediently at his side. "You are brave for one with no manhood."

Yanhamu did his bow—hands to the knees and then out.

The guard laughed. "What are you doing here?"

"*The Heliopolis Black Bull*." Yanhamu pointed to the ship. "Has everyone gone?"

"Disembarked? Yes. Why do you—?"

"Where is the palace dancing school? My sister has been taken there."

The guard laughed again. "All right, all right," he said when he could get his breath back, and then he gave directions.

As Yanhamu ran off, the watchman called out, "Since you don't have a manhood, if I see you on the military quay again, I'll let my baboon have his way with you!"

Once off the quay, Yanhamu made his way through narrow streets. The sky was fully dark now, for the moon had been awake during the day. However, this was an artisan section lit by torches. Inside buildings and sitting at tables on the street he saw men of supreme skill working glass and pottery and painting pictures that made him gape at their beauty. But he did not dally. He ran along the side of a long wall and at the end turned right past a temple. He noted that the way seemed to lead away from the centre of the town, and at first he thought he was heading for the residential area, but then he found himself on the outskirts, faced by another long wall. He worked his way around until he reached a wooden gateway with braziers burning on either side. The great Pharaoh Ahmose was said to have been more than twice the height of a normal man and even he could have walked without ducking his head through this entrance. Two soldiers knelt by the closed gates and leaned on their spears.

Yanhamu approached one. "Sir, is this the palace dancing school?"

The man laughed. "Some call it that. Now piss off!"

"But, sir…" A stone struck him. He looked at the other solider and saw he was about to let another fly.

The other soldier said, "You heard him. Piss off, dung heap!"

Yanhamu stood his ground and let the second stone strike him without flinching. The first soldier took a step forward and lowered his spear.

Yanhamu said, "Please… what do you mean by *some people call it that*?"

Both guards laughed. "It's the bloody garrison, isn't it!"

"But my sister… I was told she was here!"

"Oh she'll be here all right," the second soldier said, and he made a rude gesture and laughed again.

Yanhamu staggered backwards into the darkness. He felt the night close in as though Nut herself had come down and swallowed him whole.

THIRTY-FOUR

1336 BCE, Luxor

Yanhamu awoke before dawn, his bones aching with cold. He had dreamed of a hawk that terrorized his village, attacking the women and girls and making them cry out. It took a few moments for him to remember where he was: outside the garrison in the City of a Thousand Gates. After stretching and rubbing his limbs he climbed a tree and, as the sky lightened with morning, he could partially see over the garrison wall.

The whole enclosure was bigger than his village. The buildings inside were mostly two storey and, from what he could see, they formed an L-shape along two sides of the walls. He could hear animal sounds and guessed a third shed, with at least one horse and some buffalo, was hidden beneath the nearest wall.

Still before the sunrise, a cart laden with bread trundled through the gate and two young men unloaded it into a store and left. Soldiers began to emerge and, after a period of relative quiet, began training in the open courtyard, wrestling, some fighting with short sticks and others practising with spears. He saw no sign of any girls.

Yanhamu climbed down from the tree and retraced his steps into the town. There he asked people about the school for dancing girls. With each negative response, his heart sank further and he became convinced his sister was inside the garrison walls.

He returned to his tree and watched the soldiers, hoping to spot his sister or any of the girls he'd seen on board *The Heliopolis Black Bull*. At one point he saw the man who had taken his sister away—the man with the face like granite. The man shouted and pointed a lot and Yanhamu guessed him to be in charge. He also seemed to have a room to himself—the only part of the building that was three storeys high.

By mid-afternoon, weak with hunger, Yanhamu slipped and almost fell from his perch. He dropped down and headed to the artisan sector looking for work. He swept the floor of a potter's studio and was rewarded with bread and cheese, a pat on the head, and praise for working so hard. The kind man also insisted Yanhamu clean himself up before he left and gave him a pale blue smock.

Yanhamu explored the workshop area behind the quays. Everywhere was swept clean and organized with each section clearly demarked. In places the air smelled like flowers, not the usual acrid smell of living quarters and animals. He noticed that there were no farm animals in the town except for an area by the quay penned off for cattle.

Over the next three days he worked, returned to the garrison to watch, and spoke to everyone he met. But the answer was always the same. He was told where the palaces were, but there was no dancing school for common folk. He also learned that this was a special time. There was great excitement about the coming festival. Osiris was about to rise into the heavens, signalling the arrival of the inundation. But also, Horus had returned to human form as a boy about Yanhamu's age. They called him Tutankhaten.

On the second day a warehouseman asked him to run a message. He delivered it quickly and found he was sent on with another message. The second message took him to a bakery where he was given a scrap of bread, for it was always the receiver of the message who paid. Yanhamu was allowed to watch the baking and out of interest followed a laden cart to the warehouse of the first merchant. The man immediately recognized him as the messenger, but Yanhamu was surprised to note that the merchant didn't know the young man who pushed the cart. In the village, everyone knew everyone.

In the evening he decided to return to the garrison and confront the soldier who had taken Laret away.

The guards eyed him suspiciously as he approached.

Yanhamu did his bow, hands to the knees and then out, which made them laugh. "Are you hungry?" he asked as he straightened.

The men stopped laughing and he could see in their eyes that they were. "I have sweet bread," he said, and from the blue smock pulled two hand-sized triangles of cake.

The nearest guard reached out. "What do you want in return?"

Yanhamu stepped out of reach. "To speak to the soldier with the granite face who shouts a lot."

The second guard laughed. "You are out of luck. The captain prefers girls to keep his bed warm. And he has a new girl to do that."

Yanhamu swallowed. "What's her name?"

The first guard stepped forward. "The bread first."

Yanhamu handed over both triangles and the man tossed one to his colleague.

After they had both taken a bite, Yanhamu asked again, "What's her name?"

"Don't know," laughed the nearest guard. "But if the captain's true to form, we should get a go at her before the next season is out."

The second grabbed his groin. "Then we can show her how real men do it."

After they both finished laughing, the first guard said, "Got any more bread?"

"No."

"Then piss off."

Yanhamu stood his ground. As both men picked up stones, he said, "Wait. Just tell me when the girls come out. Tell me that and I'll bring you bread tomorrow."

The first one said, "You're a bit young to be sniffing after pretty girls."

Yanhamu forced a laugh, "Never too young, eh?"

The guard chuckled. "All right, horny boy. Sometimes they are allowed out in the morning before the men get up. Sometimes it's in the evening." He looked into Yanhamu's eyes. "You promise to bring bread?"

Yanhamu nodded.

"They'll be coming out very soon. Make sure you're downwind if you want a good sniff."

The other guard said something lewd, but Yanhamu was already running to his tree. It was barely light enough to see, but when the girls came into the courtyard he heard their voices, subdued and sad.

At the top of his lungs he shouted, "Laret!"

"Yani!"

His heart leapt. It was his sister's voice, although he couldn't see which girl had called back.

A commotion ensued, with female screams and shouting men. He thought he saw sticks being used to thrash the girls, round them up, and then they were gone.

Over the next four days, he watched and worked out the pattern of activity. He also discovered that these were known as the Hidden Days, the extra days in the calendar that Ra had provided before the rise of Osiris and the start of a new year. During this time, the wealthier people stopped working. They prayed and drank and fornicated.

Between short visits to the garrison, learning their routine, Yanhamu worked incessantly, running messages and helping at the bakery. On the day before the New Year, he delivered the morning bread to the garrison and hatched his plan. The girls exercised at the time of a watch change. The bread was delivered by two boys after the new watch.

The celebrations continued until the morning. As Yanhamu and another baker's boy walked a donkey pulling the laden bread cart through the dark streets, they saw the remnants of the night's excesses. Drunken men staggered between buildings and others lay where they had collapsed, either passed out or still praying incoherently to the sky.

The older boy moaned about them delivering too early. Truth was, he'd been up all night and had had too much beer.

"Then go home," Yanhamu said.

"And deliver on your own?" The other boy was clearly interested.

"I can manage."

The boy looked him up and down. "I'll miss out on any tips."

"I'll split them with you."

"I know you are trustworthy, but it's not fair."

"It is fair—I want to do this alone."

The other boy didn't need to hear more. He scurried off to bed calling, "Thanks. See you tonight, Yanhamu."

It was a struggle to goad the donkey the final five hundred yards, and he made it to the gate just before the watch changed. Inside, he took his time unloading the bread so that he was about done when the girls appeared. With his heart beating in his throat, he watched as they filed past. And then he saw her.

"Laret!" he whispered.

She looked at him, but her eyes were hollow and unseeing. Her lip was cut and her cheek glowed with the early stages of bruising.

"I'm getting you out," he said, and from the cart pulled a spare baker's cloak. Throwing it around her shoulders, he pulled the hood over her head. Checking that the guards weren't looking, Yanhamu gripped her arm and pulled her in the direction of the cart. "Walk!" he whispered as he struggled against her indifference. They made it to the cart and he placed her hand on the side and made her grip. He took hold of the donkey's reins and eased the empty bread cart towards the gate.

Keeping his head down, sure the guards would hear the drumbeat in his chest, he walked through the gate and past them. At that moment, the pealing of a hundred bells began, announcing the start of the New Year worship and parades.

Then one of the guards shouted, "Hey!"

Yanhamu swung around and gaped. Laret had fallen to the floor. He rushed to her side and helped her stand.

The guard shouted, "She better not have the plague."

Yanhamu grinned. "No, it's too much bread. Extra poison for you today!" He made a choking sign and then waved. "See you tomorrow."

The guards laughed.

As soon as they were out of sight, Yanhamu stopped the donkey and checked on his sister. He looked into her empty eyes. "Are you hungry? Can I get you something?" She didn't reply, and he felt tears prickle his eyes. He sat her in the shade and hugged her long and hard.

He told her he would be a short time while he returned the donkey and cart to the baker. He hurried, all the time wondering what they should do, where he could take Laret so she would get better. He decided to find a temple dedicated to Het and explain that it was his fault for taking the eggs. Laret had nothing to do with it, so he should pay the price, whatever the goddess needed to make amends.

He soon returned to the spot where he'd left his sister and his heart froze.

She was gone.

THIRTY-FIVE

Vanessa was back.

She stood at the door to her uncle's flat.

It was Sunday evening and Alex had spent the rest of the day reading and making sense of Yanhamu's story. He was pleased to see her, but he forced his face to stay neutral.

"Can I come in?"

He stepped aside. "I trusted you," he said.

"I'm sorry." She came close, reached out as though to touch him but then thought better of it. "One thing though, if you'd known my initial interest you would never have let me close, would you?"

He could smell her musk and tried to hide its impact. Keeping up the act, he kept a serious face and just said, "No."

"But I've got to know you and, aside from the name—"

"The deception."

She winced. "Apart from that, you've gotten to know me. I like you, Alex. I really like you."

He could hold back no longer and let a smile break through. "I'm glad you're back."

She grinned and hugged him. "Me too."

They sat on the sofa. "So you found the research."

"It's amazing."

"Can I see it?"

"No."

She looked crestfallen. "Oh, I thought—"

"I destroyed it." Alex told her about Ellen's letter and request that he make sure it never fell into the wrong hands. He also told her about the man in the brown suit who had pretended to be a policeman. "That gang are determined to get their hands on the research. I had to erase any evidence. I burned it."

"Oh my God!" she said. "Does that mean it was simple to remember or have you got some kind of photographic memory you've not told me about?"

"I've a good memory, but it's not that good. I checked out what was in the pack, which was quite disjointed and really a collection of her papers as she'd progressed with the research. That's what I burned. In the briefcase were a couple of secure web addresses and passwords. I've been looking at one this afternoon, following the story of a young boy called Yanhamu. From the notes I think he's the one who becomes a royal scribe called Meryra. During the Eighteenth Dynasty, it seems he recorded what was happening—only it would have been treason to openly write about what he witnessed, so he embedded his records in other documents. In ancient Egypt, word games and double meanings were commonplace, and remember, only the elite could read and write."

"And this was Ellen's research?"

"Absolutely, but it seems to have become much more than that. She referred to two components of the research. One was the story and one was about the ceremonial block. It seems the story explains the block. But, although Ellen was working on it, a large part of the research was by an Egyptian PhD student called Marek Borevsek. He was originally working in Berlin and then moved to Cairo."

"Berlin? Why Berlin?"

"Berlin Museum contains a vast Egyptian collection. In fact, of the Amarna Letters—almost four hundred clay tablet documents from the period—the majority are in the Berlin Museum. I think they must have met through a forum. He had a big piece of the puzzle with the letters but didn't know what he was looking for. Until he hooked up with Ellen about the ceremonial block that is."

"So it is all about that missing block."

"It seems to be a map."

She nodded thoughtfully. "If only we could find it. Do you think Ellen hid it? Do you know where it might be?"

"No idea, but I'm not sure I need it."

"Oh?"

"That's the other part. There's another secure site with photos and sketches of the block. Look."

He opened his laptop and logged onto a site. As he hit enter, he said, "Best that you don't know the password. If those BMW men..." He didn't need to finish. She nodded.

"It doesn't look very special," she said as he flicked through the site.

"No it doesn't. You would never guess what its real purpose was."

"Not about embalming fluids?"

"Marek called it the Map-Stone."

"It doesn't look like a map. It's more like you said, a breeze block."

Alex agreed. "From the story, Marek believed the scribe hid important documents and religious icons in Tutankhamen's tomb..." He paused and raised his eyebrows. "After the tomb was closed."

"You're saying he broke in?"

"More likely that he gained permission. Marek thinks Meryra was able to enter and have the tomb resealed. That would explain why the royal necropolis seal was dated after the tomb was originally closed."

"Was it?"

"I discovered that this afternoon."

Vanessa whistled through her teeth. "You told me that Carnarvon took artefacts. From the professor in Oxford you said it was papyrus... papers. Do you think it was actually this Map-Stone? Do you think he knew it held the secret? And what about them arguing? Did Carter want it?"

"I don't know, but my guess would be no. Carnarvon expected the *Book of the Dead* documents, and he said he saw the scrolls. If he'd just found the ceremonial block, I doubt he'd have thought anything of it. As you said, it doesn't look anything like a map."

He logged out and closed the laptop. "Are you hungry?"

They ate at a local Lebanese restaurant, the conversation jumping back and forth about what he'd learned. She listened with fascination to the story of the young Yanhamu, who rescued his sister and then lost her.

"It's hard going," Alex explained. Marek has translated the tablets but his English isn't perfect. Plus the sequence isn't quite right.

"And you said this peasant boy goes on to become a royal scribe of high status. How does he—?"

"I've not got that far. I must admit that it seems unlikely. But then again, having secret messages in clay tablets is also amazing."

She refused another glass of wine. "Not too much tonight," she said with her crooked smile. "One thing I don't get is why would he hide the story of his youth? Surely it's the stuff you called treason that he'd have disguised?"

"The early stuff isn't hidden. Marek thinks it was written by someone else. Someone who wanted to tell his story."

As they walked back, she said, "There's one burning question, one thing you've been teasing me with."

"There is?"

"The Map-Stone. It looks like a lump of rock but it's a map. The question is: can you read it?"

210

He stopped in the street. "No."

"But Ellen worked it out?"

"I don't think so. She and Marek worked out what had happened and what it was, but understanding how to read it...? I'm hoping inspiration will come."

"What about this Marek guy, can he help?"

"I emailed him this afternoon. But no reply yet."

Alex took her hand and they walked up to the flat. He opened the door, turned and put his hands on her waist.

"Are you staying tonight?" His question was laced with innuendo.

"Let's take it slow. I think we need to rebuild our friendship first. And I want you to trust me again." She kissed him lightly on the lips. "Sleep well. Let's see what tomorrow brings."

THIRTY-SIX

Alex couldn't sleep. He went back on the Map-Stone site and spent hours staring at the photos and drawing what he saw. When he could no longer think, he logged into the other site and read more of the story of the boy Yanhamu, who might have become the scribe Meryra.

1336 BCE, Luxor

Yanhamu began to run through the streets calling Laret's name. The more he looked, the more panicked he became. Finally, he made himself stop and think. There were few people in the outskirts, and when he asked everyone he met, they shook their heads. They hadn't seen a girl wandering the streets in a baker's cloak. Perhaps she'd gone to see the festival, some of them suggested.

The boy headed for the centre of the town, still looking along every road and around every corner. Before he reached the first pylon, the crowds began to gather. He was forced to wait as a procession of priests with flowing white gowns and shaven heads carried the god Amun aloft in a litter. They were followed by musicians with their tinkling bells, and then came the crowds, singing and clapping.

Yanhamu forced his way through and found himself swallowed by another crowd worshipping Tefnut, with many imitating lions with their growls and hand movements. They were followed by musicians and then the crowd swept after them clicking bone castanets and singing. He ducked between and through the snake of people only to find another crowd following Khnum, the god responsible for the Nile inundation. Past this procession, he briefly caught sight of the blue of another baker's gown standing out against the mainly white and ochre colours of the worshipers.

"Laret!"

He pushed his way through more people and found himself swept towards a temple. Inside, the priests were performing a ceremony and guards posted outside stopped people gaining access.

And then he saw the blue gown briefly again and worked his way in her direction, along the temple wall, and reached the front of the crowd. To his horror he realized the soldier was not just a guard. He was the captain. Bile leapt to his throat and he found himself heading for the man, forcing his way against the flow of people. Ahead he could hear the soldier shouting orders to his men, trying to corral the good-natured masses, preventing them from entering the temple. The crowds didn't seem to care for they sang and clapped and even when one of their number was struck with a stick it seemed to increase the fervour of their celebration.

Then, in the crowd, on the far side of the soldiers, Yanhamu saw his sister again.

"Laret!" he called, but his little voice was lost in the noise of a hundred people. The bodies moved closer, and through a gap his mind momentarily made no sense of what he saw. Weak though she was, Laret was running towards the soldier; raised in her hand was a copper grappling hook. While the soldiers were distracted, she lunged at the man who had brought her to this city, slashing at his face.

In a swift motion, the soldier pulled his short sword, twisted and plunged it deep into her belly. As she fell, the soldier kicked her away and waved to one of his men. Yanhamu forced his legs to move, although no sooner had he taken two steps than a soldier drove him back.

"No entry to the temple!"

Blind with distress, Yanhamu blinked tears from his eyes and pushed forward. His reward was a blow to the head from the soldier's stick.

He could no longer see her body. "Laret!" he cried and pushed back through the throng, circling the temple entrance to get closer to where she had fallen. When he reached the point, the blood on the ground was already vanishing under trampling feet. The granite-faced soldier was still there, although his bloodied hand was pressed to his cheek, staunching the flow from a gash caused by the grappling hook. Then Yanhamu saw another soldier carrying a body—Laret's body. The crowd parted to let him pass and then closed ranks as though he had never been.

Yanhamu elbowed his way after the soldier, desperately trying to gauge which way he'd gone. The tears had dried, replaced by a fear for his lovely sister that gripped his throat.

Finally he was through the crowds and found himself on the merchants' quay. The water had risen almost to the level of the stone blocks. The soldier was at the end by the flooded reeds. He looked at something in the water, adjusted his tunic and turned. Yanhamu shoulder-charged him with the cry of a wild hawk. He felt the impact and then he was spinning, tumbling into the river. When he came up, gasping, the soldier glowered at him from the bank before spitting a curse and hurrying away.

Yanhamu's sister lay face down in the water. He pulled her towards him and rolled her over. Her eyes had the gaze of the dead and the howl that came up from his stomach scared geese into flight. Shaking, he tried to calm himself. He knew he had to get her out of the water quickly in case her blood attracted a crocodile. He tugged her through the reeds, but the silt beneath his feet made him slip and the reeds seemed to be trying to drag her the other way. He got her to the bank but could not lift her over. He called for help but the handful of people within earshot ignored his pleas. He climbed out and ran to the nearest man.

The man waved him away. The next listened to him briefly but then excused himself. After six more failed attempts, Yanhamu collapsed. When he opened his eyes, he realized he was kneeling beside a shrine to Het. The irony of it made him scream.

He picked up a stone and threw it. With a puff of sand it disintegrated, leaving but a smudge on the red granite shrine.

"No!" he yelled, and with all his might he picked up a larger rock and charged. It thudded against the granite and fell from his hands and struck his shin as it fell. Enraged, he yelled again and struck the shrine with his fists. "It should be me!" he cried. "I'm the one who did wrong. I'm the one you should take!"

He continued to pound and shout at the stone until a hand touched his shoulder.

A kindly voice said, "You'll damage your hands if you continue much more."

Yanhamu turned, tears blurring his eyes. The man was an elder, upper class from the look of his tunic.

The man smiled kindly. "What's wrong?"

"My sister..." Yanhamu's voice caught, and suddenly the rage he had felt melted into sobs.

"Sit down," the elder said, and eased the boy to the floor. With his hand still on Yanhamu's shoulder, he continued to talk softly until the sobbing subsided. "Now tell me what is so terrible that you wish to anger the gods, my child."

"They are already angry with me, my lord."

"Perhaps, but why anger them further... unless your life is over and your *ba* longs for the Devourer."

Yanhamu studied the noble. He had a white tunic in a style different from the other nobles he had seen. He wore a scarf with gold symbols, the writing of the gods. His hair was shaved except for a ponytail on one side. He told the man his story, that his sister now lay dead in the river, killed by the soldier who had taken her.

The noble didn't question the story, just said, "I'll help you. We must be quick."

Yanhamu hurried back to the reeds by the merchants' quay with the noble following at a swift pace. When he arrived, Yanhamu's legs gave way. He sank to his knees and wailed. Through his tears he sobbed, "She's gone and her soul is lost. Anyone who drowns will not find the Field of Reeds in the afterlife!"

The noble placed his hand on the boy's shoulder. "Was she beautiful but also good?"

"Yes." Yanhamu looked up at the man, unsure why he asked. "She was the best sister... looked after me since the plague took our mother."

"Take a good look. There is no sign of her, no sign her body was taken by a crocodile. No sign an animal has dragged her body out."

"No..."

"Then I think the gods have taken her. Sometimes it is not only the *ba* that ascends to Heaven. In special cases, when the gods so choose, the body may also leave this world."

"You think?" Yanhamu stood. "You really think she is with the gods?"

"What was her name?"

"Laret."

"Come, I will walk you to a temple and you should talk to her. Tell her you will be all right and that you will think of her every day and attend to her should she need

216

anything." He steered the boy away from the river, but instead of heading for the main temple—of the god Amun, he led the way to the small temple of Isis.

"What about the soldier?" Yanhamu asked as the noble bid farewell. "What about the man who killed her?"

"You know about the law?"

Yanhamu nodded. "The matriarch of the village taught us about *ma-at*."

"Well, there is *ma-at*, but that is really the harmony and balance of the world. No, I mean the Law of Ra." He bowed his head in thought and then said, "A good man has nothing to fear of the gods or the law. A man who has spilled Egyptian blood should beware both." He nodded as though his words meant something more to him.

Before he left Yanhamu to pray, the nobleman handed the boy an amulet. Yanhamu stared in disbelief at the precious metal Eye of Horus inside a circle.

"Is it silver, my lord?"

There was a tear in the noble's eye and he placed a hand on the boy's head. In a hoarse whisper, he said, "Your face has been opened. Be true to your heart and the gods will be true to you."

THIRTY-SEVEN

Something else was playing on Alex's mind. Ellen's funeral. It was today at 1pm. Could he go? He desperately wanted to. It felt wrong to miss it and yet reporters could be there. If Milwanee still believed he was guilty, linked somehow to another gang—maybe Polish—then surely she wouldn't forego the chance to corner him?

Of course there was another possibility: the BMW guys with the guns could also be there. If they wanted the Map-Stone, they wouldn't give up until they got him. And the fake policeman in the brown suit saw him collect the briefcase. That must have looked suspicious: collecting a briefcase on a Sunday. Did they know what the Map-Stone was like? Did they know the size? Maybe they thought the ceremonial block was in his case.

No, no matter how awful he felt, he couldn't go to the funeral.

"You have to go," Vanessa said when she rang. She said she had lectures in the morning and had rung to arrange to meet later.

"I'll be spotted," he said despondently. "I can't risk it."

"Screw the lectures. I'll be over within the hour. You are going!"

When she arrived, Vanessa had a bag. She opened it with a flourish and pulled out a wig and make-up kit.

"I've an actor friend," she explained. "We can give you a proper disguise so not even your mother would recognize you."

Thirty minutes later, Alex had to agree it was an amazing transformation. With a grey hair and beard, he looked like an old man. Vanessa had lightened his skin and made his eyes look sallow.

She transformed her image too and then pulled an old suit and tasteless dress from the bag. "Now we are an old married couple," she announced. Let's find you a walking stick and we'll waltz right in there and out again and no one will be any the wiser."

Alex noticed Milwanee hanging around outside the Southampton crematorium. He guessed the six other people around her were either part of the team or more reporters. He kept an eye out for the BMW or anyone who looked like a gang member, but saw no one suspicious.

Once inside the east chapel, he could relax. The room was packed and he felt they blended with the crowd without a problem. Ellen's brother gave the eulogy and included a poem that she had written as a teenager. It was about the wonder of life and that she had her whole life ahead of her. Her brother choked at the end and left the podium with tears flowing freely.

Alex found himself shaking with emotion.

"Thank you," he said as they came out. "I did need that. I guess it's what the Americans call closure."

"Cognitive closure," Vanessa said, "is a gestalt principle of perceptual organization that explains how humans fill in visual gaps in order to perceive disconnected parts as a whole object." She shrugged. "Sorry, but we've just covered it on my course."

He nodded, "I have no idea what you said, but I'm sure it's true. I do feel I'm ready to move on."

They got into her car, but before pulling off she studied him. "Does this mean you won't be pursuing Ellen's research?"

"Of course I will! I've not got this close to stop now."

She laughed. "Phew! OK, let's get home and solve this thing."

She drove to the M3, stopped at a service station and removed the wig and used a liquid and pads to ease off his beard. It was a relief to get the itchy things off.

Vanessa put a rock CD on and he sank into the chair and relaxed.

He must have been falling asleep because he jumped when she spoke.

"I got expelled from ballet," she said.

"Sorry, what?"

"I used to go to ballet lessons, but by eight I was asked not to return. At least, Uncle Seth was asked not to bring me back."

"What did you do?"

"Ridiculously, it was just because I was a free spirit. A bit too independent."

"You mean, you didn't do what you were told."

"I guess you could see it like that. I just wanted to dance, so they decided it was best that I did it in my own time."

"And did you?"

"Of course not."

He stared out of the window for a while until she asked what he was thinking.

He said, "Why did you tell me that?"

"Busted," she said. "I wanted to rebuild our relationship. I was a bit too blatant, wasn't I?"

"A bit. So why are you doing a politics and psychology degree now? Didn't you do a degree after school?"

She sighed, as though this wasn't a story she'd expected to tell. "I was brought up by Uncle Seth and Aunt Atara. My whole life in Hendon. My whole life pretty controlled and dull. I guess that's maybe why I rebelled when I could. Well, as soon as I'd passed my A levels I was off to Israel. Like a rite of passage, I suppose. Amazingly, I got accepted into Tel Aviv University. However, I dropped out after the first year. Too much of a free spirit again, I suppose."

Alex had seen the news about the troubles: the West Bank and Gaza Strip. "Was Tel Aviv safe? What was it like?"

"It's like California. There are beautiful beaches where people surf all day. Guys go to work in shorts and flip-flops. It's a chilled place."

"And the bombs?"

She shook her head. "It's not like that. Israel is very well protected. There's a defence system called Iron Dome. While I was there, Hamas fired tonnes of missiles and mortars from Gaza. Not one of them caused any damage. I remember sitting out on a balcony with friends. It was like a firework party. Missiles soared into the night sky only to be met by a defence missile in an explosion of light and colour. Literally."

"So why leave if it's such a cool place?"

"Uncle Seth. He came to get me and took me home."

Alex waited. He could tell there was more to this story and he saw her face flush.

Quietly, she said, "I got into trouble. I was working less and less, drinking more and also some drugs. I was in with the wrong crowd. My aunt and uncle found out—someone they knew in Tel Aviv told them. One minute I was partying in one of the coolest cities in the world and the next I was in Dullsville and grounded. Shit! I was twenty-two and treated like a kid."

"Must have been tough."

"It was the right thing though," she said with half a smile. "Uncle Seth is always right. He made sure I got myself sorted. In Israel I'd worked for a paper—although clerical stuff, not the editorial team—and they didn't let me write anything. Anyway, the job experience got me into the

221

Evening Standard, and although I'm still officially clerical, they do accept articles I write. I also sell pieces to other publications."

"So why the degree?"

"Because my boss says it's the easiest way in to journalism proper. Politics provides a great foundation—and the psychology is just so I don't go out of my mind with boredom." She coughed. "Speaking of which, am I boring you?"

Alex had been looking at his phone.

"Oh my God!" he said.

"My story wasn't that dramatic."

Alex held up his phone. "I've had a reply from Marek, the student from Berlin University. He's suggested I get a flight out tomorrow. He's sent a list of flights from Heathrow to Egypt. God, he's keen. He's checked out all the details. He's hoping to meet me tomorrow in Cairo!"

That evening, over a takeaway pizza, Vanessa asked, "Is Egypt safe? It wasn't long ago that they had riots and forced President Mubarak to resign. They've also had hijackings and terrorists blowing up planes."

"It's safe enough." Even as he said it, Alex knew he didn't sound convincing.

"What does the Foreign Office say?" She was on her phone checking as she spoke.

"High threat from terrorism."

"Then you can't go."

"The tourist areas are fine. Along the Nile and Sharm el-Sheikh aren't included in the warning."

They ate their pizza for a while and she continued to check the Internet.

Finally, she said, "So you will only go to the safe areas. Nowhere else."

"Just the safe areas, I promise." Her concern made him feel good. "Thanks," he said. "I'm touched you care."

"It's more than that, Alex." She shook her head. "If you're going to Egypt, then I'm coming with you."

THIRTY-EIGHT

1336 BCE, Luxor

On the second day of prayer, clutching the silver-like amulet, Yanhamu thought he heard his sister's voice. At first it was distant and fragmented, then it became more distinct and he knew it was her *ka* speaking. She told him she had found her way to the afterlife, that Anubis had weighed her heart and let her pass. They were the seeds of the stars and she was now one of the lights in the night sky. That night, he looked and thought he saw one flash to let him know it was her.

In the morning he decided he would return to his work in the city and find out about this law the kind noble had mentioned. He ran errands and messages and helped with the baker's carts when needed, but the more he understood how the city lived and breathed, the more frustrated he became, because there was no sign of the Law of Ra and the common folk seemed to think he meant the guards themselves.

Then a week after Laret's death he ran a message to a scribe at the court. He was told to clean himself up first otherwise he would not be allowed to enter the royal grounds and he was relieved to be waved through when he arrived. When the scribe arrived, Yanhamu's first thought was that this was the man from the temple, for he wore a similar white tunic and scarf with gold symbols. But this man was much younger. Yanhamu recited the message and was rewarded with a pebble of copper, the highest payment he'd ever received. He thanked the scribe and then handed it back. "Payment if you can tell me about the Law of Ra."

The highborn waved the copper away. "You are cute," he laughed effeminately. "Has anyone told you, you look like Tutankhamen when he was your age? What, you are about three summers younger, I think?"

Yanhamu shook his head. "The Law of Ra, please, my lord."

"It's an old expression. I can't imagine where you heard it. The city magistrate is the man who executes the law. We call it the Law of the Two Lands these days. Run me a message tomorrow and I will tell you more." He raised his eyebrows and smiled girlishly. "No charge."

Yanhamu thanked him and scurried out of the royal enclosure. He didn't need the scribe to tell him more, he knew exactly who the magistrate was: the man with the shaven head and purple sash who sat under an awning. A crowd always gathered when the magistrate was sitting and Yanhamu had assumed he was just another priest telling his news from the gods or from far-flung cities.

Yanhamu spotted the magistrate's flag amidst a crowd close to the wharf. He squeezed through until he was able to squat at the front of the semicircle. The magistrate squinted over his hooked nose at two men who stood before him. Two soldiers stood either side of the magistrate and a slave with an ostrich feather fan stood behind.

Yanhamu tried to make sense of what was being said. First one man spoke, and he seemed to be the manager of a grain store. He accused the other man of stealing from the store. He called for a boy who passed a papyrus roll to the magistrate.

"See," the manager said, "the records are thorough. It shows all the grain recorded both in and out. And yet two sacks are missing. Nekbhet has taken those sacks for his personal use."

The other man shook his head violently but didn't speak until the magistrate pointed a golden rod towards him.

"I am Nekbhet. I am the record keeper of the grain store. I swear, my lord, that I did not take the sacks. I was the one who discovered the discrepancy."

The manager indicated he wanted to speak and the rod was waved towards him. "Nekbhet is the only one with access to the store, the only one with opportunity to remove the sacks."

The magistrate asked, "And what would his motive be?"

Yanhamu noticed the manager started to scoff but managed to suppress it. "Either for food or to sell, my lord."

The rod swung to the other man. Nekbhet said, "I did not take them. If I planned to steal the grain, I would have falsified the records!"

The crowd took a collective intake of breath and began to mutter. Someone close to Yanhamu said, "An admission of guilt."

The magistrate stood, "Falsification of documents is a capital offence!"

Nekbhet quaked and started to speak. One of the soldiers lunged forward, his spear levelled at the accused's chest.

"Halt!" The magistrate raised the golden rod. "I have yet to rule on this!" When everyone quieted, he waved at the soldiers and had them part the crowd. "I want to see the grain store." He began to stride away from his chair and porch.

Yanhamu was swept along by the enthusiastic mob. They stopped suddenly by a circular wall with spiral steps which descended into the dark and Yanhamu saw the manager lead the way into the depths. In his effort to see,

Yanhamu leaned over the side. A sudden surge from behind sent him over the wall. He landed heavily on the steps, rolled and found himself at the feet of the magistrate. A spear immediately prodded his side and a soldier shouted.

As he stood, his eyes met the magistrate's and he saw a kindly man. He'd planned to speak about his sister's death as soon as he could, but face-to-face with the noble, he blurted something that also troubled him.

"The accused is innocent."

The soldier with the spear prodded him again. "Get out, urchin!"

"No!" The magistrate raised his hand and bent so that his ear was close to Yanhamu's mouth. "What do you know?"

"That the accused didn't do it, my lord," Yanhamu whispered.

"How?"

"I read it in his face, my lord."

The magistrate gripped the boy's shoulders and stared into his face. "And what do you read in mine?" he said menacingly.

Yanhamu smiled. "An honest man, who would rather listen to me than see me harmed."

"That is true." The magistrate beckoned him close and turned his head again. "Now, whisper, what you have seen in the other man's face."

"My lord, the manager is hiding something. I think perhaps he knows where the grain sacks are."

The magistrate stood and motioned to the guards. "Take us to the manager's house."

They remounted the steps and the crowd once more hushed as the magistrate was led to a large house nearby. The accused and the manager were told to kneel while one soldier entered. After a few minutes, the magistrate also entered. There was no shelter in the courtyard at the front of the grain manager's house but no one moved away, too desperate to see the outcome of the case. After ten minutes, the magistrate emerged, followed by the soldier carrying a sack under each arm.

The manager and worker were told to stand. To Nekbhet, the magistrate said, "You will take these sacks back to the store. You have been negligent in your duties allowing goods entrusted to your care to have been removed. For this you will pay the price of two chickens."

Nekbhet bowed and Yanhamu thought he saw the man smile with relief.

To magistrate pointed his rod at the manager. "You have been found guilty of both the theft of the grain and perjury. The penalty for this is death."

The crowd cheered and applauded. As one soldier bound the manager's hands ready to escort him away, the magistrate beckoned to Yanhamu. "I should give you something for your service."

"I would like to learn about the law."

The magistrate was momentarily taken aback. Then he smiled and said, "Come with me."

He strode away followed by the slave, who tried to use the fan as a sun shield. Yanhamu hurried after them. The magistrate passed through a wooden door to a courtyard and told the boy to wait. Shortly after, another man, wearing the hair and clothes of a high-class slave, stepped through the doorway and snatched the amulet from Yanhamu's neck.

"What's this?"

Yanhamu explained. "It's not real silver," he added.

"No, it is electrum and very expensive. Who did you steal it from?"

Yanhamu repeated his story about the noble at the temple. In response, the slave scoffed and placed the amulet in his robe.

"Prove yourself and it shall be returned."

"Do I have your word?"

"My word is all I have." The slave looked cross for a moment. Then he smiled. "Now, remove your dirty excuse for sandals before you cross this threshold."

THIRTY-NINE

Uncle Seth took them to Heathrow in his Bentley. The car smelled of new leather and old cigars.

When he dropped them off he hugged his niece and said something to her in what Alex guessed was Yiddish. Then he shook Alex's hand. His face was a mask of concern.

"Take good care of her, young man. She's my only niece and means the world to me."

Only when Alex promised that he would, did Uncle Seth break eye contact and let go of his hand.

"I have a confession," Alex said after they had checked in. "Your uncle scares me a little."

Vanessa laughed. "Don't be silly. He's just worried for me. And it took hours for me to persuade him last night that he'd even let me come."

They made their way through security with Vanessa still talking about her uncle.

"You know," Alex said, "It's funny he should be called Seth because Seth was an Egyptian god."

"Really?"

"He was mostly known as Seth but also Set and other names. He was the second son of Ra, the sun god." Alex paused until they were together again air-side. "Did you

230

know that a lot of religious stories were taken from ancient Egyptian myths?"

"Like what?"

"Cain and Abel."

She gave him a look of disbelief.

"Cain killed Abel, right? Remember I told you the story about Osiris, the first mummy and sometimes being shown with an erect penis?"

"How could I forget?"

"Osiris was the first son of Ra. Seth was jealous of his brother and wanted the throne for himself. So he killed Osiris. And, just like Cain, Seth used a knife."

Vanessa laughed lightly. "Seriously, that's your argument? Throughout history there must have been many people killed by a brother. It doesn't make their stories the same. And Abel wasn't wrapped up like a mummy so that he could come back to life."

"Well how about this: Lucifer was cast out of Heaven because he was jealous of Michael, wasn't he? Lucifer wanted to be God's successor. Sound familiar? It's Seth again. Lucifer is Seth, the original Satan."

"Thank goodness," she said.

"What?"

"Thank goodness you didn't say that in front of my uncle or he'd never have let me come with you."

The British Airways Boeing 787 waited on the tarmac for half an hour before getting clearance and pushed off from the stand just after 7:30 in the evening.

As they taxied down the runway, Vanessa said, "I hate flying. But I deal with it by knocking myself out with sleeping pills and diazepam. I took the diazepam half an hour ago, otherwise I wouldn't be calmly sitting here."

"Afraid of flying?"

"No, it's the old joke."

"What?"

"I'm afraid of crashing."

"I don't suppose it helps to know that at any one time there are a million people in the air. The odds of crashing are infinitesimal."

"No."

"No, what?"

"It doesn't help."

Alex held her hand and she gripped so hard his knuckles whitened. The wheels left the tarmac and the plane pulled up sharply. Vanessa sucked in air.

Hoping to distract her, he said, "And the sleeping pills, how long before you're out?"

She swallowed to help her speak. "About forty minutes. I'll just about make it through dinner and then sleep the rest of the way." And then they were through the clouds and levelling out. She breathed again and held out a strip of miniature blue pills. "Join me?" she asked, as though offering something more exotic and dangerous than a sleeping pill.

Alex declined.

"There's something else I want to give you," she said mysteriously. She hesitated before handing him a piece of paper.

"What is it?"

"Like a contract. Well, actually it's exactly that, a contract."

Alex started to read it.

She said, "I wanted to make it legal that I won't publish anything unless I have your full agreement. I thought it was the best way to prove you can trust me."

"I trust you," he said handing it back.

"No." She took out a pen, dated and signed the bottom. Then she handed it back to him. "Now you sign it."

Alex made to protest but acquiesced and signed.

"Good," she said. "Now talk to me. You told me the other night that I didn't know you."

"What would you like to know?"

"Tell me about your dad."

"He was from Aberdeen and an avid football supporter. It was a disappointment to him that I never showed any interest in football."

"Fond memories?"

Alex thought for a moment. "Giving me shoulder-carries. He used to make me put my arms in the air. He'd hold on tight to my legs and run really fast."

She smiled. "That's a trust thing."

Alex was remembering now and something he had forgotten popped into his mind. "One birthday I got a bike. I'd wanted a new bike for ages and had been shown the second-hand one I was going to get. But on my birthday I was amazed to see a brand new one. It had front and back suspension. I was beside myself with joy. Dad also had a thing for castles and we liked nothing more than finding a new castle to explore. Of course, his interest was historical whereas I used to play at being Highlander: Alex MacLure of the clan MacLure!"

"So you were close, you and your dad?"

"Not really. Shortly after that we moved to Surrey. Dad was the accountant for a firm whose head office was in London. They needed him there so we moved. It was a tough time. Money was short. Dad worked long hours and seemed to get more and more uptight. I didn't understand it at the time, how the stress can change you. I just remember him going from a fun dad to a grumpy old man with no time for his family. I was eleven. I went from a small, friendly school in Aberdeen to a huge comprehensive in Woking."

When the meal arrived it included quails' eggs, and the stewardess informed them that it was a traditional Egyptian meal: quail meat and eggs were as common as chicken in the UK.

As they ate, Vanessa said, "You felt lost and alone."

He looked at her as though she could read his mind. Then he realized. Of course she'd understand. She was a student of psychology.

He said, "And then Andrew was born."

"With muscular dystrophy, right?"

"Right. Unplanned too, of course." He took a sip of wine from the tiny plastic wine glass. "It was a bad time. It just got worse and worse. Mum and Dad started to argue. I remember waking up, hearing them shouting at each other downstairs. Looking back, I can see they needed help. They were both exhausted."

Vanessa said, "And we hurt the ones we love the most." Her voice sounded a bit far away. Maybe the sleeping pills were kicking in.

"I was almost fifteen when Dad killed himself." Alex went on to explain how the company had had problems for years but the previous financial controller had hidden it. His dad had tried to sort it out without causing a crash in confidence: correct the accounting policies, find the hidden debt, remove unjustified provisions, uncover malpractice and malfeasance. And all the time trying to protect those who had caused the problems.

"And then, after everything he had done, they pointed the finger at him, accused him of being the cause." He took a long breath. "He was an honest man. There is not a chance in hell that he did what they said, and the anguish broke him. Maybe it was on top of everything else but he couldn't cope." He breathed again. "And so that's when he hanged himself."

He took a slug of wine and looked at Vanessa. She was fast asleep.

Vanessa was instantly awake when the landing announcement came on the Tannoy. He held her hand and watched as his knuckles turned white again. The pilot had made up a little time and it was after 1am when they stepped out into the pleasantly warm night air in Cairo.

They were shuttled to the terminal building and were soon inside. People milled around kiosks with unfamiliar bank names above them. Alex needed currency so he

234

queued and quickly realized people were also buying visas here. Armed with cash and two labels that looked like big postage stamps, he joined a queue for passport control. This queue moved quickly as people were sent away because they hadn't purchased visas. The stamp turned out to be almost literally that. It was peeled from a backing paper and stuck into the passport.

Immediately beyond passport control were the baggage carousels. Alex's bag arrived fairly quickly but there was another long delay before Vanessa's appeared and they could head for the exit. They emerged into the dimly lit arrivals area with the usual confusion of tired tourists in a strange town, greeted by a wall of foreign faces and booths with signs in Arabic. They were approached by locals, who pestered them with: "Where are you from? Do you need a taxi? Do you need a hotel?"

Alex waved each one away and scanned the crowd for someone who might be Marek. Then he saw it: a sign with his name, held by a wiry man with quick eyes. As they approached, he grinned, held out his hand.

"I am Marek, your friend."

Alex hesitated as he took the man in. He'd pictured someone more Germanic or Eastern European, perhaps taller with pale skin. Marek could have easily passed for a local. Alex shook his head and patted Marek on the arm.

"Great to meet you."

"You are smiling," Marek said. "You had a good flight?"

"Not really. I was just thinking how funny it is that we have an image in our heads before we meet someone but the reality can be totally different. It must happen a lot with Internet dating."

Marek looked mortified for a second. He said, "I do not Internet date."

Vanessa gave Alex a nudge and held out her hand. "Very wise. My name is Vanessa."

After shaking her hand a little awkwardly, Marek picked up Vanessa's case and led them through to a car park and an old brown Hyundai. Opening the car boot he looked apologetic. "I am sorry for the car. At least it's free transportation to your hotel!"

Vanessa said, "Don't worry, we're too tired to notice or care…" Her voice choked off. "Alex, what's up?"

"There's a man by the exit. He just ducked back inside as our eyes met." He looked at Vanessa. "Quick, in the car!"

They jumped in the rear and Marek jolted the car out of the space and sped around towards the barriers. To get there they had to pass the airport exit.

Alex instinctively ducked down. "He's still there, watching!"

"Who is he?" Marek asked.

"I don't know. There's something familiar." Alex paused in thought and then looked at Vanessa. "My God, I think it's the man from the BMW!"

Vanessa stared back at the exit. "I think I see who you mean. Are you sure it's him?"

"No, but there's something—"

Doubt crossed her face. "OK, maybe you're right, but if he's watching then he's not following us."

"And I'll drive us very fast," Marek said rather too cheerfully for Alex's liking.

The car sped away from the airport and picked up a dual carriageway. Alex glanced behind twice, but realized it was impossible for him to judge if anyone was following. The way Marek drove, Alex guessed they were travelling at between 80 and 100 miles an hour. He tried to read the speedometer and was shocked to see it wasn't working. Marek began to chat like a tourist guide. He said something about the name of the road and that it went straight through Cairo and ended at the pyramids. Alex also heard him say something about a special hotel and then Muhammad Ali. Alex looked out of the window into the darkness. He made out the vague shape of a giant mosque and, straining to make sense of the dim images he could see, he began to relax. Perhaps it wasn't the BMW man. Perhaps he hadn't been watching them. Perhaps he was innocently waiting for someone or looking for a taxi.

Vanessa broke into his thoughts by saying, "So, Marek, do you have Arabic blood?"

"I am from Hungary, where my father's family come from, but my mother's side is originally from Egypt. I think this is why I became an Egyptologist. The Egyptian people are very friendly, but you must stay aware. Do not have your Western expectations." He looked over his shoulder at Alex and nodded as though he was saying something very significant. "Do not have your expectations. Egypt is different. You must be careful with your money and barter for everything, and even after you think you have agreed the price, be careful that it doesn't change. You see, Egyptians are clever. You may agree to pay five pounds before and at the end they ask for five English pounds."

Alex said, "There are almost ten Egyptian pounds to the British pound."

"Precisely! That is just one trick, but it is done with good humour, so do not get angry. You understand that it is best not to get angry."

The road became more congested and Marek was forced to slow. As they came off the carriageway, a car with no lights cut them up. Marek did not react and Alex quickly realized this style of driving was to be expected. A cyclist, with nothing but a torch in one hand, passed them on the kerb side, squeezing between parked cars and the moving traffic.

"Crazy!" Vanessa gasped.

Marek said, "There are almost twenty million people in Cairo. It is a big problem."

"What, do you mean it's all right for some to get killed?" A figure in black ran across the road weaving between cars. "Whoa!"

Marek chuckled, "No, no, no! I mean there are so many people that it is very congested and drivers are very aware."

The roads became even more tangled with traffic and Alex noted that horns were sounded as single, short blasts as a warning rather than in anger. More people dodged between the cars, and he tried not to worry about them or the other vehicles that looked like they would hit but amazingly didn't. He focused on the purpose of their visit. He was dying to talk about the research and fill in any gaps in his knowledge.

"I've been through all the notes, Marek. It's an amazing discovery. Just incredible. You should get a prize for what you've found."

"Thank you, but let us find what it leads to first, Alex." Marek cleared his throat. "I think you have an expression in England: do not count your chickens until they are catched."

"Something like that," Alex acknowledged. "I'd like to go through your translations line by line. Not now, of course, but when you're ready."

"Of course. Tomorrow morning. Perhaps on the way."

"Where are we going?"

Marek looked across at him, confusion on his face. "I thought—"

"That I'd know where to look? To be honest I don't know. I'm hoping that being here makes sense of the Map-Stone."

No one spoke for a moment and Alex felt awkward for whipping up the excitement without having a plan. "The clay tablets were found in Amarna, in Akhenaten's ancient city."

Marek nodded. "Yes, but the Map-Stone probably came from Tutankhamen's tomb in the Valley of the Kings."

Things suddenly crystallized in Alex's mind. The map led somewhere else. It wasn't a map to the Valley of the Kings. "The starting point has to be Amarna," he said assuredly.

238

Marek reached across and patted his shoulder. "Tell el-Amarna it is. I will book us a train for tomorrow afternoon. We should have time in the morning and then perhaps on the train to go through the translations, no?"

Marek sounded his horn as a figure dodged across the road. He said, "The trains are very bad, but don't worry, I will get a first-class train and it will be very comfortable." He grinned. "Ah, we are here."

He pulled up outside Hotel Victoria. From the outside the building was a five-storey block of salmon-pink. "I hope it is all right," he said, taking their bags out and again carrying Vanessa's. "The tourist hotels are very cheap but I don't think you would like to stay there. There are, of course, the five star hotels, but I don't think you would like to stay there either!" He waved goodbye and drove away.

From the outside the hotel looked tired and dirty. If the tourist hotels were worse, then Alex judged they must be terrible. However, his concerns were allayed as they entered a foyer that looked like it had been transported from a hundred years ago. Stylish and not at all shabby.

Vanessa said, "It looks lovely... inside."

They checked in. Separate rooms. Vanessa on floor one and Alex on the other side on the top floor.

He walked her to her room. "Double-lock your door," he said. "I know Marek said the Egyptian people are friendly, but he also said to be aware. And"—he smiled—"I promised your uncle to take care."

"I'll put a chair against the door as well." She kissed him on the cheek and said goodnight.

When Alex reached his own room, his bag hadn't been delivered. After five minutes it arrived and he tipped the boy who was grateful for the notes that were worth only a few British pennies. Taking his own advice, he double-locked the door handle and put the chain across. Maybe it wouldn't delay a determined attacker for long, but hopefully the security would help him sleep.

He stripped, quickly showered, then got under the bed sheet and switched off the light. The minutes ticked by. He couldn't sleep. He stared at the ceiling and started to think about Vanessa.

She was alone in her room. Maybe she couldn't sleep either. Maybe she was worried really and would feel safer together.

He rolled over and looked at the phone. Should he call her room?

As he reached for the handset, there was a light knock on his door. He jumped out of bed, picked up his damp towel and tucked it round his waist. His heart raced. He'd once seen a film where the guy in the room looked through the peephole only to get a bullet through the eye. He faced the door, nervous and uncertain.

The knock again.

Alex said, "Who is it?"

"Me." A whisper from the other side.

Vanessa.

He took off the chain and turned the handle.

She was still dressed in her trouser suit, which made sense since she'd just crossed a lobby and come up the stairs or lift.

She said, "All right if I come in?"

He said, "I was about to call you."

"Really?"

"I couldn't sleep."

"Me neither." She stepped over to the bed and sat on the edge. He double-locked the door again and walked towards her.

"Coffee?" he asked.

"Not a good idea." She held out a couple of small wine bottles. "I got these from my mini bar."

He fetched two plastic cups from the bathroom and she poured red wine for them both.

He sat and they chinked the plastic.

"Nervous? Excited?" she asked.

Alex thought and then said, "Excited, but a touch uncomfortable, I think. I was looking forward to meeting Marek, but... I don't know, I guess it wasn't totally what I expected."

"I meant about me being here." She laughed lightly.

"Vanessa..."

"I'm sorry about what happened between us." She placed a hand on his thigh and looked into his eyes. "It's best we just remain friends."

"Yes," he said, and found himself leaning in. Their lips met.

She pulled back briefly and whispered. "We should take this slowly."

Minutes later she was out of her trouser suit and he was pleasantly surprised to discover she wore nothing underneath.

FORTY

At the gate to the magistrate's house, Yanhamu stepped out
of the bindings he wore on his feet. The slave led him to a
water trough. He was then instructed to remove all of his
clothes and immerse himself. As soon as Yanhamu
disrobed, the man scooped up the dirty clothes and tossed
them away.

When the boy was in the trough, the slave gripped his
head and roughly pushed it under the water. After a
moment of panic Yanhamu was released and then his hair
was scrubbed with a bar of natron blended with sweet-
smelling flowers. Then the slave handed the bar to him and
told him to rub it over his whole body until his skin was
pink.

A small girl came from the house and handed the slave a
simple white gown. She stared at Yanhamu in the trough,
covered her giggles and scurried back.

The slave beckoned him out of the water and handed
him the gown. "Now I will tell you two stories and I want
you to tell me which of them is the truth. Understand?"

Yanhamu wiped the last of the water from his eyes and
studied the slave's face.

The man said, "The first is: I took bread from a bakery as a teenager. My punishment was to lose my ear." He pointed to a partially severed left ear. "My second story is that I was sold into slavery as a baby, because my mother died in childbirth."

Yanhamu asked, "Your parents were not slaves?"

"No."

"What work did they do?"

When the slave answered, Yanhamu smiled. "That is the lie. Your parent's were both slaves but your mother died in childbirth as you said."

The slave did not confirm or deny Yanhamu's assertion, but told him to sit under the sycamore tree and wait. He left him there and a short time later the magistrate appeared. He no longer wore his cloak of office and had changed into a simple white tunic.

Yanhamu stood. "I did not steal the amulet, my lord."

The magistrate studied him and then asked him to open his mouth and show his teeth.

"Can you read and write?"

"No, my lord, but I can work."

The magistrate walked around him. "You do not have the look of a peasant. Where are you from?"

Yanhamu told the man about his village and the matriarch's name.

The magistrate pondered for a moment and then said, "So, you can tell when someone is being truthful. A magistrate is required to have this skill, to judge the guilty from the innocent, and it is something I... it is a talent I was born with. You want to learn the law, my boy, so be it. You will learn by being my assistant. Is that agreed?"

Yanhamu nodded enthusiastically. "You won't regret it, my lord."

"I regret it already," the magistrate said. Then, waving to the slave, called, "Paneb!"

The magistrate left and the slave told the boy to kneel and bow his head.

"Since you are staying, you need to learn your place. You are the lowliest. You do what you are told, when you are told. If I am not happy with you, you will be thrown out. Although I am a slave, you will not call me Paneb, you will always call me Master Hapuseneb. Is that understood?"

"Yes, Master Hapuseneb."

"You will never be familiar with his lordship. You will never be familiar with his family. You will avert your eyes from the ladies, including the young lady Nefer-bithia. Is that understood?"

"Yes, Master Hapuseneb."

"Now, hold still." The slave pulled a copper blade from his belt, tested it to show its sharpness, and gripped Yanhamu's hair. For an horrific moment the boy thought he was going to be cut in some sort of initiation ceremony or worse still have his throat slashed. He dug his fingers into the earth and braced himself.

Hapuseneb guffawed and pulled hard, making tears wet the boy's cheeks, but Yanhamu bit his tongue and felt a chunk of hair sliced off.

"Since you are staying here, and living in my quarters, I'm getting rid of these lice." He paused and then began to systematically cut off the tangled hair, leaving only stubble and a few bloody lines where the blade had nicked the skin.

When it was over, Yanhamu stood and shook the hair from his gown and tried hard to look as though he hadn't cried.

The slave said, "Now clean up this mess and then I will take you through your daily duties."

"Master, I would like my amulet back."

Hapuseneb raised a shaved eyebrow and turned his back. "Prove yourself to his lordship, Lord Khety, and I will believe that you did not steal the precious necklace. Until that time it will remain in my safe keeping."

That night, his hands and back aching from the work the slave had made him do, Yanhamu dreamed he was a

244

magistrate. He pulled the gown of office tightly around his shoulders and stood up tall. A circle of spectators screamed for justice. In the centre stood the captain of the guard, the one who had taken and killed Laret. Anubis was there. The crowd stopped shouting and Anubis read the list of crimes the captain had committed, telling of how he had taken a young maiden on the pretence of taking her to be trained as a royal dancer. How he had abused her and disrespected her. How he had taken her life with a short sword and had her body thrown into the Nile.

The captain said nothing as the charges were read out, his granite face impassive. But his face was different because the gouge from Laret's hook had badly scarred him and the livid mark ran over an eye and twitched with guilt.

When Anubis finished, the crowd began to shout once more. Then they were no longer just people, but demons: the devourer, the bone-crusher, the serpent, the *ba*-eater, the beheader and the water-demon. They were all there, a morass of terrible creatures all eager for death.

Yanhamu raised his hand and they fell silent. He invited the captain to speak, and as he defended himself, denying each charge, Yanhamu shouted, "Liar!"

The defendant finished, to the derision of the baying demons.

Yanhamu pronounced the death sentence and watched as the demons destroyed the guilty captain the way a hungry child might tear at a chicken carcass.

FORTY-ONE

The cigarette-smoke-heavy room produced dim blue-grey patches of light. There were three chairs and two men. The young man in one of the chairs made animated gestures between rapid puffs on his cigarette. The other man was impassive and had a walking stick propped against the arm of his chair. He wore a hat and his cigar smoke curled around its brim.

He shook his head at a complaint and was about to interrupt the younger man when there was a knock on the door.

After a hesitation the younger of the two stood and answered it.

"Yes?"

"Brotherhood."

Recognizing the password, the young man opened the door. "Joachim," he said in polite greeting, although both men knew it was merely out of necessity. This new man was the one codenamed Fox. The old man was the one known as Owl but there was no need for secret names here.

"Wael," Joachim acknowledged, and walked to the chairs and stood behind one.

The senior man leaned on his cane as though about to rise. But it was just for show and he simply nodded, welcome.

He said, "Please sit." His voice was thick with catarrh and a heavy Yiddish heritage which Joachim reckoned the old man put on for effect. He could speak good English when he wanted to.

When they were all seated, Joachim said, "Our friend is nervous."

"I was just talking about that," Wael said. "It's no wonder he's nervous after you arranged for him to be chased and have his house burgled." He looked from Joachim to the old man and back. "And you also scared him with guns!"

"It's worked, hasn't it?" Joachim shrugged dismissively. "He's here now. All you have to do, Wael, is play your role. I've done the most difficult part."

The elderly man cleared his throat and Wael swallowed the retort he was about to make.

"Enough of this petty griping," the man known as Owl snapped. "Tell us what you have learned, Joachim."

Joachim said, "I don't know why, but he's very uncomfortable with you." He returned Wael's hard stare for a second before continuing: "Something you said or didn't say, but MacLure is a little suspicious."

Wael was about to protest, but the elderly man raised his stick to indicate he should be silent, then said, "Do we have a problem?"

Joachim blinked the smoke from his eyes. "Maybe. Maybe not. The rabbit's an unusual person. His mind doesn't quite work the same as yours or mine. And he is very aware of the potential implications of the bird's discovery."

The old man said, "We can call them MacLure and Champion now."

"Our discovery," Wael said. "The research was Champion's and Marek's."

247

Joachim slammed his hand on the chair's arm and glared. "Wael, you are an idiot." Then he looked pleadingly at the old man. "I said we should find someone from Eastern Europe rather than make do with an Egyptian."

Wael shouted, "I'm in character, and how dare you call me an idiot? And then you insult my family…"

"Enough!" For the first time, the old man showed anger by gripping his walking stick and banging it on the floor. "You,"—he pointed the stick at Wael—"what do we need to do to convince the Englishman?"

Wael shook his head. "I have no idea."

Phlegm rattled in the old man's throat and he sat forward. The others waited for him to speak.

To Wael he asked, "Do you have access to the map?"

"No. I think it's in his head."

Joachim groaned.

Wael said, "What we need to do is get him to draw it."

The old man nodded thoughtfully. "This is what we will do. Joachim, you will travel with them to Dairut without Wael."

Wael began to protest but was silenced by a look before the old man continued: "We will find a good reason why Marek cannot travel. And we must not give Mr MacLure the opportunity to confirm his doubts." He looked at Wael. "You will do something to establish your credibility. Yes?"

Wael looked down and then back. "Yes, sir."

"Now go and get some sleep," the old man said. "You will need all your wits about you."

"And if I can't get the map?"

The old man lit a fresh cigar with rapid sucks and then a long draw. After he had blown out the flame, phlegm rattled as he spoke. "Then we will use Joachim's plan." He looked at the young man. "If we can't obtain the map from Mr MacLure using peaceful means, then I think Joachim is quite capable of extracting the information."

FORTY-TWO

1332 BCE, near Elephantine

Three years had passed since the magistrate had taken Yanhamu under his wing. He sat in the Chair of Justice beneath a temporary awning. Hapuseneb the slave stood behind the chair fanning him. There was a small gathering outside and, close by, a guard stood beside a beekeeper. A small group of peasants were penned in one corner and controlled by a group of twenty guards. There was an expectant hush as the people awaited the magistrate's ruling.

"What do you think?" the magistrate asked quietly of Yanhamu.

The young man, standing beside the magistrate, straightened his tunic, looked to the west and mountains that were starting to glow red in the evening sun. "It seems unfair, my lord."

The magistrate inclined his head, stood and raised his staff of office in one hand, the ostrich feather of justice in the other. He began with the traditional pronouncement: "Before the gods, before Hathor, Ma-at and Thoth, before Pharaoh and Horus, in the name of the Law of the Two Lands, I have come to my judgement.

249

"The temporary houses that have been constructed within one hundred cubits of the beekeeper's fields will be knocked down." He looked at the Clerk of the Land Registry who smiled and nodded.

The peasants gasped and a woman wailed, "This is the only fertile land!" Then she cried out as a guard struck her with his staff.

"Silence!" he yelled.

The magistrate continued, "This is my judgement. This is the law. So be it." He struck his staff of office on the ground to signal the end of the session and turned to Yanhamu.

The young man finished writing the magistrate's words on a scroll and placed them inside a tamarisk wooden box. His eyes did not look up to meet the magistrate's.

Later, in their smoky temporary quarters, Magistrate Khety said, "You have been exceptionally quiet this evening, my boy."

Yanhamu wafted the mosquito-repelling smoke from his face so that he could see his master better while he pondered his response. They had finished their meal and Lord Khety had consumed more than his usual amount of beer.

"Boy?"

"Perhaps we should talk about it tomorrow, my lord—after the final case."

The magistrate grunted. "No, I want to talk about it now. You are troubled by my judgement, aren't you? We have listened to those people all afternoon. We visited the beehives, we saw the peasant's houses, noted the presence of the bees in the air." He took another drink and looked into Yanhamu's face. "So tell me, boy, what was your judgement?"

"My lord, the beekeeper claimed to have worked this plain all his life. He told us that his family has tended bees here for six generations. We heard from the Overseer of the

Fields that honey produced here is by royal commission. We saw the white stakes that mark the honey-flower fields and walked around the perimeter and confirmed the size of the fields match the records of the land registry. The beekeeper complained that the peasants kill his bees in their village—if that is what their collective hovels can be called. He claimed they also go into his fields, disturb the bees and steal the honey."

The magistrate nodded.

"We heard from the Clerk of the Land Registry that the peasants' houses are not on the registry because they are outside the city limits and are poor and badly constructed. The people choose to live here because there is a short belt of fertile land and drainage water."

"So they have no rights."

"But they have the right to *ma-at*... and to live without injustice."

The magistrate scoffed. "They choose to live beside a field of bees. How can they complain about that? And there can be no justification for theft or destruction of anything!"

"I agree, my lord, but there has been no evidence of theft and only the beekeeper's word that they have killed and disturbed the bees, although I could read no evidence of untruth in his face. Perhaps there has been theft, but it does not mean these people are the guilty ones. Perhaps in the past there has been damage to beehives, but it could have been the wind. Perhaps bees have disappeared, but they are as likely to have been eaten by the birds."

"Perhaps. Perhaps. Perhaps! Have I taught you nothing about the Law of the Two Lands?"

"Yes, my lord, you have taught me that it is unfair." Yanhamu saw his master scowl then and knew he should not continue, but he couldn't help himself. "The law talks of harmony and justice and yet it seems to me that this justice is unbalanced, unequal."

A cough from the far end of the room reminded Yanhamu that the slave Hapuseneb was standing in attendance. He was reminded that over the years he had served the magistrate, Yanhamu had gained in status and was almost treated as one of the family. He hesitated, the frustration at the inequality of the law bubbling in his blood.

The magistrate eyed him and gulped down some more beer. "Oh don't stop now, boy. Let's hear your wise judgement."

Yanhamu swallowed and took a sip of his own cup of bitter southern beer. "The peasants should have the same rights as the beekeeper. Well, in fact, the beekeeper is merely a representation of the city and state. The overseer and the land registry clerk were not impartial witnesses because they are part of the state."

"Rubbish!"

"We both saw that the stakes had been moved over time. The area of the bee fields remains the same, but the beekeeper has undoubtedly moved them gradually over time as the desert has claimed the area to the north-west."

"The land registry does not deny the beekeeper this right."

"I do not deny that the beekeeper has rights—according to the land registry, but why should the peasants' houses not be counted. Why can't they have land rights?"

Hapuseneb came to the table, apparently to clear away dishes. He caught Yanhamu's eye and glared.

"More beer, Paneb!" the magistrate ordered from the slave and nudged him aside.

Yanhamu continued: "I would have judged that the beekeeper should move his stakes and hives one hundred cubits back and create an area between that the peasants must not encroach upon. The beekeeper can maintain his land by expanding elsewhere."

"You are a fool, boy!"

"Perhaps…"

"Ha! Perhaps. Perhaps. Perhaps!"

He quaffed another beer and yelled at Hapuseneb again.

Yanhamu felt tears prickle his eyes. He had not intended it to end this way, but he could hold back no longer. "I'm leaving," he said.

"No you are not. I need you." There was a subterranean growl full of menace in the magistrate's voice.

"You need me because you are going blind, old man." Yanhamu stood, his hands clenched in frustration. Immediately, he felt his arms pinned by the slave's strong grip.

The magistrate slapped the table. "Sit down. I have not finished. And never show me such disrespect again!"

Yanhamu was forced to sit, and although released, he knew Hapuseneb stood behind him ready for whatever happened next.

For a long time, the magistrate looked into his drink. When he looked up, the anger had dissipated and a sadness was reflected in his eyes like dull cataracts. "Yes, I need you to be my eyes. Even when you first boldly spoke to me, I knew my power to see the truth was fading, and over the past three years it has become so bad that I can no longer make out a man's features when he is more than two paces away. Without your ability, I am finished.

"Have I not fed you? Have I not taught you to read and write? Have I not pretended you are not from the gutter? Have I not let you live amongst the high class and shown you a life you would never have lived?"

Yanhamu felt like saying that the motivation had been selfish, but used a calming trick the magistrate himself frequently used; he counted to three before he said, "That is true."

"And where will you go? Back to your stinking village?"

"I will join the Medjay."

The magistrate laughed loudly as though Yanhamu had told him a great joke. "Egypt's best fighting force of Nubians. Well good luck with that!" He stopped laughing and stared, the animal growl returning to his voice, "If you leave, you leave with nothing. You are but a boy who does

253

not know how to fight. You will be the lowliest and the weakest and just padding for His Majesty's front line against the Hittites. You will be dead before a year is out."

"That may be, but I must at least try to learn to fight. I am a man now and I have my honour."

"What on earth are you talking about?"

Yanhamu stood slowly and bowed. Hapuseneb stepped back.

"Because, my lord, I have learned that the law cannot bring me justice. There is a man who must pay for the death of my sister."

FORTY-THREE

The stories of Yanhamu swirled around in his head all night. He had taken to dreaming that he was the ancient Egyptian. When Alex awoke, the sun was streaming through a gap in the curtains. Vanessa wasn't in his bed, although he couldn't recall her leaving. He had a thumping head as though he had jetlag. Which was nonsense since there was just a two hour time difference. Gingerly, he made his way into the bathroom and climbed into the shower. After five minutes of pummelling water, he began to feel alive and hungry. Getting dressed, he noted the time was midday. He picked up the phone and called Vanessa's room. There was no answer.

As he dressed, Alex spied an envelope pushed under his door. Expecting it to be a message from Vanessa, he was surprised to read a note from Marek. It said he'd found something in the texts.

I now wonder if it wasn't Meryra after all who hid the treasure! I also need to finish a review of an MRI scan for my professor, so I'll be delayed a day or so.

Inside the envelope were two train tickets and the address of a hotel in Dairut, a town Alex had never heard of.

He found Vanessa in the lobby nursing a miniature cup containing what looked like black mud. He leaned over her but she moved her head at the last minute so that his kiss landed on her cheek.

"It's a Muslim country," she said with the raising of an eyebrow. "We must be discreet."

"How are you feeling?"

"I didn't sleep much. You?"

"Too well, I think." He rubbed his face. "I don't know whether it's jetlag or what, but I only just woke up and I feel like the walking dead."

There was a silver pot on the table. She poured more mud into her cup and handed it to him. "Drink this coffee. You'll soon feel better."

He knocked back the glutinous liquid. After a couple of swallows to make sure it had gone, Alex told Vanessa about Marek's note and showed her the tickets. "We have three and a half hours before our train leaves. After we eat, I want to go to the Egyptian Museum."

"Oh?"

"I think we should check out our friend—just as a precaution."

"You're suspicious about something?"

Alex pressed his fingers around his right eye socket where the headache seemed to have found a home. "There was the thing about the research... he seemed nervous. He had shifty eyes too, didn't you think?"

"Oh, Alex, you're being paranoid! Didn't you notice his teeth?"

"No."

"They were discoloured. He's a heavy smoker and we didn't see him smoke once, did we? I think he was suffering from nicotine withdrawal—being kind to us."

From reception, Alex took a map that had a number of local eateries marked on it by the concierge. When they stepped out onto the street, the acrid air immediately

256

assaulted their noses. The road was packed with slow-moving cars.

After a short walk they found a reasonable-looking café, busy with locals and a sprinkling of tourists, and sat at a round table beside the road. Vanessa enjoyed selecting something random from the menu. It turned out to be a plate of falafel and crudités which Alex was relieved to find looked edible.

After another strong cup of coffee, washed down with a bottle of water, Alex began to feel human again. There was no bill, just a price the waiter seemed unsure about. It was much more than Alex expected and, as he dealt out the cash, he reminded himself to agree prices beforehand.

They studied the map and located the museum close to the bank of the Nile.

Vanessa said, "Too far to walk."

They looked up and down the road and a taxi driver immediately sounded his horn and waved.

Alex leaned over. "How much to the museum?"

"Fifty."

Alex looked at Vanessa. She shrugged.

Alex said, "Twenty Egyptian."

The driver shook his head, "Forty is best price."

"Thirty is my best price."

The driver shook his head. "Forty."

Alex turned away. "Let's try another."

Vanessa started to complain, when the driver shouted after them, "OK. OK. Thirty."

As they climbed into the rear, the driver said, "To the museum, thirty each."

"No! Thirty total."

"OK. OK."

"At least it's slow," Vanessa said when they realized the seat belts didn't work.

They weaved in and out and cut through many side roads, leaving Alex confused about the route. He glanced at Vanessa, who seemed perfectly happy, and he tried to dismiss worries that they were being taken somewhere to be mugged. Finally they emerged at a large roundabout they recognized from the TV coverage of the riots: Tahrir Square. Beyond, they could see the imposing building of the museum. The driver stopped by security barriers where armed soldiers stood behind movable metal screens.

"Forty," the driver said, and his face went from serious to splitting into a cheeky grin.

Alex dealt out thirty pounds.

"Tip?"

Alex laughed and gave the man another ten.

"You need a guide?" the driver asked as they climbed out.

"No thanks," Alex said, and they walked away, past the barriers, to join a queue for tickets to the museum.

The adjacent road was crammed with coaches. Security men shouted at the drivers, who responded by shouting back. Alex wondered whether they were being told to move along, but from the tone, the conversations didn't seem to be good-natured.

"Is it safe?" Vanessa asked.

Alex pulled a face. "I hope so! Let's just keep out of the way of anyone with a gun."

At the gates they filed slowly through a detector and Vanessa had her handbag checked. To the right, people queued to buy entry tickets. In front of them was a garden and the garish entrance to the museum.

Vanessa said, "What is it about Egyptians and salmon-pink buildings?"

They followed the path through the garden littered with chunks of stone, remnants of statues and broken temple blocks, like the biscuit crumbs of the gods.

A few drops of rain made them look up.

Alex said, "Now that's one thing I didn't expect. Let's hope it's not a downpour."

The entrance to the museum portico was blocked by turnstiles. Alex approached someone checking tickets.

"Excuse me, I'm looking for a researcher called Marek Borevsek."

The man didn't look up from his task.

"Could you tell me where I might find...?"

Still no response.

Alex spotted Vanessa talking to a vendor selling bottled drinks and ice creams.

She beckoned him over. "The offices are underneath apparently. There's an admin entrance at the end." She pointed to the third opening on their right.

They walked past the second entrance, through which they saw a dirty grey interior and concrete stairs. The next entrance was more in keeping with the building, and at the top of the steps, through an open door, was a full-body turnstile like the ones Alex had seen at Paris metro stations. On the far side a security man sat at a podium.

"I'm here to see Marek Borevsek," Alex said slowly through the battleship-grey bars. "He's a research fellow here."

A cigarette in the man's mouth made him squint as he looked first at Alex and then longer, approvingly, at Vanessa.

"Marek Borevsek?" Alex repeated.

The man looked down, presumably to a register below the level of the desk. He looked back up and, in passable English, said. "He's not here."

Alex's eyes widened. He looked at Vanessa.

"What, not here at all?" she asked.

The security man squinted at her. "No. Not here... today. He work at hospital."

Alex passed the map through the bars. "Could you show us where, please?"

"Research at hospital. Here." With a red pen, the security man put a cross. Then he handed them a slip of paper. "Cleopatra Hospital," he said, and pointed to Arabic writing.

They thanked him, exited the museum grounds and immediately caught a taxi.

The hospital was beyond the Victoria Hotel and took forty minutes in the cab. During the ride, the rain briefly became heavier and then abruptly stopped. The driver had spoken little English but had immediately understood the slip of paper from the security man. As he left them outside the hospital, Alex shook his head in wonderment. "That was cheaper than the first taxi and more than twice the distance!"

Vanessa said, "Let's just hope this is the right place."

They went inside the dusty—rather than salmon—pink building and were relieved to see signs in English. Vanessa headed for a desk and got directions to the radiology department.

"Good English," she said with relief as Alex joined her and they wended their way through corridors switching first right then left before a long corridor led them to double doors. On the door was a notice, the English of which said: Ancient Egyptian Research Department, Cairo Museum. Vanessa and Alex exchanged glances and nods and pushed open the door. The same sign was on the third door to the right, above which was a permanent sign: C.T. Unit. They entered to find the next door locked, with a sign asking them to ring for attention.

Vanessa pressed a doorbell, and seconds later a young lady in blue scrubs opened the door. She stepped through and smiled.

"We're looking for Marek Borevsek, Alex began. "He's a—"

"Oh yes." The woman beamed, although the waggle of her head seemed a contradiction. She asked them to wait and disappeared through the door again.

"My friends," Marek said as he appeared. He shook their hands warmly. "Sorry to keep you waiting."

"Only a few minutes."

Alex had looked over Marek's shoulder as he came through the door and was disappointed not to see anything. He said, "What are you working on? Can we take a quick look?"

Marek shook his head. "I am sorry, but you know how sensitive this is, and I must be quick. Really, there should be a security presence, but we are lucky." He opened the door so that they could see. They followed his indication and saw a room to the right filled with more people in blue scrubs. One man stood to the side, a machine gun across his chest.

"Security," Marek explained with a nod in the man's direction.

Alex recognized the main feature of the room as an MRI scanner behind which was a body on a table.

Marek said, "We are scanning a group of unnamed mummies. After the success of using it with Hatshepsut's identification, my professor has been allowed to try and identify others. I am so sorry I cannot join you on the train, but I will catch up, hopefully later tomorrow. I must just finish up here first though." He shook their hands again before darting back inside.

"Wow!" Vanessa said. "I told you I'd seen the Queen Hatshepsut documentary, right?"

"Shame we couldn't have had a closer look," Alex said as they retraced their steps.

"But you're happier now?"

"Yeah. I guess yesterday I didn't like the way he didn't acknowledge that the breakthrough with the Amarna Letters was because of me. Ellen showed me those symbols and I recognized there was a hidden numerical meaning. I'm sure she told him."

Vanessa pulled his arm so that he swung around and looked at her. She was grinning. "In history, how often do researchers and inventors complain that someone else stole their idea? Or, for that matter, didn't acknowledge their contribution?"

"All the time."

"And you are just as guilty of pride. Don't worry, I'll tell the true story, whether Marek acknowledges you or not."

"It's what we find that matters." Now it was his turn to smile. "Come on. Back to the hotel, freshen up, and then we've a train to catch."

FORTY-FOUR

1332 BCE, near Elephantine

The magistrate was subdued during prayers and his review of the scheduled case. He squinted against the morning sun, as though its rays could pierce his tender brain, and walked slowly to the scene of the incident. A damaged ferry-raft was tethered at the water's edge, and beside it a town official, Overseer of the Waterways, waited for them to approach before stepping from beneath his sun shade and bowing a greeting.

The magistrate said quietly, "Is this the ferry?"

"It is, My Lord Khety. It is of basic construction, operated by a ferryman and his junior, who pull the raft across using a rope strung from bank to bank. As you can see, the ferry can comfortably take ten people, but on the day of the accident there were at least sixteen people on board."

"How many died?"

"Four passengers and the junior ferryman."

"How many bodies were retrieved?"

"Just one. The others are unaccounted for, swallowed by the torrent of the Great River—or worse..."

In a rush of horror, Yanhamu expected the official to continue with a speculation about the deaths, and he feared the memory of his sister's death. He interrupted, saying, "My lord, we should examine the ferry."

The magistrate looked disapproving at the interruption, but he just waved his hand to indicate they should go and see the raft. He stood on the bank as Yanhamu climbed on board, paced out the size and checked the construction. He stepped off and the others waited as he wrote notes on the papyrus.

The magistrate asked, "Are there other crossings close by?"

"This is the only raft ferry. There are a number of small boats that operate along the bank here."

"And their prices?"

The overseer looked perplexed. "I do not think that is relevant. The ferryman is guilty of overfilling his craft. The guide rope was old and could not take the strain of the heavy raft in the fast-flowing waters. Please forgive my rudeness, My Lord Khety, but the case is straightforward, the ferryman is responsible and should be sentenced."

"Are you a judge now?" the magistrate bellowed, and Yanhamu saw him wince afterwards with regret at the pain caused by the effort.

"No. I just thought—"

"Then don't think!"

Yanhamu whispered, "My lord, we should see the guide rope."

The magistrate instructed the overseer to show them the rope that had once strung across the river.

"It is not here," the official responded.

The magistrate established that the rope had been taken away and disposed of. He insisted that a runner be sent to locate it and, while they waited in the shade erected by Hapuseneb, the magistrate removed his wig and used a damp cloth to wipe cool his shaved head and neck.

"What do you think, Yani?" It was the first time the magistrate had called Yanhamu by his familiar name. In fact, the last time he had heard it, his sister had been alive.

At first his voice caught with emotion. "My lord?"

"What's going on here? I would like your opinion."

"I do not like the fact that the rope has been taken away. It is important in this case. And the overseer has not filled me with trust."

"Is that your prejudice talking or your logic?"

Yanhamu thought for a moment and glanced over at the Overseer of the Waterways. The man looked worried. "My logic, I think. For the trial, I know it is not planned, but I suggest you ask the overseer to speak as well as the ferryman."

Before the magistrate commented, he pointed towards two sweating boys as they returned with the heavy coiled rope over their shoulders.

When it was laid before the magistrate, both he and Yanhamu examined it. Both ends were cut through.

The magistrate called for the overseer to account for the cuts.

The official said, "To remove the rope we had to cut it free."

"But to see evidence that the rope snapped, I would need to see the frayed end."

The official spoke urgently to an assistant, who in turn spoke to others before returning and spoke to the overseer.

"We do not know where the frayed end is."

The magistrate shook his head. "That was key evidence and there is no explanation for cutting the end that was frayed if the rope was to be destroyed. Without this evidence I will not try this case." He waved to the slave who started to dismantle the sunshade.

"But..." the official said as he scurried after the magistrate who had begun to walk back to the town. "People died and their relatives need someone to atone for the murders!"

The magistrate stopped and, with his face close, gave the official a withering stare. He whispered, "Do not press me, for you may regret the outcome of further investigation."

The overseer stepped back, bowed and stood still as the magistrate and his entourage returned to the town.

"Tell me what you think happened here," the magistrate said to Yanhamu as they packed to return home.

"I don't think there was ever a frayed end to that rope. I think it was deliberately cut and then removed so we wouldn't see it."

"Why?"

"I don't know, but a deliberate cut would mean someone intended for an incident and perhaps for the ferryman to be convicted. I would like to have asked the overseer if he was taking bribes. Perhaps the ferryman did not pay up?"

"I have no doubt the overseer is charging the operator—what I will call—a commission, but to challenge him in public without any evidence would have been a serious and unacceptable affront to his position. Of course, it could be one of the other operators..."

"Or the junior ferryman who had opportunity and whose motive may have been to take over the business."

"And yet he died."

"There is no evidence that he died, his body was not found."

"Interesting." The magistrate nodded and was deep in thought for the rest of the walk to the temporary accommodation.

After the magistrate had provided instructions for the preparation of their journey home. He readied himself for the pronouncement in the town square.

Yanhamu said, "May I ask what you will pronounce, my lord? Will you say it was an accident and that the ferryman has no case to answer for?"

The magistrate studied the young man. "That depends on you—whether you are still intending to leave."

"My lord? I don't understand."

"I could leave the case open. If you stay with me, I will let you investigate further. You learned the Wisdom Texts by rote and you write as well as any scribe of your age. You have a natural talent and eye for justice, albeit naïve at times, and to have you die by a spear in some foreign field would be a travesty."

"Are you saying I could be a magistrate one day? But I am low-born, my lord, I know I would never be accepted by society."

"I have thought about that. My plan is to either adopt you as a son or approve your marriage to my daughter, Nefer-bithia. Don't think I haven't seen the way you two look at one another!"

Yanhamu was taken aback. Never in his wildest imaginings did he see himself accepted into a higher class. After he caught his breath, he said, "You are too generous, my lord."

"No, I am a selfish old man who needs you. I need to pronounce my judgement now, so what is your answer. Will you stay?"

Yanhamu bowed and raised his hands from his knees to show extreme respect. "Master, I have made up my mind and know my destiny lies in another direction." When he looked up, the magistrate had a tear in his eye.

"So you are bent upon revenge against this soldier. Is he still in the City of a Thousand Gates?"

"Two years ago he left. A promotion, I heard, to head the fortress at the border town of Gaza. That is where I will go."

"You should learn to fight before you confront this man. Do not go to a common garrison; you are a good-looking boy and you know how soldiers can be!" Anyway, if you are to have any chance of survival in battle, you should go to the military academy in Memphis."

"But, Master, that is for officers, and they will not take someone without good provenance."

"Is there nothing I can say to change your mind?"

Yanhamu shook his head.

"Somehow I suspected not. Take this document to the military academy." The magistrate handed him a scroll, sealed with the mark of the chief magistrate of the Land of the Arch, the first nome. "With my word they will have no choice but to enrol you."

"Master." Yanhamu repeated his bow, but the magistrate quickly strode from the courtyard and past Hapuseneb, who now stood like a statue by the gate. He watched as Yanhamu finished packing his shoulder bag.

"That is a bad omen, that is!" the slave said.

A cluster of sparrows fluttered frantically and inexplicably in one corner.

Yanhamu stepped towards the gate. "I don't believe in omens."

"We have never seen eye to eye, young Yanhamu. You were born a village peasant. You are not noble or even of artisan stock. However, I have accepted your elevation above me without protest and I recognize that his lordship has seen you have a good heart. Be safe on your life journey. Remember his lordship and, when you have tired of the army, if you are still alive, come back and check on him. Will you do that?"

"I will."

The slave moved aside and let Yanhamu step into the street.

"Boy!" he called as Yanhamu started to walk away, and he ran up beside him. "You may not believe in bad omens, but I do and you'll need something to ward them off." He pulled something from his tunic and held it out, closed inside his fist. He placed a small bag into Yanhamu's hand and for a moment held it there.

"I believe this belongs to an honest man," he said.

Yanhamu opened the bag. Inside gleamed the unusual silver amulet: an eye inside a circle.

FORTY-FIVE

Ramses station—the Clapham Junction of Cairo—had twenty platforms. No one checked their tickets as they entered and, without understanding the signs, they were directed to platform eight, where their train was due. To their astonishment it arrived on time, but that wasn't all that made them stare in disbelief. The solid blue carriages had no markings except for dents; the windows were small and so dirty they could hardly see in.

Relief struck them at the same time as they realized this was not their train after all. From time to time they could see cells through the windows. It was a prison train. It stopped briefly but no one got on. And no one got off.

Another train stopped twenty minutes later and someone, Alex took him for an armed porter, waved them back. "Second class," he shouted.

Faces pressed against grimy windows. The doors opened inwards and passengers crammed into the doorways smoking heavily. As the train started to move, people still hung on to the door handles and the porter pushed them inside. The doors didn't close.

Alex began to fidget, glancing up and down the platform. Then he choked.

"Shit!"

A man stood by a wall, partly obscured by a vending cabinet. When Alex had looked in his direction, the man deliberately looked away. That in itself wasn't too alarming, but his face was hidden by a hoodie—out of place and too hot for Egypt.

Alex turned his back. "We're being watched."

Vanessa looked uncertain.

"Over my shoulder. By the wall. Man in a grey hoodie."

Vanessa glanced and widened her eyes with concern. "He's definitely out of place."

"Stay with the bags."

"I…"

Alex was already walking away. He headed towards the platform exit and descended the steps. At the bottom, he waited for a couple of minutes. When the man in the grey top didn't appear, he tagged behind a group going up the steps. As he came onto the platform, he used them as a shield and then ducked behind another group.

Ahead, the man in the hoodie had moved to the other side of the vending unit and seemed to scan along the platform, from Vanessa to the exit. Watching her and looking for me, Alex thought.

As Alex stepped behind the wall to the block of waiting rooms, he spotted white skin under the hood. He circled the building, and as he came up on the opposite side there was an odd sense of familiarity about the man's figure. And then Alex placed him.

He squeezed between two Arabs and lunged for the man in the hoodie. Grabbing the back of the hood, he jerked it away.

"Pete!"

His friend's face went from shock to crumpled submission. "Hey… er… hi, Alex."

Alex kept hold of the back of Pete's top. "What the hell are you doing here?"

"Er… watching you?"

"Following!"

Pete shrugged. "Following you."

"Why? For Christ's sake, why?"

"Why'd you think?"

Alex's head spun. Pete knew about the break-in, had helped him forge the plan, and had taken the Isis puzzle. He said, "You know Ellen hid the ceremonial block don't you? It'll be at Highclere, right? It's not in Egypt."

Pete laughed mirthlessly. "I know it's not about finding the missing chunk of stone."

"How...?"

"I know more than you think."

Vanessa joined them and gawped at Pete. "You!"

Alex said, "He's been following us. He must know."

Pete gave Vanessa a wolfish grin. "More than Alex realizes. I'm part of the team."

Alex stared at him. "What?"

A train pulled up at the platform. Vanessa and Alex picked up their bags.

As they moved, Pete followed.

"You don't think that East End gang really planned the burglary, do you? Ha! I did that when Ellen told me she'd found something. Here's the deal now, just as it was before: you let me in on this little treasure hunt of yours and I don't tell the police that I know you arranged the break-in and forced me to help you."

They looked at the train and saw it was another second-class one. Still not the right train.

Vanessa said, "I'm confused. Did you just confess to organizing the burglary?"

"Yes, but the police won't know that and my witness statement will make them question everything again." He jerked his hood out of Alex's grip.

Vanessa looked at Alex. "What do you think? Is he telling the truth?"

Alex didn't answer. He was thinking. He looked at Vanessa and back at Pete. "So was it you or your thugs who trashed my flat?"

The guards called and waved people to get on.

Vanessa pointed along the platform. "Look over there."

Alex followed her indication. A tall thin man dressed smartly in a black suit was standing near the exit, clearly staring straight at them. "The guy from the BMW! It *was* him at the airport!"

Vanessa nodded. "One of yours then, Pete?"

"What? Who?"

The man was walking quickly towards them. Something in his intense eyes gave Alex a shiver.

Pete was staring.

"Pete?"

"Never seen him before!"

The train started to move.

Vanessa grabbed Alex's arm and pulled. "Get on the train!"

Alex was momentarily mesmerized. The man started to run. Was that a gun in his hand?

Vanessa had already jumped into an open doorway, forcing her way through.

Alex and Pete walked quickly beside the train.

Vanessa shouted, "Get in, for God's sake!"

Alex glanced along the platform. The man was closing fast. Alex gripped the rail beside the door and swung in. Pete was right behind. He flung his bag on the train and reached for the handle on the opposite side.

A woman on the platform screamed.

"Alex!" Pete shouted.

Alex twisted in the mass of people by the door and saw Pete holding on but leaning back with the man holding onto his neck. The train shuddered forward and Pete's eyes bulged with desperation. His fingers started to slip and then he let go.

Alex leaned out, grabbed hold of Pete's jacket and pulled as hard as he could. The train jolted and BMW man lost his grip. Pete tumbled through the door.

Alex scrabbled to a window in time to see BMW man getting to his feet. He just stood there staring after the diminishing train as if he had all the time in the world.

FORTY-SIX

The young officer said, "I joined the army to fight, not sit in this stinking tent all day reading boring documents."

"What?" Yanhamu looked up from the clay tablet he was translating.

The other officer continued to bitch: "We spend a year learning to be officers and just because we can read and write we get lumbered with the clerical stuff. The job stinks. The tent stinks. I stink!"

The other young man was called Thayjem and, during the year they had worked together, Yanhamu had learned to tune out the complaints. He went back to his translation. Something was troubling him. The Hittite document appeared to be a list of supplies, but every now and then place names and numbers seemed out of place.

"Oh, Ra protect us!" he blurted with sudden realization.

"Hey, you're supposed to pray to Seth! We're in the Black army, remember?"

Yanhamu didn't respond; he was already heading out of the tent. He flagged a message runner. When the boy sprinted over, Yanhamu said, "Make haste to the western valley where the Fourteenth are advancing. Tell the commander he's being led into a trap—tell him to retreat!"

The boy nodded abruptly and ran to where a charioteer was readying his horse. Within seconds, the horse pounded up the dusty road as fast as the messenger could drive him.

"What the hell got into you, Yan-Khety?" Thayjem said as Yanhamu ducked back into the tent. "A mosquito go up your bum?"

"I wish." Yanhamu picked up the tablet he'd been translating and stared at it as if glaring would make the words more true. He put it on the table and slid it over to his colleague. "What do you make of this?"

After a cursory analysis Thayjem said, "A shopping list, I should say. What did you take offence to, the pork? The heathens eat the disgusting stuff, I know, but you really should control your vomit."

"Shut up and read it again!"

Thayjem translated out loud and concluded: "Still a shopping list."

"And this one?" Yanhamu slid over a tablet they had translated the night before: the message that spoke of a sneak manoeuvre to outflank one of the Black units and cut them off.

"You know this was a great coup. The Fourteenth has been sent to ambush the enemy. If that Amurru messenger hadn't defected, we would not have known and we could now be handing out Hittite shopping lists to our men." Thayjem laughed and then stopped when he saw Yanhamu had not smiled.

Thayjem said, "Are you all right? You look sick."

"I'm going for a walk." Yanhamu slipped out of the tent and squatted in the shade. Across the plain he could see a stream of soldiers heading towards the main encampment. He tried to judge the number of men and horses but lost count in the confusion of heat haze and dust. Beyond the hill he knew the Blacks' leader had his command tent. It was said that General Horemheb himself had given the

276

leader his name: Apephotep—son of the serpent who fought Ra beyond the horizon. The name was both a challenge to the gods and a reflection of the soldier's fierce reputation.

It was said that Horemheb had been sent to Qadesh by Pharaoh as an emissary with promises of funding and military support, but no one in the army believed there was a chance of a lasting allegiance. The city-state was too important and too used to playing a political game to commit to one side. There was also talk that Horemheb had the Reds—the army of Ra—moving north from the Egyptian–Syrian border. He didn't expect peace.

From inside the tent, Yanhamu heard his colleague fart and then laugh. Thayjem may bitch about not fighting, but they had both seen the dreadful result of battle, and being away from the front line meant they had a good chance of getting out of the army alive. It wasn't until Yanhamu had joined the academy that he realized old soldiers were a rarity. Most of the time the men were fed reasonably and there was always beer to drink, and they all seemed to think that they would be the exception—the soldier who would return home a hero and make love to all the young girls. Yanhamu wondered then what Nefer-bithia was doing, and the thought of her made his heart heavy. He could have accepted the magistrate's offer and married her. At sixteen, she was undoubtedly married to another now and he was stuck in a foreign land with only the promise that, should he die here, his body would be returned to Egypt. It was a promise made to all the men, for everyone knew that you had to be buried beneath the soil of the Two Lands to find your way to the afterlife and the Field of Reeds.

He shook the morbid thoughts from his head, collected two cups of beer and returned to the tent. He handed the beer to his colleague and began translating the clay tablets again.

The light was fading and braziers had been lit when a chariot pulled up outside their tent and a mid-ranking officer charged in. He looked the two translators up and down disparagingly.

"Which of you girls is responsible for the message to the Fourteenth this afternoon?"

"Yan-Khety," Thayjem said, and pointed with excessive vigour.

Yanhamu stood to attention, a hand on each thigh. "It was me, sir."

"And you ordered a retreat?"

Thayjem gasped.

The mid-ranking officer continued: "You are to come with me immediately. The commander wants to see you." He turned, marched to his chariot and pulled himself athletically beside a driver. Yanhamu slung his scribe's satchel over his shoulder and squeezed beside the officer on the footplate.

The charioteer lashed at his horse and it jolted into a gallop. Yanhamu clung to the rail as they were driven at speed along the dusty track, leaving their tents in the supply section and heading for the Seth commander's encampment nearer the front line. During the twenty-minute journey, Yanhamu shivered. The evening air had a chill, but he realized it was more than the drop in temperature that cooled his skin. As they neared, he could see the long flowing black pennants against the dying embers of the sky and he thought of serpent's tongues tasting the air and judging his fear.

When the chariot pulled up at the massive tent, bigger than most noble's houses, they jumped off. Beside two giant Nubian guards, with faces blacker than river mud, the mid-ranking officer told him to wait until he was called. Yanhamu wiped dust from his tunic and shoes and, taking a damp cloth from a slave, cleaned dirt from his face.

The wait was so long that Yanhamu became thirsty and wondered whether he had been forgotten. Finally, an attractive boy wearing kohl around his eyes stepped between the guards and said he should follow.

He was led into a section of the tent and Yanhamu knew immediately that this was Apephotep, a large man with a charisma that seemed to fill the air like an invisible cloak. Yanhamu thought the air shimmered, although this could have been the effect of the fading light and torches around the tent. To his side stood a scribe and behind the commander were six slaves with the markings of deaf mutes who encouraged the air to circulate by moving their ostrich feather fans like the rhythm of a gentle sea. He stepped forward, eyes down and bowed, lowering his hands to his knees and out.

Apephotep growled, "So you are the imbecile who ordered the retreat."

"Sir, I found something that suggested our intelligence was false. I did not mean to order a retreat, merely to prevent an attack that would have left our men exposed. I believe we were the victims of misinformation."

"Look at me!" The big man slammed his fist on the table. "Do you realize the punishment for such a loss of face? The Blacks are the most fearless of Horemheb's armies. We do not retreat!" He calmed but continued to glare. "Your job is to use your head, is it not? How would your clever head feel if it was separated from that pretty neck?"

Yanhamu did not answer.

"But you were lucky. The message got to the Seth Fourteen just in time. There was a fight and we were victorious." The officer studied Yanhamu for a while as though deciding his fate, before he said, "Glory to Pharaoh, the living god, he who unites the Two Lands."

"May he live for eternity in the palace of Ra," Yanhamu recited.

"Glory to Horemheb, our beloved general who will make our great nation powerful once more and drive the usurper from our beloved land, the land of the true gods."

Yanhamu was unsure how to respond. Men whispered ill feelings towards the pharaoh and said terrible things in the stupor of their beer, but he had never heard Pharaoh Ay referred to as the usurper before. It was tantamount to treason.

Apephotep watched his reaction and then said, "What are your politics?"

Yanhamu shook his head. "I have no politics, sir."

"Is Horemheb your leader, no matter what? Would you lay down your life for him?"

"In this foreign field, My Lord Horemheb is Egypt." Yanhamu kept his face straight. He knew there was only one answer he could give and prayed he could mask his feelings as well as he could read others. He said, "Of course, sir, without question."

Apephotep nodded thoughtfully and let Yanhamu sweat before saying, "Your life shall be spared, although I must tell you my decision was a close one. If you had realized the subterfuge before, the leader of the Fourteenth would not be wounded and now lying in the care of the priests of Bast."

Apephotep beckoned him forward and the scribe indicated he should kneel. To Yanhamu's surprise, the commander reached forward and, over his head, placed a collar of office with gold embroidery and trim and lapis lazuli beads. "You are to report to Serq, the leader of the Fourteenth, as his personal strategist and officer second class. You will be responsible for his personal safety and you will take a blade in his place if the time comes."

As he stood, Yanhamu noticed a few specks of dried blood on the collar and couldn't help himself.

"What happened to his last one?"

"He asked too many fucking questions!" Apephotep guffawed. "Now, the captain's boy is here and will take you to the temple."

Yanhamu entered the area that had been designated as a temple of Bast. A statue of the cat goddess had been placed in each corner of the yard and between them bundles of papyrus flowers represented the walls of the temple. Torches burned all around and bowls of incense smouldered and fed a layer of smoke that hung below the awning. Of the thirty or forty wounded, either seated or lying here, Yanhamu knew that none of them would be lower class and all would have Egyptian blood. The gods of health were for the higher classes and were ministered by priests who walked between them chanting and rattling their sistra.

Yanhamu knew of the commander of Seth Fourteen by reputation. One story was that he had gained the name Serq because of the speed of his aggression, like the strike of a scorpion. Others said it was just because a scorpion had stung him in childhood, leaving its mark on his face.

The boy, who had led the way from the Seth encampment, pointed to a chair at the rear of the yard. Yanhamu walked over and bowed his head to avert his eyes and stopped just short of the captain's chair.

"My new strategist," Serq said in a voice that was rough but slightly higher pitched than Yanhamu had anticipated. "What's your name?"

"Yan-Khety, sir."

"I knew of a Khety once. A magistrate from Thebes. Are you related?"

Yanhamu hesitated. When he enrolled at the military academy in Memphis he had been surprised at the magistrate's letter. Instead of an introduction, it was a statement of Yanhamu's heritage. His acceptance had been guaranteed and the enrolling officer had noted the name.

Yanhamu said, "I am his son, sir."

"Gods protect me, a strategist and a judge!" He laughed mirthlessly. "Let me see your face."

Yanhamu looked up and choked. The light was poor, but the evidence was clear: the man in the chair had a hard face with a small scar on his left cheek that looked like his namesake—Serq, the Scorpion. Yanhamu's legs buckled. He grabbed the chair for balance. After more than two

years in the army, he had finally come face-to-face with
Captain Ani.

FORTY-SEVEN

The train rumbled slowly on tracks that creaked and groaned and they began to pick up speed.

Vanessa glared at Pete. "You're not coming with us," she said, her voice clear and final.

Pete laughed. "As I said, lady, I know too much and can make Alex look guilty. In fact, for all you know, he *is* guilty. I'm part of this whether you like it or not."

"You've got nothing," Alex said.

Pete pushed someone aside and picked up his bag. He placed his hand inside. "It's all in my notebook in here. The whole sordid truth."

Alex reached towards the bag. As he started to move, Pete withdrew his hand and, in a smooth motion, slapped Alex across the face. At precisely the same time, the train jolted and began to slow. Vanessa used the sudden move to grab and spin Pete around. She slammed him hard against the carriage wall, twisting his arm behind him.

Other passengers moved aside as she strong-armed him to the lavatory. They disappeared inside, and moments later Vanessa reappeared on her own.

The train was pulling alongside platforms at Giza, Cairo's second station.

Vanessa said, "We need to get off and switch trains."

Alex nodded dumbly.

She looked into his eyes. "You OK?"

He took a long breath and noticed all the dark faces close by watching him intently.

"Yes."

"Have you got the notebook?"

He held up Pete's bag.

The train stopped and Vanessa beckoned to Alex, saying, "Keep your eyes open for the BMW man." She looked up and down the platform and stepped off. Then she waved him over to a wall. They followed it around the side so they were away from the platform, with a good view, but shielded from anyone not at the far end of the station. Only one man could see them clearly and he appeared to be security. It was a small station with two platforms. A rail flyover swept overhead. The sound of wheels drew their attention and they shrank back as a cleaner pushed his trolley past them.

Alex put his hand on his heart. "God, it's doing ten to the dozen."

A minute later a train stopped on their platform. The engine was identical to all the others: a square block of dirty petrol blue, like an oversized container but with small windows behind metal grills. The carriages, on the other hand, were much better. Some cream with green stripes, others blue with a grey stripe. All first class.

An announcement in Arabic was followed by a series of places in English ending with "Dairut".

"Our train? Only an hour late."

A few locals got on, but most of the orderly queues at the carriages were backpackers. Alex and Vanessa waited until everyone was on and then ran to the open door, jumped in and shut it behind them. Vanessa waited by the window and watched the platform until the train began to move.

"No sign of anyone suspicious," she said.

* * *

They found their allocated seats in a compartment although the numbers were handwritten in Arabic above the seats and Alex had to ask which were twenty-five and twenty-six.

Alex held up Pete's bag. "What did you do to Pete?"

"Helped him sleep for thirty minutes or so." When Alex frowned, she added, "Like you, I had some martial arts training. Uncle Seth insisted before I was allowed to go to Israel on my own. Self-defence really, but I know how to make someone go to sleep." She studied Alex's reaction and shook her head. "Don't you dare be concerned for him. He wasn't a friend. He was using you."

"I guess."

"There's no guessing about it."

Alex opened the bag. Inside were mostly clothes, but there was Pete's passport and a tatty black notebook.

Vanessa held out her hand. "Let me see?"

Alex handed it to her and placed Pete's bag under the seat. He'd point it out to a guard and say someone had left it. Hopefully Pete would get his passport back.

After a long anxious wait, the train finally pulled away and, through a window that looked like it had been sandblasted, they watched the outskirts of Cairo pass by. Houses looked unfinished, with concrete-encased metal rods on most roofs. Most were unpainted and rugs dangled from windows.

"Look at that!" Alex said, pointing to a bicycle hanging from a window ledge. "Saves space, I suppose."

She didn't look up; she had her head buried in the notebook.

Alex was disappointed that he couldn't see the pyramids from the train, and they were soon in the countryside, running along an irrigation channel, heading south. It must have been parallel to the Nile, Alex reasoned, although there was no sense of where it lay. On both sides he could see fields, occasional buildings, palm trees and, in the distance every now and again, sandstone mountains.

The main crop appeared to be sugar cane. Some shacks had dried cane propped against the side and Alex wondered whether it was used for shelter as well as food. They passed many pickups with so much sugar cane loaded on top that the drivers must have had trouble seeing the way. Heavily laden bony donkeys were also prevalent. He saw a dead donkey in the ditch between the road and channel and Alex was glad Vanessa wasn't looking.

The train had bursts of speed and, in places, stopped for no apparent reason. An Australian passenger in their carriage commented that the track was in poor condition and the slow sections were due to a fear of derailment. Great.

Vanessa finally put the notebook down. "Well," she said. There was a strange glint in her eyes.

"Well what?"

"All has been revealed." She tapped the book. "Your friend Pete has kept good notes, luckily for you."

"Stop being so cryptic and tell me what you've learned."

She smiled. "Well, firstly it confirms that you weren't involved in the break-in at Highclere. Pete planned it all, even as far as getting a gang to execute the burglary. It seems he has contacts through the security firm he works for." She smiled again. "He was playing two angles. Pete was working on Ellen to find out what the treasure was and was also hoping for a payoff from the burglars if they got away with it."

"You said 'firstly'. Is there something else?"

"There's a list of things from the exhibition. He marked the genuine and the fake, such as Tutankhamen's headdress."

Alex reached for the book. Vanessa held it out but didn't immediately let go. "This is gold dust. It's great news for both of us. For you because we have evidence it was Pete and not you. Secondly, there's another story with a different angle. It's better than I thought. With this, maybe I can write something award-winning." As he opened the book she added, "So let me have it back, because I'm guarding that with my life."

He grinned and began to read the plans and outcomes Pete had kept note of.

In the evening they were offered dinner, which consisted of different types of bread and a cup of Nescafe. When Alex asked for a glass of wine, the waiter just scowled at him.

"No sense of humour, that one."

Vanessa said, "Muslim country with strict rules. They obviously do have a sense of humour, it's just different to ours. Remember, Marek said not to have expectations."

"Did you notice Marek said it twice? In ancient Egypt they used to repeat spells over and over. Like in the *Book of the Dead*. Telling a god something again and again made it more truthful. It struck me that maybe they still do it."

Vanessa went in search of the lavatory. When she returned she was pulling a sour expression. "They certainly don't have any expectations about clean toilets." She sat and looked at what Alex had been doing.

He'd drawn some symbols on a napkin.

"What's this?"

"I don't know if you are aware but they found these symbols in a Sinai cave. They're thought to be almost four thousand years old. A professor of archaeology presented his findings to a conference in Paris." Alex pointed to the first symbol. "The professor began by saying that it was clearly representative of a woman and this is possibly representative of the matriarch. The next is a small bird, a

287

quail perhaps, possibly being the primary source of meat or—as is more likely—part of a town's name. The next symbol is sometimes representative of bread, but here the professor said there were two hills nearby, so thought the bird and hills meant a town known as *Quail and Two Hills*. The next symbol is a horse. Well, you'll have to excuse my sketch!"

"I'll use my imagination."

"OK, horses were thought to have been introduced by the Hyksos, who ruled Egypt between the Old and New Kingdoms, and may either represent her importance as a leader or perhaps her wealth as a horse owner. The professor then pointed to the next symbol and said some people thought it to be a plough, symbolizing that the society was not at war, but was one of peaceful farmers. However, the professor thought it was a bellows, meaning to get air and to be able to live. And since the next is obviously a fish, he interpreted this as meaning they turned from being farmers to fishermen to stay alive. Perhaps this is a story about a female leader at a time when food wouldn't grow—she then showed them how to fish so that they would not grow hungry.

"The professor paused and then pointed to the final symbol and said it was the universal sign for a star. From this he concluded that the society was religious, worshipping the stars or perhaps a single star."

Vanessa said, "The final shape is the Star of David. The symbol of the Jews."

"Ah." Alex took another sip. "You're one step ahead of me. The audience were very impressed by the professor's interpretation, that was until a Rabbi stood up and asked for the microphone. When he could finally speak he said, 'Professor, I am afraid your interpretation is incorrect. You see, overall we have a woman. The next symbol in the row is a chick, then we have two mounds and a donkey—or, more specifically, an ass. The plough symbolizes to dig. I would say the fish is a mackerel and, of course, the final symbol is the Star of David. You see, this is Hebrew. And Hebrew should be read from right to left. What this actually says is the equivalent of holy mackerel, dig the ass and boobs on that chick!'"

Vanessa laughed and clapped. "Very good. Of course, I knew it was a joke immediately."

"You did?"

"There was a flaw in your story. The Star of David didn't become a symbol of Judaism until about four hundred years ago."

Alex drew an upside-down triangle on the napkin so that it was the right way round for Vanessa. "A pyramid," he said. He then drew another triangle, this time the wrong way for Vanessa. "It's been argued that a right way up pyramid is a symbol of God's power coming down to Earth—you know, like the sun's rays."

"Like the famous painting by William Blake—with God reaching down from the clouds."

"Right. And the inverted pyramid is man reaching up to Heaven." He raised his arms forming a Y. Then he drew the two triangles together, forming the Star of David. "What you might not know is that ancient Egyptians used the hexagram to represent Sirius, the most important star and constellation in the ancient Egyptian night sky. Its rise each year coincided with the Nile inundation. Some people believe the pyramids of Giza are aligned to represent the stars of Sirius. One of the shafts from the Great Pyramid actually points to Sirius, as though it's a guide for the dead pharaoh to reach the afterlife. Most people think the Egyptian afterlife was underground, but it wasn't. It was in the night sky—and principally the constellation of Orion, where Osiris dwelt. The belt lines up with Sirius which was linked with Isis."

"It's interesting, but there's still a long gap before being adopted as the Jewish symbol." She poured them both more water. "Let's not talk religion anymore. It's all speculation. At least what Ellen and Marek have discovered can be proved."

"I hope."

"If you become famous, what will you do?"

"I don't know. I hadn't thought that far. I don't think I'll make a fortune. If there's anything valuable, I'm happy for it to stay in Egypt. I'll be proud to see it in the Cairo Museum." He thought for a while. "I guess fame is its own reward."

She checked her watch. "Almost three hours to go. God, I could sleep for England!"

He rubbed his face, suddenly overcome with fatigue.

Vanessa said, "We arrive after ten, so I'm going to catch a few zeds."

When the waiter cleared their trays, he stopped at the next compartment. Joachim stood, looked through the waste on the trays and lifted out the napkin with the symbols. He walked to the next carriage, pulled out his mobile phone and pressed a speed-dial number.

"Yes," a gravelly voice answered.

"They've been discussing symbols," Joachim said, his voice expressing his excitement. "And I'm looking at some right now. MacLure wrote them on a napkin."

"And just left them for you to find?"

"You're dubious?"

"I'm realistic. What are the symbols?"

Joachim described what he was looking at.

The old man was silent.

"Gershom?"

The old man said, "The last one worries me... the Star of David."

"If it is from the map, then the clue may not be as cryptic as we suspected."

Gershom scoffed, "It is not from the map. The star symbol is far too modern to have come from ancient Egypt.

No, my worry is that if it came from the artefact then it may be a fake."

"Or perhaps MacLure has made a mistake."

"Perhaps." Gershom coughed and Joachim waited for him to speak again.

Gershom said, "There is another possibility—Mr MacLure is on to us and playing a silly game."

"Then I will put a gun to his head and just get him to tell me the truth."

"No. You know we promised no killing, Joachim."

"I won't kill him, just threaten."

"And if the threat doesn't work? No, Joachim, you will wait and only use that as a last resort. You will follow him again tomorrow and let me know as soon as you learn something more."

They ended the connection. Joachim stared at the row of symbols and thought about what the old man had said. Tomorrow, he decided. Tomorrow is a day that could change the world.

FORTY-EIGHT

1325 BCE, Ugarit

Serq snapped, "What's wrong with you? I hope you're not squeamish at the sight of blood!"

Yanhamu tried to compose himself. The man he hated—the man who had spoiled and killed his sister—was here. After leaving the academy Yanhamu had requested a posting to Gaza, but the captain wasn't there, and after searching local records, he could find no proof Captain Ani had ever been there. Now he looked down into the face that had haunted his nightmares for the past eleven years.

"I asked you what is wrong!" Serq shouted.

Yanhamu covered his mouth and ran from the makeshift temple. Beyond the bales of papyrus flowers he bent double and vomited. A priest enquired if he needed a prayer but Yanhamu waved the man away. He stood straight and gulped in the air, trying to force himself to return. As he looked around, he watched the priest he had waved away. The man occasionally placed a bowl beside a wounded man and encouraged him to drink from it. As he watched the priest collect another bowl and fill it with something white from a jug, an idea came to him. A scribe always carried the tools for writing, which included arsenic, the substance that rich women used to whiten their skin and doctors as part of a remedy. Yanhamu also knew it could be used as a poison. He walked to the bowls, and after first tasting the milky substance he poured it into a bowl and then surreptitiously emptied his pot of arsenic paint into the liquid.

He carried it carefully to Serq, who eyed him suspiciously.

"A thousand apologies, sir." Yanhamu bowed, averting his eyes and feeling better for it. "The incense—I think it was affecting me." He placed the bowl on a table beside Serq's chair. "Sir, this is goats' milk, if you are feeling up to drinking it."

Serq looked disdainful. "I've only got a slight leg wound, Khety. I'm only here to ensure the goddess favours me and prevents infection. Now tell me how you knew there was to be an ambush today."

"I knew we had information about troop movements of the enemy that had been obtained from documents in the possession of a messenger. I was translating a tablet that seemed to be list—a food order—but I got suspicious. There seemed to be code. There were numbers and town names in the wrong places, sir. They were in the same places in the other document, which I recall had the same numbers which couldn't be explained."

"So you couldn't be sure it was a trap?"

"No, sir."

Serq thought for a moment, staring at one of the braziers. "Then it was very bold of you to send the message to my force. If you had been mistaken, the loss of face would have been unacceptable. And you know the punishment for that."

Yanhamu nodded and noticed Serq still seemed to be deep in thought.

Eventually, the leader of the Fourteenth said what was on his mind: he began to talk through strategies and battles he had fought. Yanhamu found himself only half listening.

He kept staring at the bowl, wondering what would happen if Serq drank it; was there enough arsenic to kill? He had heard of men foaming at the mouth and writhing with terrible gut pain after being poisoned. He touched the electrum amulet he now wore around his left wrist and thought of his sister. She would be in the Field of Reeds, he was certain. He was also certain that Laret watched over him at night like she had as a child after their mother had died and father left. He smiled at the memory of her pretty face and generous heart. She was waiting for him but, if he murdered this man, there was no way he would be allowed through the Gates of Judgement. Ammut would destroy his *ba* and it would be an eternity of nothingness.

Serq picked up the bowl. He continued to talk about victories and the glory of war, especially under General Horemheb.

Yanhamu stared at the white liquid as it swirled with the man's gestures. And then Serq placed it to his lips.

In that instant, Yanhamu saw a priest behind shake his head. The man had a Bast mask and, as Yanhamu looked closely at the cat's face, he saw his sister's eyes looking back, pleading with him.

"No!" Yanhamu struck the bowl from Serq's hand.

The leader roared with fury and Yanhamu fell to his knees. "Your pardon, sir! I saw an evil bug drop into the liquid." His voice trembled as much as his hands and he gripped the amulet and prayed for strength. He could not kill the man like this. His sister had given him a sign that this was not meant to be, but now he knew his life clung to his body like a spider dangles on a thread.

Yanhamu waited, prostrate before his new leader.

Serq stood.

The whole temple became filled with chattering. The occasional moan, chanting and sound of the sistra was gone. Yanhamu glanced up and realized Serq was looking west. Everyone who could stand did so. Everyone was looking west.

The night sky had a bright orange patch tinged with purple.

"It's Ra!" someone shouted. "Ra has returned from the underworld!" There were more shouts and chanting and bowing in supplication.

Yanhamu stood and stared at the strange light. The purple edges looked like cloud, billowing, forcing its way up against the night's dark cloak.

And then the ground trembled—a weak shake at first and then it was like being on the footplate of a chariot driven fast over rutted soil. Men cried out. The shrine to Bast tumbled. A fire started on the ground where a brazier had fallen and then caught a bale of papyrus.

Yanhamu fell and pulled himself up next to Serq, who was holding onto his chair.

"That is not Ra," Serq said quietly and, as if in response, the air was filled with a terrible roar, like a thunderclap, only this didn't end.

A group of men, closest to the fire, pushed the burning bale away and stamped down the flames on the ground. The head priest composed himself and began to lead prayers. Yanhamu and the others kneeled and extended their arms towards the light.

Serq knelt beside him and muttered again, "That is not Ra."

Yanhamu braced himself for another reaction to Serq's heresy, but if anything the roar began to diminish. They stayed like that for a long time, the priests lamenting and Serq occasionally grumbling his doubts. Yanhamu noted the moon had travelled a full house—an eighth of the night sky—when he heard another far-off sound. At first it was a whisper in the air and then the sound of a million locusts heading towards them. The priests stopped and everyone stood and stared west again. The glow was still there, more faint and purple as though the dark clouds were building and pushing the sun back into the underworld.

295

Then they saw it, a wall of water rushing into the valley, tearing up trees and ploughing through the earth like a river breaking a child's mud dam. Almost as soon as they spotted it and started to wonder what it was, the tidal wave crashed through the temple and swept them away.

It took two days for the men to reunite into the semblance of an army. They had been ten miles from the sea and yet the tsunami had travelled far beyond the temple of Bast. Apephotep had toured his bedraggled forces and proclaimed the gods were on their side because large numbers of the enemy had been destroyed in places. They were on the verge of a great victory. Yanhamu didn't see Serq after the wave struck. He was assigned a unit of twenty and, for the first time in his military career, found himself at the front line. Initially, there was trepidation, but as they marched north through the hills they saw the enemy was routed. Everywhere they went was destruction; whole towns were swept away and in their place was a fetid land covered in jetsam. By the time the horns sounded to signal the end, Yanhamu was relieved that he hadn't drawn blood even once. He gathered his men in one of the main encampments and they celebrated long into the night with beer, singing and dancing. Animals were butchered and roasted, for there was certainty they would be returning home. And when they were tired of talking about all the women they would make love to, they talked of how they would spend the gold they would earn as the heroes who defeated the Hittites.

In the morning, the leaders and high priests returned from a meeting with the general. They moved amongst the units and reported the news that the great victory had been in the name of Ra who had spoken to Horemheb and told him it was time to return to the Two Lands and drive out the usurper of the crown. They would also receive twice their allotment of gold. A ripple of cheers ran through the legions as they heard the news and then the whole army began to chant the name Horemheb.

FORTY-NINE

Alex felt Yanhamu's frustration at being so close to taking the life of his nemesis. And yet at the last minute he couldn't go through with it. If he'd had the chance to kill Ellen's murderer would he have done it? He imagined it was the guy from the Thames who had attacked them. He imagined standing over him with a gun, his finger tightening on the trigger.

"Alex, we're here."

For a moment he was disorientated. He opened his eyes. "Vanessa?"

"We've arrived in Dairut. Time to get off."

The first-class carriage chairs reclined to a reasonable angle and the gentle rattle of the train had quickly lulled Alex into a deep sleep. He returned the seat to vertical with a jerk and put his head in his hands for a moment. He had a headache and quick movements caused a throb in his right eye.

Vanessa held her case and stood over him, urging him to hurry. He stood gingerly, not wanting to jar his head again, collected his bag and followed her.

"What next?" she asked as they stood on the platform and watched as the final passengers disembarked and hurried away. The train pulled off, and within a minute they were alone on the platform.

Alex pulled out the note from Marek. "We're to take a taxi to Deir Mawas. I don't know if that's a place or hotel. I guess we find a taxi and ask."

They left the platform and cut through the ticketing and waiting area. One man sat reading a newspaper, cigarette in mouth. He looked up as they passed and then jumped to his feet.

"MacLure?"

"Yes."

The man beamed, folded his paper under his arm and pointed to his chest. "I driver. I take you and wife."

"Not wife," Alex explained, but when the man pulled an uncomprehending face, he said, "Fine. Deir Mawas?"

The man grinned and nodded again and said something Alex assumed to be the same place. Then he led them to an old silver Nissan estate, loaded the bags in the rear and held open the doors.

Alex wasn't happy with the bags being loaded before the price had been agreed. "How much?"

"No, no. No price. All paid."

Alex looked at Vanessa, who just shrugged and got in. They buckled up and exchanged glances, relieved to find these seat belts worked.

The driver glanced back. "English? Where from?" he said, and they set off at speed.

"London," they replied in unison.

"Yes, London. Arsenal. Chelsea. Manchester United! Lovely jubbly."

With the intermittent flashes from street lights and then darkness, Alex found himself nodding off again. He heard Vanessa say: "Well he seems to know where he's going even if we don't." And the next thing he knew, they were bundling out, registering and staggering up to bedrooms.

His hotel room was very basic: a single bed with a cotton sheet that smelled dusty, a tiled floor partially covered with a thin rug, and a wardrobe, the wood of which didn't match the headboard or solitary chair or small table with a kettle and mug. Alex's mind played through the hieroglyphs and other symbols on the Map-Stone. He pictured the majesty that would have been Akhetaten, the ancient city of Amarna, and imagined finding the clues. He was unsure of when his thoughts shifted from consciousness into dreams, but his night was filled with grand images and the gods of ancient Egypt. He was Yanhamu descending a long shaft into darkness, led by the jackal-headed Anubis. At the end he saw an orange glow of burning torches. The tunnel ended in a chamber. In the centre, lit by the torches, he saw a small gathering. Around the outside, he sensed people watching, but couldn't quite see them. Anubis guided him to giant golden scales. Thoth, the ibis-headed god, said something and Anubis responded. Alex heard them chanting "Yanhamu. Yanhamu." And he saw Anubis place his heart on one side of the scales and a feather on the other. He heard teeth grind and realized Ammut, the terrifying Devourer, part crocodile, part lion, part hippopotamus, sat under the scales like an expectant dog at a dinner table. If Yanhamu's heart was found to weigh more than the feather, it would be fed to Ammut, and his soul, his *ba*, would not find the afterlife. There was no such thing as Hell, just oblivion. He wouldn't see Ellen again.

It was time to say the spells of the *Book of the Dead*. Yanhamu knew it. He had to pronounce his worthiness to the gods. Patiently, Anubis pointed to the far side of the chamber, and Yanhamu thought he could make out a throne lit by a green luminosity upon which a mummy sat—Osiris. As Yanhamu, he began to recite the magical words. He didn't know how he knew them, he just did. However, when he came to the part about not committing murder, Thoth interrupted and asked him to explain. Yanhamu recounted the story of meeting Serq, the Scorpion, at the temple of Bast. How he had poisoned the milk but didn't administer it. Thoth took notes and shook his head. "That's not the story."

"He killed my sister," Yanhamu said, and then stared in horror as his heart twitched on the scales.

Thoth said, "And how do you explain the theft?"

The heart twitched, moving perilously close to the edge, to the waiting jaws of the Devourer.

"I didn't steal anything. The Map-Stone is hidden. I didn't steal it!" he pleaded.

Ammut smacked her lips and Yanhamu shouted, "I haven't done anything wrong!"

Alex sat up in bed, covered in cold sweat.

When they met the driver in the morning, he pointed outside. "Not good."

Alex and Vanessa exchanged glances. What did he mean? Their appearance? The Nissan? The weather?

They followed him onto the road beside the Nissan estate. This time the driver pointed to the sky, a blemish-free azure.

Alex said, "A bit windy?"

The driver nodded and raised both hands as if weighing the air. "Not good."

Vanessa opened a local map she was holding. "Can you take us to Tell el-Amarna?"

The driver pulled a concerned face but waved them into the Nissan and raced them through the town of Deir Mawas.

Vanessa had found it on the map over breakfast and they knew Amarna was a short journey north along the Nile, before a crossing point. She'd said, "We don't need to wait for Marek to visit the ruins, right?"

"Not really. He seems to have done the hard part for us—organizing getting here."

"So what was on the block that Lord Carnarvon took— the one Ellen's hidden?"

"Symbols that make up a kind of map."

301

"Could you draw them for me so I can understand? So I know what we're looking for?" When he reluctantly nodded, she pulled a pen and paper from a side pocket of her bag.

He laughed, "Typical journalist—always comes prepared."

He drew a rectangle and then added sides so that it looked three dimensional. He shrugged. "I'm not very good at this. I can see it in my mind but drawing is another matter. You see, the ancient Egyptians were not only masters of disguising language and double meaning, but they would draw two-dimensional figures that folded into three."

She studied what he had drawn. "So what is it—a room?"

"This is a palace or temple, I think. These symbols represent the scale but there may also be images. A flying goose, for example, may literally be a giant wall painting of a goose that confirms we have the right place." He drew a square with concentric lines and illustrated levels. "This, I think, represents the tomb, with steps here and here"—he indicated both sides and then pointed to the middle of one—"and here is a hidden section. I think that's what we're looking for."

Vanessa frowned. "I don't want to be rude, Alex, but that's not much of a map. Perhaps we do need Marek to interpret."

It felt like a challenge, and Alex had pointed out they had no idea how long Marek would take to join them. They had nothing to lose by visiting the site and they may even get inspiration from what they found.

He was about to respond when the Nissan jolted. They had left the main road and were now thundering along a minor one, its surface in dire need of repair. Between bumps, Alex said, "A rally-cum-Formula One driver!"

From the front the driver laughed. "Formula One. Michael Schumacher. Yes, that is me!" Then, as if to prove it, he oversteered around the next bend before halting. Outside, through swirling sand, they could see that the potholed road became a hardstanding that led to a moored flatbed ferry.

A man, with a billowing galabia and face wrapped in a scarf so that only his eyes showed, came to the window. When Schumacher wound it down, the passengers heard a rushing sound. At first Alex thought it was the Nile but realized the river was choppy rather than fast-flowing.

"That's the wind," Vanessa said.

Schumacher wound up the window after a brief animated conversation. He looked back at the passengers, weighed the air again and said, "Sand."

Alex pointed to the ferry. "Let's go."

The driver shrugged, pulled across the hardstanding and onto the ferry.

There were no gates at either end, just drive-on, drive-off ramps, and Alex estimated it would take eight cars, maybe four trucks. Their Nissan was the only vehicle and, as soon as they stopped, the diesel funnel belched smoke and they began to trundle across the hundred-metre gap.

The western side of the river had been lush fields, but the town of Tell el-Amarna on the opposite bank had a narrow strip of cultivated land before desert stretched towards the eastern hills that jutted abruptly from the plain like a jagged limestone perimeter wall. The blur caused by sand in the air made the landscape look like a watercolour painting.

In the town, Schumacher stopped and briefly scanned left and right as though looking or waiting for someone. No one appeared, and after a few seconds he continued.

Alex leaned forward and handed a piece of paper to the driver. He pointed to a rectangle. "The Great Temple," he said. "Please take us to this place."

While waiting for Vanessa at the hotel, Alex had managed to get on to the Internet and copied out the layout of the ruins that were once the great city of Akhetaten. It had been five kilometres long and housed over twenty thousand people. The modern town was just beyond the northern reaches of the old city and the taxi driver followed the road east out of town before turning south on a dusty track and following the boundary between farmland and desert. A large modern cemetery ran along their left and ended abruptly. Beyond were the ruins of a city destroyed more than three thousand years ago.

"Here." The driver stopped the car. "Sand," he said, and made the gesture of something painful striking his face. Then he handed them each a scarf and demonstrated how they should wrap it around their heads.

Alex opened the door and felt the blast of the dry hot air. They stood in the lee of the vehicle, the river to their backs. Before them were desolate, sand-covered ruins, a once great city reduced to fragments of stone, with nothing more than a few feet high. They moved forward and felt the first rush of airborne sand which stung their exposed hands.

Alex pointed ahead and they trudged across compact dusty ground that crunched under their boots. He stopped at a wall, the only remaining external section of the temple where Akhenaten was said to act as high priest in his daily worship of the sun god, Aten. The enormity of it took Alex's breath away. He looked at Vanessa and saw her eyes wide with wonderment.

She placed her head close to his so he could hear. "I never imagined I could feel this way about ruins," she shouted. "It's both awe-inspiring and devastatingly sad."

He nodded. "It must have been spectacular. This temple was unlike any other. It was both vast and open." They walked over a wall and into the first section. The second section was more open, with hundreds of stumps of what Alex had read were once offering tables.

Vanessa pointed out the steps in the central area. "This isn't the same as your diagram."

He said, "Too big, I think." He found a little shelter and checked his sketch and took them through a side wall. "I can't make it out, but the Royal Palace was here. Maybe part of it was the right size, but nothing distinct I can get a bearing on."

From there they walked through sections of wall and followed paths past stumps that were once pillars and seemed to have been removed with modern-day tools.

Alex headed for the tallest landmark, a pinkish pillar in the shape of bundled reeds.

"The smaller temple," he explained as they reached it. Like the Great Temple, the walls were clearly defined. There was a central section and then the remnants of pillars at the far end.

Alex sat on the ground, sheltered by the wall.

Vanessa pulled two bottles of mineral water from her handbag and handed him one.

After a long drink, he said, "I just don't know."

They sat looking at the stones with sand swirling around until the Nissan pulled up close by. They jumped in, grateful for the respite.

"Good?" the driver asked.

"Not good," Alex said, studying the diagram. "Is there another palace?"

The driver beamed. "Ah!"

He U-turned and followed the track back to the modern cemetery and then retraced their route to the town. But instead of heading for the ferry he continued north. At the end of the town there was a triangular section of desert. More ruins, but this time surrounded by agricultural land.

Alex and Vanessa jumped out, braced themselves against the wind and walked over to the foot-high exterior wall. Alex paced it out.

Against the wind, he said, "About the right dimensions. No sign of any flying geese." He quickly counted the shallow stumps of identical height—pillars removed mechanically, he surmised. "Forty pillars. It was a special number for the ancient Egyptians as well as the Jews."

Vanessa asked, "So that was the forty you were interested in?"

"It's one of the numbers on the Map-Stone—four hoops symbolizing forty and a pillar. So my guess is we're looking for forty pillars." Alex walked around the walls ending at steps at the far side.

Vanessa stood beside him. "OK, so if this is the first area in your map. Where's the next? Where's the square with the steps on either side and the hidden area?"

Alex looked around. If this was the location, the starting point, then it was a disaster. He signalled for them to get back to the shelter of the Nissan. Once inside, he removed the scarf and grimaced. "If this is the place, then we've a problem. The area we're looking for will be over there." He waved a hand towards a field of sweetcorn. "If it is, it's going to be damned hard to find it now."

FIFTY

Yanhamu walked through the rubble of Akhetaten and tried to imagine what it had been like. He had seen a unit of the Medjay heading to the northern quarter where they would be looting and destroying anything that remained. The mercenaries had swept through the city killing everyone they found.

Except for the swarms of flies, feeding off decaying bodies, nothing stirred.

Thayjem came up beside him and said, "What are you thinking?"

"This is more terrible than war. Did these people really deserve this? They were Egyptians after all, and no man has the right to spill Egyptian blood."

"Well that's debatable—not that our blood isn't sacred, of course it is, but it is questionable whether these people were true Egyptians. Pharaoh has declared them outlaws and their kind must be eradicated throughout the land if *ma'at* is to be restored, the gods satisfied and the Two Lands be the great power it once was."

"You sound like a propaganda merchant."

307

Thayjem scoffed. "I just want to finish this stupid task and go home. What is it, twenty months since we had our victory parade in Memphis? And more than two years since Ra created the great wave that destroyed our enemies. We thought it was over then, but who could have known that we would march to Thebes?"

Yanhamu nodded. He was studying the architecture and trying to work out where the King's House ended and the Hall of Records began.

Thayjem continued: "I thought Ay would be declared the false pharaoh. I thought there would be a fight akin to the battle of Osiris and Seth." He laughed. "Did you notice the irony since we were in the Seth Army, but on the side of the true pharaoh?" He stopped abruptly. "What are you doing?"

Yanhamu wasn't listening. He felt along the damaged wall. "This city was the greatest in the world and now it is going to be systematically torn down, stone by stone." He patted Thayjem on the shoulder. "Take the men up to the royal tombs and get started. I'm just going to take a look at the records—if there are any still here. You know, for a while, not only the treasury records, but all written texts were brought here. It is said that Ra told Pharaoh Akhenaten to build a library for all the wisdom in the world."

Thayjem waved to the motley band of ten soldiers who squatted lazily in the shade. They reluctantly assembled themselves and led their horse and carriage back to the Royal Drive. Thayjem turned back and gripped Yanhamu's shoulder. "Don't be long and don't let the Medjay mistake you for an outlaw! If you get killed here, I'm not searching through the bodies to find you."

"Thanks!" Yanhamu grinned. "And, if I find a Wisdom Text, I won't share it with you."

He watched the unit go and then returned to studying the walls, their murals and occasional hieroglyphs. He found a short flight of descending steps where the wall was

308

damaged and a hieroglyph appeared to have been chiselled out. At the bottom, he heaved a wooden door aside and found a passage which led to an antechamber.

He heard a noise and was surprised to see light ahead.

"Is someone there?"

He walked through to a main chamber lit by lanterns and he saw desks and hundreds of earthenware pots, from jug-size to the size of a small man, the sort used to store papyri and clay tablets. The room had been disturbed, tables knocked over and most of the pots broken. He moved shards of pottery aside and picked up a scroll. It was a record of food and animals transported from the Delta during a month. He picked out another: a schedule of activities of a tax collector and the payments due. Reading through another and another, he became disappointed by their mundane nature.

He sniffed the air and wondered if it had become more smoky and then jumped as he heard voices echo along the stone passageways. Yanhamu drew his sword and headed towards the sound. The air became acrid with smoke. He passed through two small rooms and then ascended stairs and could now hear the voices clearly. It was an argument.

Yanhamu shouted, "Who's there?"

He entered a chamber lined with shelves, each with pigeonholes stuffed with papyri. A soldier appeared to have lit some of the scrolls, the fire of which spread rapidly. Another man was frantically trying to stop the destruction but was struck to the ground.

The soldier looked across the chamber towards Yanhamu at the same time as raising his sword arm to drive it into the man on the floor.

The soldier growled, "Piss off!"

"Stop!" Yanhamu clashed his sword against metal and, through the smoke, took in more of the scene: the man on the ground was a noble, possibly by royal appointment; the soldier wore the blood-red cloak of a mercenary.

"I said, piss…" The mercenary turned towards him with the glower of a cornered jackal. "You!"

The shock made Yanhamu drop his sword. "You… Captain Ani…" he stammered. "Serq, you're alive!"

The man on the ground rolled, but Serq slashed at him with his blade, splashing scarlet across the old man's white gown. He stepped and prepared again for a death blow, but all the time his eyes were fixed on Yanhamu.

"Ani?" He laughed mirthlessly. "I haven't been called that for a long, long time. Did I know you from somewhere else?"

"You came to my village and took my sister."

Serq shook his head, uncomprehending. "It's the way of war. So you survived the great wave but stayed with the Seth. Good for you. I, on the other hand, recognized an opportunity and formed my own elite unit. Much more—"

"You took her to your garrison. You used her and you killed her."

A thought crossed Serq's hard face. The scorpion-like scar seemed to twitch with life and Yanhamu was sure then that the man suddenly remembered who Laret had been. Serq looked down and then up, attempting to mask his true thoughts. He said, "Look, you're a smart lad. You can join us. There's enough gold here to share. Once I despatch this old crone." He slashed down with his sword but struck wood as the old man diverted it. Serq tore his eyes from Yanhamu and struck again, this time tearing through the old man's gown.

Yanhamu bent and felt for his sword but grasped a metal rod instead. In a smooth movement he had it in his hand and was charging and screeching. "No…!"

The rod struck Serq in the chest but didn't stop. Yanhamu drove forward with all the force he could muster.

Serq staggered backwards and then tripped over a bag on the floor. His eyes stared, glass-cold, and his mouth opened as if to shout but only air rushed between his lips. His sword clattered to the ground and then he toppled.

Yanhamu stood over Serq, his rod raised to strike again should the man rise. But he didn't. Instead, he checked for a pulse in Serq's neck, found none and turned to the man on the floor.

The old man tried to lever himself up but then slumped. His gown was splashed with scarlet, his face pale, and when he spoke his voice trembled. "Pray, don't kill me."

"We've got to get out of here—now!"

Yanhamu pulled the man to his feet and dragged him from the chamber of burning scrolls. The old man nodded and pointed in directions and they zigzagged through corridors into a small courtyard. Here, Yanhamu carefully helped the old man to sit and inspected his wounds. A deep slash to his left arm was causing most blood loss although a stab to the side concerned him more. Yanhamu staunched the bleeding and gave him water.

The man said, "The records..."

"It's too late to save the scrolls," Yanhamu said. "You saw how fast they were burning. What were you doing in there anyway?"

The man ignored the question and looked at his bloodied gown. "I need the apothecary. Please help me. I can show you where it is."

Yanhamu helped him up and supported the old man as they went through the corridors of the King's House and out onto the street. They checked for mercenaries before Yanhamu helped the man find the shop he was looking for. Inside, everything had been broken or knocked to the floor. While the old man searched through bottles and jars, Yanhamu went through other shops until he found clothing. When he returned with a couple of gowns, the old man finished applying a poultice to his wounds and smiled.

"Yanhamu." He held out his hand. "Second officer and on a royal mission."

The old man studied him as he dressed. "My name is Meryra, also on a royal mission. Did you notice the sack in the records chamber? The mercenaries are stealing

311

anything of worth. They are not collecting royal treasures for Pharaoh but for themselves."

Yanhamu nodded. So that's what Serq and his mercenaries were up to: appear to act for Horemheb but profit in the process.

Meryra interrupted his thoughts: "When you say royal mission, I presume this is also in the name of Horemheb?"

Yanhamu pulled a scroll from his satchel bearing the mark of the Office of Pharaoh Horemheb. It was authority to collect the mummy of Akhenaten and treasures from the royal tombs and move them to the safety of the Valley of the Kings.

Meryra nodded. "I expected it would be so. While Horemheb tries to rid the country of the people he calls the outlaws—Akhenaten's and his queen's followers—he must also be seen to do the right thing by the priesthood and the gods. Each pharaoh has a duty to protect all pharaohs who have gone before." There was a deep sadness in Meryra's dark eyes as he added, "This is the same king who removed the guards from royal tombs. Even the tyrant Ay did not dare encourage the desecration of holy sites."

"And your mission?" Yanhamu said sceptically, having registered the old man's criticism of Pharaoh.

"I will explain fully later. Clearly, you have been sent by the gods and we must move as quickly as we can. How are you to move the royal coffin?"

Yanhamu told Meryra about the carriage and his small armed unit he had sent ahead. They would travel during the night and find cool places to leave the body during the daylight hours.

The old man said, "Excellent. Go to them and collect me when you return this evening. On the road by the Great River, the last building in the south has an animal enclosure. I will be in the hut behind it. Oh, and in Akhenaten's tomb you will find a coffin. It is empty but you should take it back as evidence. Do not bother looking for any mummies. They have gone."

FIFTY-ONE

Free your mind of the problem and the solution may appear: the concept of *aha moments* problem solving. From Alex's experience all his insights came this way. He needed a distraction.

He said, "Let's go."

The driver said, "Hotel?"

"The Royal Wadi." Alex pointed to the hills. "Can you take us there?"

The driver grinned and swung the Nissan around to head south once more.

"Are you all right?" Vanessa touched Alex's arm.

"Akhenaten's tomb," he said. "Since we're here we must go see his tomb."

Vanessa looked confused but sat in silence as they drove back through the town, picked up the main road and followed it to the hills and into a valley. The road looked new with drainage channels.

"Wadi means riverbed, I think you told me?"

Alex nodded. "But a long time dry, even in Akhenaten's time. This was his equivalent of the Valley of the Kings but radical because it was to the east to greet the rising sun rather than where it went at night—the underworld. There are five royal tombs here, although it's unclear who they were for. In fact, only one was completed."

They drove through the valley until the road ended in a parking area. There were four other cars already parked. Alex and Vanessa got out and followed a track into a side valley. Here they were sheltered from the storm, and the trek to the gated entrance to the tomb took only five minutes. Beside a ticket booth, two men in black uniforms and carbines scowled at them.

Alex said, "The Antiquities Service—no wonder Carter had so much trouble with the authorities. What a tourist-friendly bunch!" He paid for their tickets and they walked to the farthest tomb and then followed a path to the entrance.

An Asian couple, with what looked like a police escort, came out and down the ramp. Alex and Vanessa stood to one side to let them pass and exchanged polite nods. Once clear, they walked up the ramp and into the tomb.

The cool air was an immediate relief from the arid heat outside. They were standing in a corridor perhaps twenty yards long, hewn from the rock. Vanessa ran her hand over the smooth surface.

"How did they do this? It's near perfect, like they used a modern angle grinder."

Alex didn't answer. He half closed his eyes, breathed in the dusty air and imagined he was here over three thousand years ago, walking in the footsteps of a pharaoh.

To the right a small opening led to a roughly cut tunnel. It was barricaded with a no entry sign. Alex continued straight and then stopped where the corridor narrowed.

"This would be where the door to the outer chamber was." He hesitated and took a long stride through. Immediately to the right was another passageway. Ahead, twenty stone steps took them down. A string of weak lights created a pinkish limestone glow that somehow added to the sense of travelling back through time.

314

They heard a male voice echo from the right and followed the sound through one chamber directly into another. An American guide was explaining to a group of four that the side chamber had contained the coffin of Meketaten, the second of Akhenaten's and Nefertiti's daughters.

He said, "As you can see from the very realistic style of art of the time, her death caused the pharaoh and his queen extreme distress. This is the first time such imagery had been used. She was born in year four of Akhenaten's reign and some believe she died in childbirth." He pointed to the image of a young woman with a child strangely facing away from the mourners. "Some people say that this is Meketaten with her child. But let's see who can work out why that's nonsense. We know the princess died in year fourteen." The guide hesitated and then nodded. "Yes, that's right, she was only ten. My own theory is that this child is Tutankhamen."

The guide waited for this suggestion to be appreciated before continuing. "Back to Meketaten, what is much more likely is that a plague spread through the land, possibly also killing Queen Nefertiti, who herself disappears from the records shortly after this event."

"Where is the queen buried?" one of the tourists asked.

The guide beamed. "No one knows. It is a mystery what happened to the royal family. Even Akhenaten's body has not been found and maybe was never buried here."

Alex pitched in, "Do you think his mummy is one from KV55?"

The guide looked at Alex and then back to his group. "Ah, the mysterious KV55. This is a tomb in the Valley of the Kings—KV—that was discovered in 1907, very close to where Tutankhamen's tomb was later found. It is small, simple and unadorned, and at some point was damaged by flooding. There is a great deal of evidence to suggest the mummy is someone from the Akhenaten royal house and that it had been relocated." He looked back at Alex. "It seems to fit but the jury is still out."

The guide led them out and Alex and Vanessa tagged along behind. One by one, they descended steps and, when they were all gathered at the bottom, he turned them around and pointed out to where the door would have been sealed with a limestone block.

"This is known as the Well Room and"—he shone his torch slowly over the walls—"these are the famous reliefs showing Ahkenaten and the royal family worshipping the Aten."

From there he led them into Akhenaten's burial chamber, about ten paces square with two pillars and a low platform. The guide explained that the rock walls here were of poor quality so were plastered and then chiselled. Unlike Meketaten's burial chamber, most of the decoration was gone except for the names of Akhenaten, Nefertiti and Aten, which he pointed out near the ceiling.

"On this plinth would have been Akhenaten's pink granite sarcophagus. Unfortunately it's damaged, having been found in pieces and is now outside the Cairo Museum. One interesting thing is Nefertiti features on each corner as a protector. The accepted wisdom is that Nefertiti died before Akhenaten, but I think this tells us a different story." He placed a hand on a wall. "If only we could see what was painted here, it would tell us so much. For example, who performed the Opening of the Mouth ceremony? This would have told us who Akhenaten's successor was. This is also fascinating." The guide pointed to a small alcove and the group peered in. "This side chamber was never completed."

Alex stopped listening. He was thinking about what the guide had said earlier about the body in KV55: *There is a great deal of evidence to suggest the mummy is someone from the Akhenaten royal house and that it had been relocated.* Perhaps this was the *aha moment*, the idea he needed to solve the problem with the map. Perhaps the

316

map wasn't found here. Perhaps the map pointed to somewhere else entirely.

The group began to leave, ascending to the main burial corridor. Vanessa followed and Alex took the rear. As they passed the halfway point of the corridor, Alex stopped and grabbed her.

"Shit!" he whispered, then raised his hand to stop her talking.

The guide and his group neared the entrance. Alex looked behind and then at the barricaded side opening. "This way," he hissed.

He lifted the tape strung across the entrance and together they ducked through. He was still holding her arm and pulled her quickly along the side passage. The illumination faded quickly and, after ten yards, when it opened up into a small chamber, they could barely make out the opening on their right. This was a rough and curved passage.

Alex slowed. His breathing sounded loud in the confined space. He swallowed and whispered into Vanessa's ear, "There was a tall man at the entrance." He breathed deeply trying to calm his racing heart. "Vanessa, I'm pretty sure it's the guy who's after us—the BMW man!"

Vanessa said nothing.

They stood in the darkness for five minutes.

Distant voices echoed through the passageways. The American tour guide started again. Feet moved down the main hall. They faded. Then more footsteps, only this time coming towards them.

A flashlight played across the chamber they had left.

Alex and Vanessa backed into the darkness, feeling the wall. It smoothed and opened up. They felt their way into another burial chamber, round it and through to yet another. At the far end they felt it open into another doorway. The ground dropped and Vanessa stumbled. They both froze as the scuffing sound echoed loud.

Footsteps behind them again.

They pressed on into the pitch-black. Then the flashlight briefly lit the room they were in. An unfinished chamber. They could go no further.

Alex pulled Vanessa to the side and crouched beside the entrance. He held her hand.

The light bobbed and flashed across the room, growing brighter. Feet crunched, heavy on the sand-coated stone. The person paused and then stepped through into their chamber. The torch, attached to a gun, swung towards where they crouched.

FIFTY-TWO

Yanhamu rode at the front of the carriage beside the old man. Four of the foot soldiers carried lanterns and another swung above the heads of the two men on the carriage seat. They had been travelling for an hour, making slower progress in the dark than Yanhamu had hoped.

"You've some explaining to do," he said, and was surprised by Meryra's expression. "Why are you looking at me like that?"

"You don't recognize me, do you?" Meryra said, and pulled a dull silver necklace from beneath the gown. "You have the same amulet on your wrist. Where did you get it?"

"Many years ago... a gentleman in Thebes..." Yanhamu stared long and hard. "Was it you?"

"You're the boy who raged against the gods... the one who lost his sister. And you've grown into a fine young man."

"You told me I would find justice through the law. I studied for years under the Thebes magistrate and found it to be at times unfair and biased against the common people."

319

Meryra shook his head. "I was referring to the Law of Ra—God's justice, the Two Truths—not the crooked laws of mankind. It seems that you have had your revenge after all."

"But I have killed a man—an Egyptian—and my soul is doomed now anyway."

"You did not spill his blood. It seems that blow to the chest stopped his heart, and anyway, I believe when Anubis weighs your heart, he will find it a good one. The gods are not stupid, my son. They know good from evil—and I can help you. All you need to know is the language of the gods so you can speak the truth that they will understand."

"You can?"

"I was Akhenaten's Chief Scribe. I later became Keeper of the Secrets and when Ay took power, he could have either killed me or used me. The consummate politician, he decided it was better to keep me close and made me treasurer. I arranged Akhenaten's burial and was a witness to Tutankhamen's. I know the secrets and I know the ancient words." He reached behind to pull something from his satchel. His movement was awkward, as though the cut in his side troubled him. When he turned back he had a leather tube from which he pulled a papyrus scroll.

Handed the scroll, Yanhamu carefully opened it and held it under the lantern. After a few minutes he said, "This is some of the finest writing I've ever seen. It's the prayer to the gods—the Proclamation of Innocence—isn't it? But who is it for, my lord?"

Meryra's face dropped in an expression of deep sorrow. "It is a long story, but this is for Pharaoh Tutankhamen. Yes, I know he is already entombed in the Great Field, west of Thebes, but his *ba* is trapped for eternity unless I can get these spells to him."

"I don't understand." He handed back the precious scroll. "But first tell me how you knew I would find Akhenaten's coffin empty."

"Because that was part of *my* royal mission. Only my mission did not come from your king. I suspected that, as Pharaoh, Horemheb would continue what Ay had started—to regain support from the priesthood, rebuild the confidence in the old gods and to erase all memory of the city of Akhetaten and Akhenaten's incredible initiative. You have learned of the injustice and inequality in the land—well Akhenaten tried to change that. He gave the common people rights—even non-Egyptians—and they loved him and his queen, Nefertiti. The irony is that the old establishment hated Akhenaten for what he did. Ay persecuted his followers and branded them traitors and outlaws. Now, Horemheb has vowed to eradicate them from the land. And yet Akhenaten and Tutankhamen were buried with full honours and prepared for their journey to the afterlife. The reason? Because each pharaoh knows that he has to be seen to do the right thing for his predecessor since he needs the next pharaoh to show him the same respect. The family tombs are in the Great Field west of Thebes. Ay, in the name of Tutankhamen, moved it back there and Horemheb removed the protection of the royal tombs in Akhetaten and appeared to do the right thing—I knew he would move the coffins—once the robbers had taken everything they could.

"I could not let Horemheb take Akhenaten's body. I did not trust Ay and I trust Horemheb even less. So I took Akhenaten's coffin. Do not ask where I have hidden it, for I will not tell. I made a sacred vow to his wife, in this world and the next, to protect it."

"I saw Akhenaten's broken sarcophagus, but the coffin was not within. The empty coffin was in another chamber."

"So you have realized the empty coffin is not Akhenaten's." Meryra smiled. "You may not know this, but in the time of the ancients, a thousand years ago, the pharaohs were buried twice, once in sacred land of the south and again in the north of the Two Lands. Only one coffin contained the body, and it was believed that the soul could travel between both tombs." He laughed mirthlessly. "The truth is, they were covering their options in case they picked the wrong place. In modern times we know you can be buried anywhere in this sacred country."

"And this explains the empty coffin?"

"No." Meryra dropped his voice so none of the walking soldiers could overhear. "The coffin belongs to Smenkhkare. It was a symbolic burial for a pharaoh that never was."

Yanhamu waited and then said, "Will you not explain?"

"I have kept a secret record and I fear your life would be at risk should I tell you. I have hidden the truth within the records in the Hall at Akhetaten. My only regret is having too little time and nerve to write them in the language of the gods for them to know the terrible truth when men are judged."

Yanhamu tried to get Meryra to say more but only learned that his records were encoded. He also refused to provide more information about Smenkhkare. But after a long silence the old man whispered, "What I will tell you is that Ay killed Tutankhamen, his own grandson."

"But he died on a lion hunt. The tellers said he fell from the chariot while spearing his quarry. He died bravely, did he not?"

Meryra shook his head and paused as though the words were hard to speak. "It is true that he fell from his chariot. He had a bad foot and his balance could betray him sometimes, but the fall did not kill him and he killed no lion that day. He was bedridden, with his good leg broken above the knee. He died of malaria, but it was no fatal fly that bit him. I am certain Ay fed the young king that poison over many days, even before the fall, until the toxin in his blood made his heart fail."

Yanhamu leaned close, whispering, "I can't believe it. No one would dare kill a living god!"

"Ay did not view Tutankhamen as a god. As the priest of Amun he believed he was closest to God and the chosen one." Meryra clutched his amulet to ward off any demons that may overhear his hushed voice and added, "Ay told me that Amun spoke to him every night. It is a shame he didn't hear him warn of Horemheb's treachery."

Meryra would say no more and tried to sleep as the soldiers walked through the night. Just before daybreak, the old scribe asked to be helped down from the carriage and knelt. With arms outstretched along the ground, he prayed until the sun had risen over the eastern hills.

The men were reluctant to continue, but Yanhamu had reckoned on a five-day trek to Thebes and he needed them to cover another eight miles before they rested. Meryra struggled back onto the seat and Yanhamu noticed pain in the old man's eyes.

"How are you?"

Meryra said, "My side hurts, but I will complete my mission."

"To take the scroll to the necropolis for Tutankhamen? Yesterday you said his *ba* was trapped. You talk in riddles and I still don't understand."

Beside the coffin was a wooden trunk that Meryra had them load onto the cart. He cast his eyes towards it. "Years of practice I am afraid. I am too used to keeping secrets and now I find it difficult even when I want to be clear." He smiled weakly. "My satchel contains my writing. The trunk contains precious things for Tutankhamen, from a time when he was known as Tutankhaten, a name Ay did not wish to go with the boy to the afterlife—if indeed he can get there. You see, I believe Ay did not prepare the king for his journey. The embalmers were paid to do a poor job on him and his stillborn daughters. I know that the tomb was completed in a hurry because Ay claimed Tutankhamen's official tomb for his own. Ay also carried out the Opening of the Mouth ceremony without the other priests, and I later found the scrolls—the Proclamation of

Innocence and the Proclamation of Worthiness—both destroyed. So my mission is to give him his childhood toys, remind him of his true name and provide him with the spells so that his *ba* can reach the Field of Reeds and reside in the court of Osiris."

Later, Yanhamu said, "Lord..." He paused, taken aback at how dull the old man's eyes now looked. "Lord, there's something I've always wondered. Why did you help me on that festival day in Thebes? I was a peasant and you a noble, a royal scribe."

"You were riling against the gods, and on that day I felt the same. Your status meant nothing to me. What mattered was you were a sign, a sign that my duty was to stay close to Ay and feign my support."

"And you gave me the amulet..."

"Because..." Meryra coughed and winced. When Yanhamu reached out to give support, the old man held up his hand. "I'm all right. The amulet... it was instinct. Perhaps it was my way of acknowledging Ra's message to me. Or perhaps I sensed our destinies were entwined."

After the day's rest, Yanhamu was shocked to see how much Meryra's condition had deteriorated. The man's face was grey and his skin clammy. Yanhamu helped him onto the seat, but at sunset, after Meryra prayed, he was too weak to sit unsupported and was laid on a bed beside the empty coffin.

In the morning, when Yanhamu gave him water, Meryra's voice trembled with effort. "I must make it to the tomb... I promised her."

"Promised who?"

Meryra did not respond.

Yanhamu wiped the sweat from the old man's face and looked up the road. Thebes was at least two days and a night away. He knew that the old scribe would not last. He said, "Just one more day. Hold on, lord, we can make it."

They walked all through the day with a short break when the sun reached its zenith. The soldiers took it in turns to rest on the carriage and Yanhamu walked alongside, providing Meryra with water and trying to keep the mounting fever at bay.

By the evening the old scribe was muttering incoherently and could no longer drink without support and considerable spillage. When they stopped at a village Meryra seemed to be sleeping fitfully, but Yanhamu could not rouse him. Later, as Yanhamu wet the old man's mouth, Meryra mumbled something. Yanhamu didn't understand but he answered anyway and talked about anything he could think of until the old man fell asleep.

As the first rays of sunlight touched the mountain ridge, Meryra partially opened his eyes. He tried to speak but couldn't. His eyelids fluttered with the last movements of his life. Yanhamu held his hand and called a stop to the carriage. He leaned over to whisper into Meryra's ear.

"I will complete your mission, my lord, and ensure Tutankhamen has everything he needs. I will also make sure you are buried with honour. I will, however, also find out your secrets."

FIFTY-THREE

The man with the torch was a security guard. He beckoned with his weapon, indicating they should stand and come out. Into a walkie-talkie, he barked something in Arabic and it hissed back static. Then he snapped at them and motioned with the gun for them to lead the way out.

Conscious that the BMW man was somewhere behind them with a gun, they followed the chambers and passages back to the main hall. Here the security man tried the walkie-talkie again and exchanged a few terse words with the person on the other end. Where the side passage joined the main hall, he made them wait while he reattached the no entry barrier and sign.

They blinked in the dazzling sun as they emerged from the tomb. The security man made them wait again as he first exchanged words with the other guard at the entrance and then on the walkie-talkie.

"What do you think?" Vanessa asked as they sat on a stone bench in the shade.

"I don't think they know what to do with us." He glanced around and down the valley. "One good thing—the BMW guy isn't here." It was a feeble attempt to be positive because he knew the man was probably waiting for them somewhere.

When he finished on the walkie-talkie, the security man grunted at them and waved his gun. They marched down the track, single file, to the parking area.

As they neared the road, Alex looked for the Nissan and Schumacher. A hundred yards ahead he spotted the driver standing beside the car. Alex waved frantically, trying to get him to come up, to talk to the security man and explain. But the driver did the opposite. He got into his car and, casually as you like, K-turned and drove away.

"Hey!" Alex called and waved, but he was silenced with a push in the back from the man with the gun.

When they reached the parking area, they were made to wait. A few minutes later a white van turned in to the valley and approached at speed; it was a Toyota with "Police" written in reverse on the front. Two policemen with long batons climbed out, one from the passenger seat, one from the rear.

The security man nudged Alex in the back so that he staggered towards the van, and the policeman by the side door said, "Get in... both of you."

They did as they were told, climbing into the rear. The policeman followed, slid the door shut and sat opposite.

Alex reached for his pocket and stopped as the policeman tapped him with the stick.

"No."

"It's just my passport." Alex slowly retrieved it and held it out. "We're English."

The policeman took the passport but didn't look. "You have been arrested. You were in a forbidden area."

Alex started to protest, but the policeman impassively shook his head.

"Why did you not have a police escort?"

Alex said, "We had a local driver."

The policeman shook his head once more. "You will be taken to the station at Mallawi."

The Toyota jumped the queue at the ferry, pulled on, and one of the men upfront shouted something to the

327

ferryman. Moments later the flatbed was crossing the river. On the other side they headed along the bumpy road then turned north on the main road, away from Deir Mawas, away from their hotel.

In under ten minutes they were being escorted into a shabby police station and providing a desk sergeant with name and address details. Vanessa handed over her passport. There was no discussion, just registration. They were patted down before being escorted into separate eight-by-ten-foot cells.

Alex sat on a hard wooden bench, uncomfortable, hot and hungry. There was a toilet and sink in the room behind a screen and Alex thought about how luxurious their last hotel had been in comparison.

After an hour the jailer opened Vanessa's cell and she glanced in as she walked by.

"Ask for the British embassy," Alex called after her.

She was gone twenty minutes and didn't look in as she passed back. As soon as her cell door was locked once more, the jailer stepped to his cell and opened the gate.

"Where am I being taken?" Alex asked as he was ushered out of the cell.

The jailer simply grunted, "This way." He prodded Alex in the back to provide incentive and guided him along a series of corridors to a room with a table. An officer with a pencil moustache sat behind a desk and pointed to a chair opposite.

"Sit down, please," he said in accent-less English.

Alex sat. "I'm a British citizen and demand—"

The officer shook his head as he interrupted. He spoke softly but with authority. "You are in my country, Mr MacLure, and you do not make demands. Now, I would like to take your statement. I want you to explain why you were wandering around the ruins at Tell el-Amarna without a tourist police escort."

"I didn't know we needed an escort."

"I do not believe you, I am afraid. I think you avoided an escort because you were looking for artefacts or perhaps a trophy."

"No! We were not looking to steal anything."

"Then why were you hiding in the tomb? You went into an area that was clearly forbidden."

"I thought I saw someone… someone I was afraid of. I thought we were being followed."

The officer rubbed his forehead as if pushing away a developing ache. Alex noticed that the man winced as he listened, and Alex reminded himself that this was not the man's first language. He took a long breath and tried to speak calmly.

"Let me start at the beginning," he said, and began to tell him about the journey from Cairo. He mentioned Marek and the association with the museum, but said they were just tourists interested in Pharaoh Akhenaten. As he spoke, the police officer wrote meticulous notes. He stopped Alex now and again, questioning details such as train times, the name of the hotel in Deir Mawas, the name of the taxi driver. When Alex said *Schumacher*, the police officer noted it with a scoffing grunt. He shook his head many times during the story, which made Alex doubt Vanessa had told the same story. However, when he finished, the officer looked into his eyes, assessing for a while.

The man eventually closed his notepad and said, "Go back to the cell."

Alex was escorted back and asked for water as he re-entered. Moments later, he and Vanessa were given a bottle of water each. The seal was broken but he was too thirsty to worry about the hygiene and gulped the water down.

He could see it was dark outside when the cell door was opened again, and he was given a plate of something that looked like mashed potato. It was gritty and tasteless.

The next time the door clunked open, Alex sat up with a jolt. He'd fallen asleep. He massaged the stiffness from his neck and looked at his watch. They'd been in custody for over seven hours. Vanessa stood in the corridor outside and looked equally dishevelled.

The jailer said, "You go now."

Uncertainly, they followed him back to the reception and were handed their passports.

"Alex, my friend!"

Alex swivelled. Marek had been sitting in the police station waiting area. He jumped up and rushed over, gripping Alex by the shoulders. He looked the Englishman up and down and then at Vanessa. "You are all right, yes?"

"I've been better... and worse," Alex said, putting on a brave face. He stopped mid step as they left the station. There was the Nissan and driver.

"That bloody driver!" Alex said to Marek. "He just left us at the tombs in Amarna. He could have translated and got us out of the situation."

Marek shook his head. "I don't think so, my friend. Ahmed—the driver—would not have been able to persuade them against arresting you. In fact, he risked being arrested too. He did the right thing. He went back to Deir Mawas, to the hotel, and this evening picked me up from Dairut. I've come straight here."

Ahmed sheepishly opened the door and climbed out. He placed his right hand on his chest and bowed. "Schumacher is sorry," he said.

In the car, Marek explained that security were concerned that the prohibited area had been breached. The fact Ahmed hadn't registered with the tourist police after crossing the river made them especially suspicious. "You would be amazed at how many things are still stolen from the sites."

For the rest of the journey, Alex updated Marek on what they'd found at Amarna. "I thought it would be more obvious when we got there but the city is mostly destroyed. You know, I foolishly expected to find a wall painting or an engraving of flying geese."

330

Marek thought for a moment. "Flying geese? There's a section of wall in the Cairo Museum taken from the Royal Palace at Amarna. It has flying geese. But I must tell you, wild geese were a common symbol of an ideal life. And the accession of a new pharaoh was announced by releasing four wild geese to the four corners of the world to bless his reign with prosperity. Perhaps, before we do anything else, we should go through what we know."

Vanessa scoffed. "Before we do anything else, we need a bath and something decent to eat!"

FIFTY-FOUR

1322 BCE, Thebes

When they arrived on the western bank of Thebes, Thayjem was surprised by Yanhamu's orders. The plans had changed. They would not transfer the coffin straight to the tomb, but Thayjem and one soldier would remain with it. They would also guard the old man's trunk and the items they'd collected from Akhenaten's tomb. Thayjem was also surprised by the instruction to have the old man mummified at the temple of Osiris and not to worry about the cost.

Thayjem said, "Yan-Khety, I know the man seems to have meant a lot to you but only the richest of the rich can afford to pay the extortionate fees of the priests. How could you possibly—?"

Yanhamu opened Meryra's trunk and showed Thayjem what he himself had suspected: the childhood toys were no ordinary items. They were incredible treasures made of gold, silver, electrum, ivory and lapis lazuli.

"Guard these treasures with your life, Thayjem, because they belong to a god."

After providing full instructions, Yanhamu went to the quay and found passage on a cargo vessel returning to the

Delta, and within two days he was dropped a discreet distance south of Akhetaten. Although he still had royal papers permitting him to be there, Yanhamu dreaded meeting the Medjay mercenaries. But by the time he reached the Hall of Records, the only life he saw was a pack of jackals wandering through the broken and deserted city.

Inside the building, he barricaded the doors so that he could work without fear and began to systematically check the urns. He emptied one at a time and read through their contents. When he finished he replaced the clay tablets or scrolls and marked the pot as having been reviewed. After many hours, he took a break and ate bread and onions washed down with beer. He counted all the pots and estimated the time it would take to review every pot and every document in the Hall. It would take weeks.

And then a thought struck him: Meryra's secret documents were precious. He would not have put them in a broken or unsealed pot. Yanhamu walked around and looked at a few unbroken and sealed urns. Most of them were covered with dust as if they hadn't been opened in years. He also considered that the old man had encoded the messages so that the casual eye would not notice them. This had to mean clay tablets, since papyrus was used for official documents and would be scrutinized. He worked his way through the chamber and used a series of marks to exclude old pots, ones too big to be moved and ones containing papyri. He knew he might have to go back and re-evaluate, but the number remaining was manageable in a day. He decided to start with the ones that looked most recently sealed and within an hour had found something interesting. What first caught his attention was the randomness of the documents. Most purported to be letters from state officials and vassal kings, but such documents should have been separated by category. Communications to Amenhotep should not have been stored with a letter to Akhenaten's treasurer.

He read through the letters and then, placing three side by side, he spotted the unusual marks: a numbering system that should not have been there. From each line he read the word that corresponded with the number and immediately knew he had the right documents and the code. The first document he decoded explained something that had recently happened. After the sign of the flood and the victory parade in Memphis, General Horemheb had marched them to Thebes. The army had camped all around the city limits while Horemheb and his attendants confronted Ay. The soldiers had expected some sort of fight and the Egyptians amongst them feared drawing Egyptian blood. But it had never happened. Within days, most of the army was split to defend the borders, although this had been for show, because the majority returned to the garrisons of Memphis and the fearsome Medjay stayed at Thebes' city limits.

Within four months, Pharaoh Ay had died, was buried with full honour, and Horemheb proclaimed Pharaoh. There had been much rejoicing in Memphis when the tellers proclaimed there would be a festival to celebrate the confirmation that Horemheb was descended from the Great Ahmose and that Tutankhamen's wife, Queen Ankhesenamun, recognized him as the living god.

Now Yanhamu read a tablet with a very different account. Horemheb's claimed lineage was a lie and Ankhesenamun married him only to preserve the true royal line. Yanhamu found another tablet that said Queen Ankhesenamun did not wish to marry a commoner and had sent a message to the Hittite king asking him to send a son as her husband.

Yanhamu could not believe what he was reading. The thought that a Hittite prince might have become pharaoh shocked him to the core. Avidly, he read on and discovered that Ay had consented to leave in the *old way*. Yanhamu could not be certain but he guessed Ay had agreed to die as a pharaoh rather than be overthrown. Ay had also been allowed to use the tomb that he had stolen from Tutankhamen.

Yanhamu found another tablet that confirmed that Tutankhamen had been buried hurriedly in the tomb with a shortened service led by Ay and without the scripts to provide instructions to the dead pharaoh's *ba*. So this was why Meryra had produced the papyrus of spells for Tutankhamen. Yanhamu stopped interpreting the tablet, reached for the leather tube he'd placed in his bag and carefully removed the scroll from its sheath. As he started to unroll it he realized there was another document inside, a short a message and then hieroglyphs.

Yanhamu, I am sorry the quality of this is poor. My health is declining and I wanted to give you this so that you can face Anubis in the Hall of the Two Truths without fear. You are a good man and the gods will recognize you. Have the priest who writes your book use this spell.

Below this was text written in the old language, that the gods had taught them, explaining that his heart was pure; he could have killed a man in cold blood before, and that would have been murder. He stopped the man killing another and in doing that the man had died. It ended with the repetition:

I am pure. I am pure. I am pure. I am pure.

Emotion overcame Yanhamu then, and he cried for the first time since he had lost his sister.

FIFTY-FIVE

Alex and Marek were talking in the hotel's dining area. They were discussing Nefertiti and whether she had become Pharaoh. Marek believed she was only ever co-regent.

The names of Akhenaten and his successors were erased from history until Tutankhamen allegedly ruled, although his grandfather-in-law, Ay, was really in control.

Marek said, "I can accept that Nefertiti was the same person as Neferneferuaten but I do not believe she was Smenkhkare. When you were in Tell el-Amarna, did you visit the tomb of Merye the Second today?"

They exchanged startled looks.

"You don't think...?" Alex waited expectantly.

Marek exhaled. "That Merye was our Meryra? It could be!"

"What can you tell me about him?"

"Not a lot. I was just going to say he was a high official at the time of Akhenaten. In his tomb is the painting of Smenkhkare and his wife. The cartouche for his wife is that of the King's Great Royal Wife, Merytaten—who you will know was the daughter of Akhenaten and Nefertiti. So if you are right that Smenkhkare was Nefertiti, then she married her own daughter."

"But you said tomb. Based on the painting, it suggests he died during the reign of Smenkhkare."

Marek poured himself some water. "Yes that would be a problem. Our Meryra was alive when the city was destroyed by the mercenaries."

Alex clapped his hands in realization. "Unless the tomb was never occupied. Didn't the higher classes have their tombs built before they died?"

Marek creased his face in thought. "That is true, and there was no evidence of funerary objects or his sarcophagus. You are certainly becoming an expert in this area, Mr MacLure."

"It's called the Internet."

Marek looked confused and then understood what he was saying. "And as you know, there is no one checking the information. We live in a strange time when communication of gossip is more important than the facts."

Alex smiled. This reminded him of something Ellen had said about the communication in the New Kingdom, how the official records were trivial but the true messages—the facts—were hard to find.

"Each night I've read and re-read your translations of the Amarna Letters. I think you were mistaken about Yanhamu being Meryra."

"You think they were two people?"

"Yes, I think Meryra was the scribe with the secrets but it is the boy's story."

Marek thought for a while and sipped his water. Then he inclined his head. "You could be right, my friend. Two different messages."

"The way the messages are hidden by Meryra is quite different to the story about Yanhamu. In fact, the boy's story is barely disguised until the end."

Marek said nothing. He sipped his water.

Alex wondered what the other man was thinking. Was he embarrassed that Alex had seen something he hadn't? "Did Ellen ever discuss it?" He prompted.

337

Marek shrugged and looked around as though hearing someone approach. There was no one there. He shrugged again. "I have had many conversations on many subjects. I think perhaps we did have an exchange on this one. She was certainly obsessed with the Amarna period."

Alex remembered something. "I was going through her emails and found one from you telling her to delete your communication and switch to the webmail account."

"Right."

"I couldn't find it. I have no idea what the account is."

Marek hesitated and looked up. Vanessa walked into the room. Her hair was still damp, but she looked fresh. There was a charge in the air as she joined them with a smile.

"What have you guys been discussing?"

Marek said, "The mystery of Nefertiti. Alex thinks she became a pharaoh and married her own daughter."

"Really?"

"That might not be as strange as it sounds," Alex said. "Perhaps it was for appearances. Maybe Nefertiti's plan was to protect the lineage by pretending to be a male pharaoh. After all, at this time there was a movement to suggest that, like the gods, the pharaoh was a hermaphrodite—or at least, he could be both male and female."

Vanessa sat and picked up a menu. "Is it frustrating that you'll never know the truth?"

The men both vigorously shook their heads. "Oh no," Marek said, "that is the allure of Egyptology—the hope that one day we will find the answers."

Alex added, "As long as there are clues and progress, there is hope."

Food arrived and Marek explained he had ordered the special for everyone. "I hope you don't mind. Always have what they recommend," he said with a knowing nod.

As they were served, Vanessa said, "About the clues, what I don't understand is what the letters told you. What

338

made you realize there was a map to find? And how do you know what the map is for?"

Marek answered, "The code in the letters didn't tell us everything. Ellen and I thought perhaps half is missing. We know something happened to make Nefertiti leave Amarna. Some people stayed, but many left with her. Alex thinks she was the pharaoh, but certainly she was seen as the leader."

Vanessa prompted, "OK, so Akhenaten had died and Nefertiti may have been a pharaoh, then what, she stood down in favour of another?"

"King Tut?" Marek said, nodding. "There's a gap here. We don't know what happened, but Meryra was unhappy. He also stayed in Akhetaten—Tell el-Amarna—to protect the library and maybe also guard the royal tombs. Royal cemeteries like the Valley of the Kings would have been guarded by the army, but the pharaoh took away any financial and military support for Akhetaten."

Alex said, "Then sometime later—we're not sure when—a character known as the Scorpion razed the city to the ground."

"Meryra tells us he needed to confess to the gods about what he had done," Marek said. "He wrote his own special *Book of the Dead* to explain. He says he went into Tutankhamen's tomb. It looks like he was also directed to go there to make reparations, possibly for Nefertiti's or Tutankhamen's treatment. Everlasting life could only be achieved by convincing the gods that you were worthy."

Vanessa's eyes flashed understanding. "Alex has told me the *Book of the Dead* included some gruesome bits, like a prayer to the *Eater of Entrails*."

When she said this, Alex had a flashback to his dream as Yanhamu having his heart weighed and trying to convince Thoth he hadn't stolen the Map-Stone. He said, "For me, the most important hidden message is the one at the end where Meryra talks of burying the treasure in a tomb and taking a map to Pharaoh Akhenaten."

"But you said Akhenaten was dead by then." She looked from Alex to Marek and back. "I don't understand."

Marek shook his head. "It's probably symbolic. Remember, in their eyes the pharaoh was a god and only his physical form had died—his *ha*. The *ba*—the personality and *ka*—the life spark or spirit, go on and can still be communicated with. Meryra would have believed Akhenaten was still present."

Vanessa nodded and looked at Alex. "So how did Ellen know that the ceremonial block thing was the map?"

Alex said, "She didn't say. Marek?"

"No, she didn't tell me."

Alex said, "Well, from the clay tablet letters it was described as a spiritual guide. The ceremonial block and the letter include the same expression: **To reunite the house of the Aten.**

"I think Ellen also realized that the symbols on the block were linked to the letters."

"That's right," Marek said. Although Alex thought he detected a little doubt.

"Can you show us what's on the block?" Vanessa asked, enthusiastically. "I'm dying to see what it says."

Alex considered it for a moment. Up until now he hadn't produced too much of what he'd seen from Ellen's notes on the Map-Stone. He'd been concerned for anyone who knew. But now they were here. And it was just the three of them. It felt like a relief to finally agree to share what he knew. "Can you ask for a pen and paper?"

Marek called the waitress over and spoke in Arabic. Moments later, Alex had a pad of paper and a pen. First he drew the block as it physically appeared and pointed out the lines he'd drawn for Vanessa, the concentric lines and steps.

Vanessa said, "It looks a bit like a maze."

Alex stared at it and realized that the lines did indeed look like a sort of maze. He agreed and then drew the images around the sides, and then on a separate piece of paper he tried to show them in three dimensions—as though they were written on six sides of a box.

He pointed to a hieroglyph like a rectangle missing part of a side. "This means a building, especially a palace."

To Vanessa, Marek explained, "It's what is called a determinative. The symbols before it are the sounds confirming it is a palace." Then to Alex he said, "Some of these symbols aren't hieroglyphs, you know?" He pointed to lines and marks that Alex had drawn.

"I'll come to that," Alex said, agreeing. "There's another with a flag and a god or pharaoh. I think this refers to a temple. In Ellen's notes she thought the next block of symbols refers to a location. There are two parts: water and gold."

Vanessa said, "Gold. No wonder Pete was interested."

Alex continued: "Then we have lines forming a right angle—a triangle with a side missing. There is a spiral and there is a hoop followed by two reeds—the number twelve."

Marek said, "The ancient Egyptian builders used a continuous rope with twelve equally spaced knots."

"Yes, and here we see a line with twelve knots." Alex turned to Vanessa to explain. "You'll remember I asked your uncle about twelve and three, four and five, in case their meaning in Hebrew was important. But I see now I think it represents the perfect triangle and infinity. If you cut through a pyramid and draw a line down the middle you'd have two triangles each with a base of three, height four and side of five." He looked back to Marek for acknowledgement and added, "So, I think we are looking for a palace with dimensions of three-four-five—the magic triangle."

The others nodded their understanding.

Alex said, "Yesterday, I realized we have a problem. With ruins, we don't know how tall the buildings were. I also don't know which dimension is which. The other symbols I think will make sense when we find the right location." He pointed to the four hoops and a column.

Marek said, "But the hoops—the heel bones—are facing in different directions."

"Just the effect of combining the diagram, I think," Alex said. "Four hoops is forty."

"And then a pillar. So the forty pillars?" Vanessa asked.

"Exactly," Alex agreed, impressed that she was following. "And the flying geese next to that. The Northern Palace we saw used to have forty pillars. I didn't spot anywhere else that had forty of anything. But we saw no flying geese."

Marek said, "There were geese at the Royal Palace of Amarna."

"But the forty pillars were at the Northern Palace."

Marek frowned. "There's another possibility. Geese could symbolize the journey to the afterlife or the rise of a new pharaoh."

Vanessa said, "We don't seem to be getting anywhere."

"What about this symbol?" He pointed to something that looked like a portcullis. "You said you'd explain the ones that were hieroglyphs."

"The number eight. It's cuneiform."

"And how does that fit in?"

"I have no idea. But there is something else. Remember what I said about 2D and 3D? I realized something while we were in the police station last night." Alex pointed to the corners of the original drawing of the block.

"Four corners. Four directions." He picked up the second piece of paper and folded the corners together and redrew what he saw:

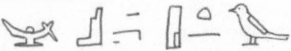

Vanessa looked at both men. "Can either of you translate this?"

Alex shook his head.

Marek said, "Is it possible this is incomplete?"

"Highly likely. The paint was very faded so I'm not even a hundred per cent sure about this."

Marek took the pen and added to the picture. "I believe it may be this."

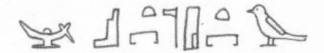

He pointed to the first symbol. "This is clearly a boat and could be a determinative—telling us the rest is the name of the boat. The next is a throne—it's not normally on its own, but it doesn't go with the rectangle."

Alex said, "Could there be a symbol missing in front of the throne? I should have mentioned that after the geese there was also this." He drew a small circle followed by the reverse L-shape.

Marek studied both and shook his head. "No, that would make it a word. With the extra two symbols after the throne, the transliteration is *st*, meaning place. I then added the flag to the next three because this would mean temple— *hw t ntr*. I think the bird is a swallow representing the sound *wr*."

Vanessa said, "So what does it all mean?"

"*Khd st hw t ntr wr*—sails to the place of the Great Temple. But it's odd because this could be written in half the number of symbols." Marek shrugged. "To be honest, I don't know if it makes sense, but I know someone who will." He took the paper and stood, saying he would find a fax machine and wouldn't be long.

He returned after ten minutes looking frustrated. "My friend in Cairo isn't answering his phone, but the fax went through. All we can do is wait. In the meantime, tomorrow morning we should go back to Amarna. There is something I want to show you."

FIFTY-SIX

1322 BCE, Thebes

Meryra's secret clay tablets were not safe in the Hall of Records. If Horemheb could destroy so much of the city, what was to prevent him from razing it to the ground? So Yanhamu buried them in a sacred spot on the outskirts of Akhetaten. He returned to Thebes and found the secure house where Thayjem guarded the treasure and coffin. He could recall every word and, as soon as he arrived, he locked himself away and began to write.

Starting with the papyrus intended for Tutankhamen, Yanhamu copied the declaration with meticulous care, replacing the pharaoh's name with Meryra's. When he had finished he started on another, this time inserting his own name and the spell Meryra had written for him. After a week's work, he took a break and went into the artisan sector of Thebes. He bought fresh writing materials and ordered ten of the highest grade sheets of papyrus. Later he instructed Thayjem to purchase another ten and to discreetly source ten more.

When he returned to his writing desk he sat for a long time contemplating what he was about to do. The knowledge he had gained from Meryra's tablets was dangerous, but writing the stories down was tantamount to treason. In the small hours of the night, he began to write. It was an obsession and an obligation to tell the truth, although he was unsure whether he was telling the gods or merely exorcizing the demons of a suppressed truth. In the morning and every morning after each writing session, he hid the documents beneath the floor.

After Meryra had been taken to the priests, it took seventy-five days for his mummy to be ready. At Akhet, the hour before dawn, Yanhamu instructed Thayjem to load the empty royal coffin onto the carriage and wait for him before sight of the entrance to the valley.

The temple of Osiris looked mystical in the torchlight. As Yanhamu arrived he could hear the incantations of the priests. He smelled frankincense in the cold morning air and the sound of sistra were like a chorus of birds. He peered inside and saw the high priest in a leopard skin placing the four symbols of protection for the afterlife on a mummy: the scarab, the djed, the Isis knot, and the ankh.

The temple bursar came over to him and after introductions Yanhamu handed him a package.

The man opened it, glanced and nodded with a half-smile. "This indeed covers the cost of the best materials. Rather than a pottery coffin you can choose the finest tamarisk wooden one."

Yanhamu bowed. "I am grateful, but no coffin is required, thank you."

As the mummy was placed on Yanhamu's cart, the priests looked surprised, but they made no comment at the lack of a coffin. They loaded the canopic chest and a shroud was used to cover them both. After the final sign, the high priest bade Yanhamu a safe journey to the tombs of the nobles. But Yanhamu had other plans.

The hill of the pharaohs, shaped like a natural pyramid, glowed orange in the first rays of morning as he left the temple. He circled around the area where the nobles were buried and took the track to the pharaoh's tombs. As instructed, Thayjem was waiting at the bend before the necropolis gates.

As the soldiers kept watch, the two officers transferred Meryra's mummy and canopic chest to the other carriage. When they were finished, the troop formed a formal guard around the carriage, Yanhamu lead the way and Thayjem guided the pony.

"Papers!"

In the half-light of dawn it was possible the guard couldn't see Yanhamu's second officer insignia and he let the rudeness pass. He handed over the papers he'd been given more than four months earlier. With authority he said, "By order of Pharaoh Horemheb, I have brought the king from Akhetaten, where lawlessness has jeopardized his safety."

The guard saluted. "My apologies, sir," he said, although his gruffness continued to show little respect. "It has been a difficult night and a long shift." He studied the document under torchlight and the way he ran his finger around the seal of the pharaoh made Yanhamu wonder if the man even bothered to read the document.

The guard saluted again and stepped back to let the strange cortege through the gates, waved two colleagues to lead the way to the tomb and then followed.

Although the top of the pyramid hill now shone like the sun itself, the ancient wadi that carved its way through the centre had such a chill in the air that Yanhamu questioned whether this was death itself. No wonder the necropolis guards were so well paid. They spent their nights with the souls and no doubt the demons that preyed upon them. He was relieved that the walk up the gentle slope soon ended by an open tomb.

"Pharaoh Akhenaten's," the guard said gruffly, and Yanhamu caught him making a slight hawking gesture as though the pharaoh's very name left a bad taste in his mouth. "Let's get this coffin in there and we can seal it up finally." As he spoke, he went to pull the coffin from the back of the carriage.

"I'll take it," Yanhamu said, stepping in the way of the guards. He signalled for Thayjem to help and the two officers lifted the coffin from the carriage. He nodded to the guards. "You can bring the canopic jars and the loose items, but don't touch the trunk."

Compared with the royal tombs in Akhetaten, he could see this one was simple and unfinished. With lanterns along the walls, they eased their way down steps into the antechamber and from there into the burial chamber. They placed the coffin of Smenkhkare into a golden shrine that seemed lost without a sarcophagus.

The guards hurried back and forth with the other items that Yanhamu had brought from the royal tombs at Akhetaten. There was little of value, just family memorabilia from a different time and culture.

When they finished, Yanhamu joined them at the entrance and handed the necropolis guard a second document. This was the one Meryra had shown him. He said, "I also have an order to take some old stuff into Tutankhamen's tomb." He hoped the guard wouldn't study the document too well. It had the pharaoh's seal, only this time it was the old pharaoh's and not Horemheb's.

"It's sealed," the guard said.

Yanhamu snapped back, "Then get it unsealed, man!"

He left Thayjem to supervise and returned to the coffin in Akhenaten's simple tomb. He listened for a while to be sure he was alone and then lifted the coffin lid and said a prayer to Meryra lying within. He adjusted the scarab on the mummy's chest and placed the electrum amulet beside it. His final act was to remove the scroll identical to Tutankhamen's from his satchel and whisper. "Go find your god, old friend."

The entrance to Tutankhamen's tomb was close to Akhenaten's. When Yanhamu emerged into the valley he saw Thayjem arguing with the guard and stonemason responsible for closing the tombs. The entrance had been opened but there was only a small access hole in the doorway to the antechamber and the stonemason was refusing to make it any larger.

Yanhamu inspected it. There was barely enough of a gap to crawl through. From his satchel he took a small gold comb and palmed it to the stonemason. He added, "I don't need to get into the king's burial chamber. I'm just responsible for taking some funerary items for him."

There was a moment of hesitation and then the man nodded and turned to hammer and chisel more of the door away.

When he was happy the space was big enough, Yanhamu said, "It's fine." He put a hand on Thayjem's shoulder and instructed him to fetch the trunk Meryra had brought from Akhetaten. He took a torch and gripped his amulet, said a prayer to the dead and then clambered through into the room. The light from the flames danced off the golden furniture crammed in the small space. He cast his eyes around at the astounding sight of more wealth than he could imagine and then jumped. The light caught two large figures: black men standing either side of the burial chamber door. It took a moment to register that they were statues, and he laughed at his skittishness.

Thayjem called through the hole, "Sir?"

Yanhamu fixed the torch to a wall mount and took the first item that Thayjem passed to him. Working quickly, they emptied the sack of the items, many of which had Tutankhamen's original Aten name engraved on them. After placing all the items around the room, Yanhamu bowed to the two statues and apologized for using the faience necklace to pay for Meryra's mummification and the gold comb to pay the stonemason. He also promised that everything else Meryra had put in the sack for the king was now in the tomb.

Thayjem was back at the hole and called as he pushed a wooden chest into the space. Yanhamu pulled it through and pushed it over to the statues. He opened the chest to show them the papyri within. "Your path to eternity is here, my lord," he whispered, and at that moment he was certain the boy king's *ba* was present. Rather than a chill in the icy chamber, Yanhamu felt a surge of warmth and a sense of fulfilment. Beneath the *Book of the Dead*, he showed the statues the pile of papyri that were the words he had translated from Meryra's tablets. He closed the lid and dropped to his knees, arms outstretched in supplication.

"My Lord Tutankhamen, who wore the crowns and bound the Two Lands together, who pleases the gods and is the son of Ra, I bring you the truth so that the gods may know the truth of your father and his queen and"—the words were formed by the quiet sound of his breath—"the rulers who came after who do not have pure hearts."

FIFTY-SEVEN

After the jail, the dusty hotel room felt luxurious. Alex lay in bed, but a day of inactivity and thoughts spinning through his mind made sleep impossible. He sat up, took out his laptop and tried to go online. He called down to reception and eventually managed to communicate that he required the access key for the Wi-Fi. Once on the Internet he searched for an explanation of the combination of hieroglyphs.

He knew the broken horizontal rectangle was the determinative for a building, so it pointed to the word or name being that of a house. The vertical rectangle seemed to confirm this. The semicircle was typically the sound *t*, the bird was the sound *oo* or *w*. The boat was often the boat of the gods, and this being followed by a building seemed to confirm that Alex was looking for a palace or temple, although Alex knew a temple was typically indicated by a flag. That's why Marek had drawn one before the building symbol.

He was still trying to make sense of it when his email registered that new mail had arrived. He'd neglected to check his email since leaving the UK and amongst the marketing communications there was one from his mother. It was a short note, hoping he was all right, letting him know that he could come and stay if he needed. She also told him that Topsy was fine. There was nothing sentimental but he found himself feeling emotional. He rubbed his face. Perhaps he was tired after all. According to his watch it was 2:30 in the morning. He fired off a quick reply to his mum and decided to quickly scan through the other mail for anything important and then hit the sack.

One email caught his attention. It was from Mutnodjemet, another of the names from the forum.

Hi, Senemut. Thanks for your email. Been lying low for a while after the warnings from Sinuhe. God, it's scary what happened to him. It can't be a coincidence, can it? Anyway, glad you're OK—are you coming back to the forum? Mutnodjemet x

Sinuhe was Marek. Mutnodjemet was a female name. Assuming this person was female, why was she saying something had happened to Marek? A shiver ran across Alex's chest. If something had happened to Marek, then who was the man who had picked them up at the airport— the man they'd just had dinner with? It had to be him, didn't it?

Alex fired off a quick reply to the email, asking what had happened and what she meant about a coincidence. Then he searched the Internet for Marek Borevsek and found the usual references to his research. It confirmed what Marek had told him about his transfer to Cairo and the research team there working on the identity of the cache of mummies found in Amenhotep the Second's tomb. Nothing suspicious there.

He returned to bed and left his laptop on in case Mutnodjemet replied. Sleep still refused to come. Over and over, he replayed conversations with Marek. The man was definitely suspicious. He didn't seem to recall telling Ellen to use a webmail account. He didn't know about the message on the Map-Stone about uniting the House of Aten. And he had called Tutankhamen King Tut. No student of Egyptology would do that, would they?

The guy didn't seem that academic and yet he was supposed to be a leading PhD student.

Or was Alex just being paranoid? Was he turning into Ellen?

Ten minutes later Alex made a decision. He picked up the room phone and dialled Vanessa. After eight rings she answered, her voice groggy with sleep.

"We've got to get out of here."

"Alex? What time is it?"

"Look, don't worry about that, just pack your things."

"What's wrong?" She was awake now.

He told her what he'd found out and suspected about Marek.

She said, "Are you sure? It sounds—"

"Paranoid, I know, but better safe than sorry. What if he is working for the bad guys?" He let that sink in for a moment then said, "Get packed. We've got to go—Now!"

"OK, OK, I'll be at your room as soon as I can."

Immediately after putting down the phone, he switched off the laptop, dressed and stuffed everything into his bag. A couple of minutes later there was a light knock on his door.

"Alex?" Vanessa whispered from the other side.

He started to open the door, his bag held ready to go, but instead of leaving, Vanessa pushed him back into the room and shut the door behind her.

She said, "Are you sure about this?"

"Yes!"

"Let me see the email."

He'd already packed, but reluctantly he opened up the laptop, switched on and waited for the connection. "We're wasting time."

She waited.

Then when the email was open she read it quickly. "It says nothing."

"But I was suspicious of him right from the start when he collected us at the airport and seemed nervous."

Vanessa pointed to the bed. "Sit down and breathe." When he did she continued. "He's a heavy smoker, addicted to nicotine. We discussed this, Alex."

"But he also made a mistake when telling you about the letters. And earlier I asked him about a webmail account and I could swear he knew nothing about it."

"What did he say?"

"He didn't. You arrived and he changed the subject."

"Maybe my arrival distracted him. People sometimes forget what they are talking about. True?"

"I guess."

"Ask him again in the morning. I bet you haven't slept, have you? You're tired and it's been very stressful what with being chased in the tombs and held overnight in prison."

"You do think I'm being paranoid."

"Just take slow, deep breaths and then let's see how we feel."

Alex gradually calmed himself while Vanessa made him a cup of tea.

"You think you've got a map that might lead to treasure. Anyone would be nervous having that," she said, handing him the tea and smiling. "Anyway, you've told Marek everything now, so it's too late to worry. He knows what you know, so if he's not genuine he won't be here in the morning."

Now it was Alex's turn to smile. "Well, to be honest, he doesn't know something."

"You didn't draw all the symbols?"

"I drew what I could make out." He put down his cup, feeling more relaxed, and hoped Vanessa would think him smart. "You see, this evening I suddenly realized the Map-Stone is more than just a map. It's also partly a mathematical code."

The Fourth

FIFTY-EIGHT

Alex and Vanessa spent an hour debating what to do.

"Tell me again why you think it's a mathematical code," Vanessa said.

"I think there are three parts: the name of the building, the lines—which make up the map of a maze—and the code."

Vanessa waited.

"Two reasons I think there's a code: firstly because I think Ellen worked it out. I told her the numbers and she knew they were significant. If it had been word-based then it wouldn't have required my contribution."

"But why does that—"

"Oh sorry. When they wrote something that meant something other than the obvious, they would use modified hieroglyphs—ideograms that weren't hieroglyphs. Like the number eight in cuneiform."

"The grid-like thing."

"Yes. And the thing that I didn't show Marek. The geese surrounding a throne. That's not normal. Geese on their own, yes. Throne on its own, yes. But geese around a throne means something else."

She got it. "So what does it mean?"

"I don't know."

"And what does the building part mean? Do you think we've seen the right place now?"

"I don't know," Alex said again.

"Then we do need Marek, whether you trust him or not. If he can work out the first part—"

"I'll work out the rest." Alex nodded. "OK, when we've got the right building, we somehow ditch him."

They stood at the front of the ferry to Amarna. Marek had asked about the symbols but Alex didn't say any more. He simply repeated everything he'd already told the man. Now he stared ahead.

Marek broke the silence. "My best guess is that the symbols refer to the Great Palace somehow." The sun was over the ochre hills already shimmering in the heat. The Royal Wadi, the valley of his tomb, cut a V in the hill like the reverse pyramid—a supplication to the sun god.

Alex turned away from the view and looked at Marek. "So, the hieroglyph of the boat refers to the solar barque?"

"Exactly." Marek grinned. "We are thinking the same thing."

Alex glanced at Vanessa, who had stayed in the Nissan, then back at Marek, and said, "I've been wanting to ask you something."

"Oh?" Marek lit a cigarette and sucked long and hard before blowing a jet of smoke.

"You first met Ellen on the EgyptConfidential forum and then exchanged emails."

Marek inclined his head.

Alex continued: "But then you said to delete the emails and switch to a webmail account."

"Yes."

He couldn't help it. Maybe he wanted Marek to be genuine or maybe he wanted Marek to admit he was a fraud. Alex asked, "Why was that?"

Marek smiled. The ferry docked and he stepped ashore. "We must register with the transport police this time, Alex, do you not think?"

"Marek!" Alex hurried after the wiry man, took hold of his arm and stopped him mid stride. "What was the reason?"

"Is it not obvious? I was afraid someone would uncover our research. There is a great deal at stake here, both money and reputation. Since Ellen and I were partners then so are we. I do not mind sharing with you. Fifty-fifty." He patted Alex on the shoulder and grinned. Then he looked more serious. "There have been suspicious people—men who I do not trust. They ask a lot of questions and I think my email was hacked into."

It made sense. Marek's experiences sounded similar to his own, but Alex was still unclear about the answer. "So what is the webmail account?"

Marek shook his head. "My friend, you must understand. After Ellen's death and the burglary at Lord Carnarvon's exhibition, I knew there was a problem. Was it not fair for me to be more worried? When you got in touch afterwards... to be honest, I was a little concerned you were perhaps not who you said you were, or perhaps were now working for someone else, so I deleted the webmail account."

Alex began to protest his innocence but Marek asked him to wait and disappeared inside a building. He emerged a few minutes later with an armed policeman in tow.

For a second, Alex panicked: Marek with an armed man! But then Marek grinned and waved to Ahmed to pick them up.

Marek said, "So, I was saying I was unsure about you, no?" He finished his cigarette and flicked it away. "Last night you told me everything about the Map-Stone and so now I am happy." He patted Alex's arm. "Come on. Let's take a look at the palace."

They climbed into the Nissan. The policeman had them wind down the window so that he could stand on the step and hold onto the car through the door. They followed the route taken the day before, around the town and then south along the modern cemetery. Ahmed stopped beside the Great Aten Temple.

They stood by the ruined wall and Marek faced south and swept his arms up and down. "This wide strip we now know as the Royal Road. At the end was a giant bridge spanning the road from the palace on the right to the King's House on the left. Beyond the bridge was the Small Aten Temple." He looked back at the Nissan and grinned. "The car would have been in the river because the Nile came close to the Great Temple and then around the Great Palace. Unfortunately the right-hand half of the palace is where the fields are now, and even geo-imaging has failed to provide any details." Looking back towards the Great Temple, he said, "Most of the area inside the Great Aten Temple was open space. From the outside it is believed that it would have appeared like a traditional temple, with pylon towers and flagpoles, but rather than dark covered halls, even the two interior temples were open to the sky."

Vanessa asked, "There were a lot of altars?"

"Offering tables," Marek answered. "An amazing nine hundred tables in a grid, and from the wall reliefs we believe these would have been piled high with food offerings to the Aten."

"So not the forty pillars?"

"I'll come to that," Marek said, and led them south to the wall on the right of the Royal Road. "So this was the Great Palace, the entrance wall forming a right angle with the side of the temple. The Great Temple was about half a mile long, the Great Palace over a thousand yards with pylons and colossal statues." The group walked forward about a hundred paces to a section that included a wall crossing their path. "Up until now we have been in the outer courtyard. Now, we know from the stone foundations that there were unusually long ramps running along the wall. There is a theory that the structure here must have been monumental, probably a pylon that could be seen for many miles. It's a tragedy we don't know what it was, because it was intended to inspire and impress—maybe something as incredible as the great pyramids." They walked on and Marek explained that the second section was an inner courtyard, probably with gardens and ponds. As they neared the final third, Marek's phone rang. He answered excitedly.

"I can't hear you," he said after a few moments. "The signal here is poor. Could you try a text?" He gave up and shrugged at the others. "That was my friend in Cairo. Maybe he has translated the hieroglyphs." He laughed. "Looks like we beat him to it."

Alex asked, "But the only clues we have are the forty pillars and geese."

Marek nodded. "Perhaps..." he said mysteriously.

The policeman intervened as they approached a network of stone walls and made them skirt around the side.

Marek explained that the section was the main building of the palace. At the water's edge would have been the Royal Quay. He raised his eyebrows knowingly. "Here, close to where we are standing, could be where the royal barge would have been moored. We have a typical double meaning of the boat hieroglyph, I think. The royal boat and referring to the palace of the sun. The bridge goes to the King's House, as I said. Beyond that was the library. That is probably where the Amarna Letters were found."

Vanessa asked, "Oh, you don't know where the clay tablets were actually found?"

"No. They were found by a village woman in 1887. She sold them to a neighbour after destroying some. The neighbour sold the letters on the antiquities market and they were bought by an Egyptologist who thought they were fakes but had them checked. Luckily, the assistant curator of the British Museum realized their significance."

"But it was too late—" Alex started to add, but Marek was in full flow.

"And so no one knows exactly where the woman found them. Now let me show you the Small Aten Temple, because I think I have worked something out." He took them past the end walls of the palace and the King's House to another east–west aligned temple. With a long thin courtyard described by Marek, it was approximately half as wide and half as long as the Great Temple. However it was divided in two with three sets of pylons still clear in the ruins.

Vanessa whispered, "See, he knew about the letters."

"Maybe. It is supposed to be his expertise."

"Exactly, and he was suspicious of you. I think you are both paranoid."

Marek frowned at them. "Am I missing something?"

"No, no!" Alex faked a laugh. "I was just saying about the three pylons. They probably relate to the three pharaohs: Akhenaten, Neferneferuaten and Tutankhamen."

"Yes. A pylon was a statement to the gods and associated with the investiture of the pharaoh," Marek explained for Vanessa's benefit. "Although Tutankhamen was called Tutankhaten at the time—after the god Aten, of course."

"So?" Alex said, looking around. "What are you showing us? What have you worked out?"

Marek faced them west. "Through the courtyard ran a straight path to the river's edge. You'll see there are a few trees spotted around? Well, they're more regularly spaced than appears now. There's a clear pattern and the excavation team who have modelled this believe there were... forty."

Alex said nothing. The forty was part of the numerical code, not the location. He was sure of it.

"Forty trees would be the forty pillars! The royal barge would be to the right beside the Great Palace of the Aten... or god's sun boat."

Vanessa asked, "And the geese?"

"To the south we have a stone quay where the main working city began. So the end of the courtyard would have been the start of a more natural setting. It is thought there would have been a garden and reed bed. As you know, geese played an important part in ancient Egyptian life and undoubtedly this is where the royal geese would have lived. Also, of course, close by we have the records office where Meryra the scribe would have worked. This section would have had great significance." Marek turned back to the pylons. They were standing at the second. "And here is Nefertiti's gateway. Alex, what do you think? Am I right?"

Alex walked forward to a square area at the back of the temple. The policeman waved him away from the walls.

Alex asked, "What's this?"

Marek wasn't paying attention. He was studying his phone. "Sorry, Alex. What did you say?"

"This area—what was it?"

Marek seemed to shake some thoughts from his head but continued to look thoughtful. "Er... the sanctuary. In fact, it was a small version of the one in the Great Temple." He looked back at his phone.

Alex said, "What's up?"

"I am mistaken," Marek said, but instead of being disappointed, his eyes flashed with excitement. "I get it! My expert friend has decoded the name we worked out last night. He's convinced the order was wrong. It is not the name of a royal boat." He held out his phone so that Alex could see what was written.

"In transliteration," Marek said, "the sounds are *Hw-t-wr-t.*"

Alex frowned. "OK, what does it mean?"

"The Palace of the Great Barque."

Vanessa said what Alex was thinking, "Isn't that effectively the same thing?"

Marek needed a cigarette and made them wait as he led them back to the Nissan. He was grinning at their faces when he finally removed the cigarette from his mouth. "Still not worked it out?"

When they shook their heads, Marek said. "It is not so much what it means, because it is a name. A place known as Hut-waret—somewhere of amazing historical importance. The Greeks later called it Avaris, the city of the Hyksos, when they ruled Lower Egypt around the Thirteenth Dynasty."

"But that's the wrong period," Alex said, disappointed. "How does this help us?"

Marek laughed. "Well, if it was a couple of years ago, then no it would not help, but recently an Austrian archaeological team thought they'd found Avaris. It is in the Delta, a place now called Tell el-Daba. And there is evidence of New Kingdom settlements. That, my friends, is where we need to go."

Joachim hadn't followed the group back to Amarna. After the Englishman had spotted him in Akhenaten's tomb, he knew he had to keep out of sight. He sat in a bar and sipped coffee awaiting instructions.

His phone rang. It was the old man. Gershom.

"Yes?"

Gershom said, "It is not Amarna. They are looking in the wrong location."

"Where is it?"

"Tell el-Daba."

Joachim didn't know the place and the old man explained roughly where it was in the Delta.

He said, "If we know where it is then we don't need MacLure anymore. If you're still saying we can't get rid of him, then let's just leave him. There's more than one way to stop him being a nuisance."

The old man cleared his throat.

Joachim prompted, "Is that a yes?"

"It's a no. Firstly because I promised and secondly because we can't be sure we know everything. Last night, apparently, Mr MacLure said it was mathematical. We don't know what he's worked out."

"Tell el-Daba then. I should leave straight away."

"One other thing. We have a problem with the site," Gershom said. "There's a village and an excavation team working the area. We need a diversion."

"You have an idea?"

Gershom explained his plan.

Joachim was dubious. "It is a good idea, but can you arrange for that?"

The old man may have been offended but he grunted, suggesting humour. "Leave that to me, Joachim. By the time you get there it should be in place." There was a pause then he added, "And if it's not, then you will need to improvise."

FIFTY-NINE

Ahmed estimated the drive would take three and a half hours, and Alex dozed most of the way in the back with Vanessa, until a jolt of brakes woke him. They were outside Cairo and Marek explained an accident had blocked the first bridge over the Nile. In laborious single file, the traffic made its way beside the river and crossed at the next bridge then doubled back to pick up the ring road.

Alex managed to piggyback off a variable Wi-Fi signal and killed some time by browsing the Internet for information on Hut-waret. Uncle Seth had mentioned two ancient Egyptian places referred to in the Bible: Pithom and Pi-Ramesses. Alex discovered that Pithom was believed to be the place the Greeks later called Avaris, the capital of the Hyksos invaders who ruled Lower Egypt for a hundred years. Then Ahmose, founder of the Eighteenth Dynasty, defeated them.

An archaeology team from Vienna University had been working the Tell el-Daba area for almost fifty years but had made their big breakthrough in 2009 when they discovered eight-metre-thick fortified walls under cultivated land that had once been almost surrounded by a Nile tributary. The structure matched expectations for Avaris, and the discovery of a warrior's mud-brick tomb seemed to be confirmation of the Hyksos period.

The connection became more intermittent, but Alex managed to read that a number of palaces and temples had been identified. The discovery of horse burials again appeared to point to pre-New Kingdom occupation. The team had also discovered Eighteenth Dynasty groundworks, although the Austrian team concluded this was restoration by Pharaoh Horemheb.

An email arrived. He saw the name Mutnodjemet—the member of the EgyptConfidential forum—but the connection failed completely before he could open the email.

Once off the ring road and on a motorway, they made good progress. When Ahmed pulled into a service area, Marek announced he desperately needed a cigarette, so they stopped and both he and Ahmed hungrily sucked in the nicotine.

Alex and Vanessa stretched their legs. He located a shop selling mobile devices and purchased a dongle with prepaid Internet browsing.

"How much further?" he asked Marek when he returned to the car.

"We are already in the Delta, about forty miles north of Cairo. Not long now—about half an hour perhaps."

It took considerably longer. Ahmed clearly didn't know the way, and the warren of roads that criss-crossed the green canals seemed to confuse him. Finally, after following a major canal and driving through a small town, Marek announced they were on the right track. And track it became, because they bumped along a dirt road through fields.

Ahmed pointed ahead at a small hill. "Tell el-Daba."

Vanessa said, "Tell means hill, right?"

Marek swivelled in his seat. "Yes, yes, a very important and strategic point here in the Delta."

"But," Vanessa responded, "Amarna is called Tell el-Amarna—that town wasn't on a hill."

"You are right!" Marek laughed. "It is one of the great mysteries... no, actually I asked Ahmed yesterday and he said it is a mistake that dates back to British rule. Some British bureaucrat mistakenly added the Tell part to the name."

Alex asked, "Do modern Egyptians despise the British for that period?"

Marek spoke to Ahmed in Arabic and they both laughed. Looking to the rear seats, Marek relayed the conversation that Egyptians had thousands of years of foreign rulers, including the Hyksos, the Hittites, the Persians, the French, the Romans and the Greeks. In fact, the most prosperous times were under the foreigners, as opposed to King Farouk, who had had only his self-interest at heart.

Alex asked, "What made you laugh?"

"Ahmed used a phrase," Marek explained. "It translates something like 'It is better to trust the foreigner you know, than the brother you know you cannot trust.'"

"Here," Ahmed announced, and stopped the Nissan.

They had passed through a cluster of houses and had pulled up outside a building that looked something like a low-lying block of flats.

Alex noticed a large number of blue signs as they climbed out. They had the word *Danger*, with Arabic beneath. "What do they say?" he asked Marek.

"There has been a gas leak." Marek headed for the building's entrance. "I will ask at the hotel."

Vanessa raised an eyebrow. "Hotel?"

Minutes later, Marek returned, a wide grin splitting his face. "It is all right, the problem is over. It seems the village was cleared but the hotel owner refused to go and the leak was fixed last night. He is very angry with the local government—his main business is linked to the archaeological dig and he doesn't know when the team will

366

return. But in case we need to stay, I have negotiated a very good price."

A surly looking man came out of the entrance and headed for them.

"One of the local excavation workers. He stayed behind when the others left," Marek explained. "He is called Tariq and"—Marek rubbed his fingers together indicating baksheesh—"he's kindly volunteered to show us the site."

Marek instructed Ahmed to wait at the hotel and he took the driver's seat. Tariq climbed in beside him and spoke in Arabic.

Marek said, "I will have to translate because he claims to speak little English." He dropped his voice. "The truth is, I suspect he can't be bothered." He started the engine and pulled away from the hotel and skirted the hill. "It's a large area, over a square mile of excavations—and that is excluding the Pi-Ramesses site to the north."

Tariq directed Marek to drive along a farm track until they reached the canal that ran east of the hill. They crossed the canal and then a road to pick up a lane that started well, as it headed east, but became a track again as it bent north through cultivated land. After the bend, Tariq pointed vigorously to the right.

Marek translated. "This is the site of the recently discovered giant palace. Our guide here calls it a citadel." He pulled to a stop and the group got out. In the fields ahead, Alex could see ruins and clear signs of excavation.

Tariq handed each of them a sheet of paper with a map, only the layout was nothing like what they were looking at here. On the diagram, a wide river ran south to the north-east corner of the page. Tell el-Daba was clearly marked but it was almost completely surrounded by water and Alex counted a further seven islands. A high proportion of the area had been under water, unlike now. The modern-day canal followed the line of the main river, but cut through the area they were now standing in.

Tariq spoke and Marek then explained. "This palace was bordered to the east and north by water. The modern canal and road we crossed on the west now slice off one corner of the area."

Vanessa looked around. "Just how big was this palace?"

After a discussion, Marek said, "It is actually complicated, as I'll explain, but the outer wall is almost square, each side about three hundred yards long."

Tariq talked as he walked.

Marek translated, "The old citadel is probably Twelfth Dynasty. The main buildings were limestone. On the ground you will see mud-brick pavements, typical of the period." They stopped by a section of wall with straight lines painted on it, horizontal in blue, white and red. "Simple decoration," Marek said. "They think the ceilings were probably more elaborately painted with hieroglyphs, because chunks with partials have been unearthed. Unfortunately, nothing complete enough to be interpreted."

Alex pointed to some columns. "Are these from a later period?"

Marek grinned. "Yes, my friend, this is what we are looking for. This is New Kingdom."

SIXTY

Tariq described the area in Arabic to Marek, who then relayed the message. "It is quite complicated here. The columns were for platforms. They're New Kingdom—Eighteenth Dynasty—and where we are now was a smaller palace on stilts."

Tariq led them across an area without excavation and into the main ruins.

Marek said, "The area we've crossed may have been a lake, or perhaps the stilts were due to flooding. Pumice from the eruption of Thera, the island now called Santorini, was found here and no doubt a tsunami followed. The buildings were an amazing seven metres off the ground!"

They walked through the section Marek had been told was the main palace. Its length was almost the whole side of the enclosure and Alex paced out ninety-two strides for its width.

Tariq pointed out part of the enclosure towards the end of the palace and said it had been a monumental doorway with pylons.

Alex looked at Marek. "Pylons suggest a temple."

Marek asked and shook his head at the response. "The excavation team has found no evidence of a temple here.

369

We have a large courtyard followed by walls running along the whole width. It's unclear why they would have long thin rooms like that, but after six, the main dwelling seems to start. Behind the large palace, Tariq said, was another palace but, from the look of it, I think they're administrative offices."

Alex said, "The orientation looks like it's south-west to north-east, correct?"

"Yes, but interestingly the later buildings were not aligned with the earlier ones. It's as though the earlier giant palace was obliterated before the Eighteenth Dynasty palaces on platforms were built."

They had looped around with Tariq throwing in commentary and Marek translating the titbits.

"What do you think?" Marek asked Alex as they reached the Nissan.

"I think we should see all the sites first."

Marek spoke to the hotel owner and indicted they should get back in the car. "Next stop, a temple," he said.

They crossed the canal and headed north, just short of a modern village called Ezbet Rushdi South. Again the ruins were in a field.

Marek translated as they got out. "This was the high point of the island north of Tell el-Daba and thought to have been a Twelfth Dynasty town centre."

Tariq led them through the field and pointed at the walls of a north-facing building. Alex estimated the entrance walls to be four metres thick and noted the blocks were limestone.

"What makes Tariq say it's Twelfth Dynasty?" he asked. "The construction looks older."

After a moment of questioning, Marek said that a fragment of a stele with Amenemhat the First's Horus name on it had been discovered, however there was some doubt because the temple was cut into an older structure beneath.

After the temple, they drove south over the hill to the southern edge of what would have been the island. They stopped by a large excavated area showing a network of stone walls and bricks.

As they walked around, Alex noted many houses loosely scattered, like a village without any palace or temple. The lack of structure suggested a period much earlier than the New Kingdom he was interested in.

Tariq kept talking and pointed out a number of tombs, but Alex waved his arms and signalled for them to return to the vehicle.

Their next stop was on the top of the hill just above the hotel. Here the ground had never been cultivated and the excavation had uncovered large sections of wall. Tariq suggested the cluster of buildings comprised four temples. They started with the largest, which Alex paced out at twenty by thirty. He found the structure difficult to judge and the offering area, with its remnant of a stone alter, seemed less linear than the temple. Beyond this, Tariq pointed out a building to the left, after which he said there was a defence tower. On the right he indicated a small house.

Alongside the large temple, Tariq said there was another temple, although Alex couldn't make this out. Next to this was a cemetery.

They walked north, through areas Tariq said were more cemeteries, until he came to the fourth temple. This was aligned with the others on the hill, and although fewer walls remained there was a clear similarity in design with the one on the adjacent island hill.

They returned to the Nissan and Tariq asked if they wanted to see the next site—a small group of simple houses. Alex recognized the name of Amenemhat the Third as Tariq said it, and agreed they should take a look.

When they stopped, Tariq didn't get out of the car, and Marek translated. "At one stage this was under water. There has been limited excavation so there's little to see.

There may have been one palace here or a couple connected. Magnetometry has shown two large courtyards, one with rooms on one side, almost the mirror of the other. There was a fortified wall with a tower and possibly a staircase leading up to it.

"How big are we talking?" Vanessa asked. She squinted out of the window as if trying to picture what Marek was relaying.

"Not all of it is clear, but so far at least a thousand square yards. A fair size, but overall about a quarter of the size of the first palace area we saw."

"So that's it then," Alex said, feeling a little frustrated. He'd hoped the building they were looking for would have been obvious.

"One more," Marek said with a shrug. "Looks like our friend here doesn't count this one."

They skirted a farm building and followed another track and stopped at a T-junction. Ahead was a vast area of excavation with clear ruins. The sun was on the horizon, its lower part shimmering red as though melting into the land.

They got out and Marek translated. "This area was on the edge of the hill overlooking the river and the citadel."

Alex said, "There's a lattice of walls. What are we looking at here?"

Marek translated then responded, "They are not totally sure. It appears to either be a large residence or a series of regular houses in rows within an enclosure."

"Twelve in a row," Vanessa said, having walked along the line. "Do they know how many rows?"

Marek said, "No, and there's an interesting structure in the north-east corner. It could be a tower, but the foundations are partial."

"Eighteenth Dynasty?"

Tariq waved his hand, indicating *maybe*.

"So that's it," Marek said. "Any insights, Alex?"

"Could I get a more detailed map of the three sites that could be from the New Kingdom? The first, this one, and the cluster of four temples near the hotel?"

Marek spoke with Tariq and said they should go back to the hotel. The light would soon fade and the owner had some charts that could be useful. "Although it'll undoubtedly cost us some more," Marek added with a rueful shrug.

In his hotel room, Alex studied the detailed diagrams provided by the owner. He'd expected a temple to be orientated east–west like Akhenaten's, but not one of the temples was like that. The group of four nearest the hotel interested him the most. He studied the layout. There was something that he couldn't put his finger on.

He took a break from staring at the outlines and thought about the symbols written on Meryra's Map-Stone.

He decided to browse the Internet for inspiration, although it took him fifteen minutes to work out how to sign on using the prepaid dongle because it was in Arabic. When he finally gained access, he logged onto Ellen's secure site about the Map-Stone.

He studied the images and sketched them. As he looked at the throne he noticed a mark. *Could there be a symbol missing in front of the throne?* Changing the order had provided the location of the ancient city, but there was still the mysterious throne. Alex knew the symbol was often associated with Isis, but he had known enough to realize it was a separate clue within the code he'd shared with Marek. He looked at the image in a number of photographs. None of Ellen's drawings had the mark, but he was sure it was there. It wasn't an indentation or a natural discolouration of the stone. Either it had been deliberately painted and faded or it was a mark added at some later point.

He drew it and wondered whether the symbol could be a disc that represented Ra. He searched the Internet for anything similar and came up blank. He then decided to research the three-four-five triangle. He spent twenty minutes reading nothing new about the *golden triangle*, when the term *golden rectangle* appeared in an article.

Alex sat back as though poleaxed. That was it! He read some more and then studied the map of the excavations. Certain he'd found it, he traced out a simple version of one of the temples: Temple IV.

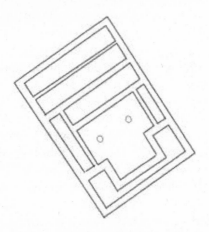

Drawing only the foundations, he saw it immediately: the Isis throne was clearly part of the structure. The plan showed that the bottom right corner was subtly based on her throne. The dot on the Map-Stone appeared to correspond to the object Marek had assumed was a building sign. From the foundation diagram it looked like one of two pillars.

Excited, he texted Vanessa:

It's the temple closest to the hotel!

As he put down his phone he remembered to check the email from Mutnodjemet. He clicked on it and saw there was no message, just a link. He followed that and a new window opened with a private posted message. As he started to read, his heart seized.

Didn't you know? Marek was found dead in his flat in Cairo. Suicide, the report said, with foul play ruled out. Strange, I can't find the link now. Could someone have removed it?

SIXTY-ONE

Marek wasn't who he claimed to be.

The room phone rang.

"Alex"—it was Vanessa—"are you coming down for dinner?"

He could hear noises in the background. Could Marek—whoever he was—overhear? "Are you alone?" Alex eventually asked.

"No, Marek and Ahmed are here. We've been waiting for you."

"Don't react to what I say."

"What?"

That reaction in itself may alert the imposter. His head was spinning. How could he say this?

"Look, sorry, tell them I've got whatever they call Montezuma's revenge. I'm not feeling well. Tell Marek I'm not well. Say I'll be all right after a good night's sleep. OK?"

"Alex...?"

He repeated the instruction and ended the call.

At 3am he packed his things and rang Vanessa's room.

"Alex, what's going on?"

"Get dressed. I'm coming to your room."

She said something, but he didn't listen as he put the phone down. As quietly as he could, he opened the bedroom door and stepped out into the dimly lit corridor. He placed a pen between the door and jamb so that it wouldn't slam closed and took a step. The floor creaked slightly. He stopped and listened.

Nothing.

He stepped again, and again. Slow and hesitant. Three more paces and he was at Marek's door. Here he paused, took deep breaths and stepped past. Beyond the door he listened again. From somewhere in the hotel the low rumble of snoring reached his ears. Alex hoped it was Marek.

He walked forward, still slowly, trying to glide over the rugs. At a corner he turned and five more steps put him outside Vanessa's room. He knocked on the door, gently, but in the still of the night it sounded loud.

No response.

He was about to knock again when he thought better of it. He took out his phone and texted her. **Open your door. I'm outside. Quiet!**

The wait seemed interminably long but, just as he thought he would have to knock again, sounds of movement came from the other side.

She opened the door a crack and he immediately pushed into the room, took the handle from her and closed it. He winced as it clunked shut and then turned to Vanessa. She was in her pyjamas.

"Vanessa!" he whispered, hearing frustration and urgency in his own voice.

She walked backwards to the bed, sat and patted it.

"Get dressed now!" Alex whispered again. "We need to get away. I was right about Marek."

"Alex…"

He waved at her to speak quietly.

"Alex…" She patted the bed again. "I think you should calm down. I'm worried about you."

"No, no! Look—" He pulled out his laptop and showed her the email from Mutnodjemet. Then the second message with the link. "I was right not to trust him. All those signs that he didn't know everything. That really isn't Marek."

She shook her head as if trying to process what he was saying. "But the message doesn't give any details. How do you know this isn't just a windup? Or maybe this is a conspiracy nut. Maybe they're just as paranoid…"

He held her shoulders and looked into her eyes. "I'm convinced. I'm telling you there have been too many inconsistencies. And today, at the first temple, there was a partial stele—the stone with writing. That's Marek's specialization, for God's sake! It was only this evening I realized he should have been interested even though it's nothing to do with why we're here."

Vanessa stood. "All right, we'll get out of here." She dressed quickly and Alex helped her cram things into her case.

As she closed it, he said, "We should go to the police. Agreed?"

She nodded.

"There's no chance of a taxi, so we'll have to take the Nissan. I guess we'll need to hot-wire it."

"It's been a while, but I should be able to."

He was astounded.

She grinned. "The wrong crowd and a misspent youth, remember?"

They crept out into the corridor and he did the same trick to stop the door slamming shut. They walked lightly in the opposite direction of Marek's room, down a flight of stairs and into a lounge area. Most of the lights here were out and there was no one around, no night porter and no receptionist. Finally, they needed to cross the foyer before they would reach the front door.

378

Alex wondered whether a small hotel like this would lock the front door at night. But when he reached for the handle, it turned and the door opened easily.

Outside the air was cool. They stood and scanned for movement. In the moon's creamy light everything appeared tranquil. Nothing stirred. The Nissan was parked only fifteen metres away. There was no cover, but no one was around. With an exchange of nods, Alex and Vanessa started towards it.

A man stepped out from beside the vehicle, his handgun pointed at the centre of Alex's chest. The light caught his face and Alex knew then that it was the man from the BMW and the tomb, the man who had grabbed Pete from the train.

There was a noise behind them. Alex spun around to see Marek approach.

Marek smiled and pointed his gun at Vanessa's head. "Drop the bags," he said, his voice shockingly loud in the still night.

Vanessa let go of her case and put down her handbag. Alex let his bag fall to the floor.

"On your knees. Hands behind your backs."

They knelt.

The blow to the back of Alex's head was immediate. He crumpled, his world suddenly black.

SIXTY-TWO

As Alex came round, he had flashes of images and for a few minutes he was confused. Then he became aware of being uncomfortable, the air was warm and it was hard to breathe. Cigarette smoke. His hands and feet were tied.

He opened his eyes. The first thing he saw was the back of a seat. He was squashed on the floor in the back of a big vehicle, possibly a four-by-four. Awkwardly and gradually, he manoeuvred into a kneeling position and then fell sideways onto the seat and sat up.

"Good morning," Marek said in a friendly voice as though nothing had happened. He sat in the passenger's seat and breathed out smoke into the already dense atmosphere.

Alex coughed. "Where's Vanessa?"

Marek gave a slight chuckle and indicated with his thumb. "She's in the hotel. My friend Joachim is keeping her company."

Alex said, "You bastard. If you hurt her, I'll—"

"Then you had better hope we can follow your map. My friend has a very bad temper and he always gets his way."

Alex stared out of the window towards the hotel and then back at the man he knew as Marek.

"Who are you?" Alex asked.

"My real name—Wael."

"You seem to know a great deal."

"I am a real Egyptologist."

"Did you kill Marek?"

"No."

"Who did?"

At that moment, the side door jerked open and the BMW man, Joachim, took hold of Alex's collar and pulled him out. "Enough chat." When the three of them were standing beside a Land Rover, Joachim gripped Alex's shoulder.

"The girl has told me it is the temple on this hill we are interested in."

"You bastard," Alex hissed, fighting against the bindings. "If you've hurt her—"

The man slapped him. "Don't worry about what I've done, worry about what I will do. If you don't help us then I shall just have to have some fun, won't I?"

Wael said, "Who is keeping an eye on her?"

"Ahmed," Joachim said dismissively. He took a piece of paper from a pocket and showed a diagram to Wael and then Alex.

Wael said, "Why this temple, Alex?"

"The dimensions."

Wael shrugged. "And that means?"

"The short end is twenty-two and a half metres long. The side is thirty metres and if I draw a diagonal line across the temple, the triangle I have is thirty-seven and a half metres," Alex said, proudly unable to restrain himself. "It's in the ratio three, four and five."

"So it's the magical ratio of numbers we are looking for." Wael grinned for a moment then frowned. "This helps us how?"

"Why should I tell you?"

The other man growled, "Because of the girl."

Wael pulled the other man aside. Alex couldn't understand what they said, but it was urgent and angry. He figured the men despised one another. Could he use that to his advantage somehow?

They stopped talking and Wael turned to Alex and spoke calmly. "It is for your professional pride, Alex. My people only want the treasure that is here. If you want, you can have the all the glory. Perhaps we may allow you to keep something valuable."

Alex thought, but there seemed no option but to cooperate.

He said, "All right. Let's go up to the temple, but I have two conditions. Firstly you cut these bindings—after all, I won't be able to walk with my legs tied and I need my hands to draw."

Joachim cut the bindings with a knife and returned it to a sheath on his belt. All the time he kept his cold eyes on Alex, like a snake trying to mesmerize a trapped rodent.

"All right," Wael said. "See, we are reasonable. What is your second condition?"

Alex said, "Let Vanessa go."

"You are in no position to bargain," Joachim scoffed, but then he waved towards the hotel. Back to Alex, he said, "I will let her join us. Perhaps it will add to the incentive."

Vanessa appeared at the entrance, her hands tied in front of her. Ahmed had hold of her arm, but when he let go she ran to Alex. He put his arms around her. "Are you all right?"

She nodded and he told her everything was going to be all right.

"Let's go," Joachim said, and pointed up the hill.

They walked up the sand and gravel path to the summit. Wael led the way. Ahmed and Joachim walked behind them.

"Marek's real name is Wael. Claims he's an Egyptologist," Alex said to Vanessa. Then, calling to Wael,

"The mummy research in Cairo was fake—to convince us you were genuine, right?"

"Yes."

"But when we asked for you at the museum..." Alex nodded at the sudden realization. "You paid the security guard."

"Of course." Wael stopped and pointed to the ground where paths converged. Most of the area was bald, but there were a few stones to depict the ruins.

Alex was dismayed. "You know this is impossible! How can I possibly make sense of this? Where are the forty columns? Where are the geese?"

Joachim placed his arm across Vanessa's chest, pulling her close and placing his gun against her temple. "I think you know how to read the map. You are a smart guy. I suggest you think hard and work it out."

Alex took the paper from Wael and studied it. Immediately north of the temple was believed to have been an offering area, beyond that another temple. The walls of the second, smaller temple were less regular and his thoughts were that this was from a much earlier period. This location was the focal point of the area. There should only have been one temple. He walked to the south-eastern corner and looked around and then studied the diagram. The previous night he had realized this was not just a series of walls with the magical triangular ratio, the walls weren't symmetrical—they were deliberately different lengths.

He asked, "How long was an Egyptian standard measure?"

"A cubit was the standard measure. It is the length of a forearm to the fingertip," Wael said. "Not very standard."

Alex knelt and measured the smallest gap with his arm, then the next biggest. Then he walked around and estimated the rest and laughed.

Wael joined him. "What is it, my friend?"

Alex returned to the south-eastern corner of the ruined temple. "What do four hoops—heel bones—mean?"

"Forty." Wael shrugged as if it were obvious. "And then the pillar. We agreed we are looking for the forty pillars."

Alex shook his head. "No. We made a mistake. They aren't hoops, they're ropes—coiled ropes. And normally they would mean one hundred."

"So we're looking for four hundred pillars?" Weal asked.

"Normally, yes, but here the coil relates to the triangle not the pillar. Ellen either didn't recognize it or knew it wasn't a number but a..." Alex drew a spiral in the dirt. Under different circumstances he would have grinned.

Joachim snapped, "What?"

"More double meaning. The spiral doesn't just represent one hundred, it also shows—"

"The Fibonacci sequence?" Wael asked.

"Precisely! And what does the Fibonacci sequence do?" Alex paused a beat before answering his own question. "It gives us *sectio aurea*—the golden section. In the Fibonacci sequence the ratio of two consecutive numbers tends towards phi. 1.61803399. So it's similar to pi."

Joachim huffed but Wael held up a hand to stop him interrupting.

Wael said, "Go on, Alex."

"The proportions of the Parthenon are famously based on this ratio. This temple's proportions aren't perfect, perhaps something is missing from the diagram, perhaps we need the full 3D effect, but this is very clever. The proportions here are both the three-four-five ratio and close to the Fibonacci sequence."

Joachim said, "I don't care what it means. Just get on with it!"

384

Wael glared at his companion and immediately said, "And that helps us how, Alex?"

"Well, I think of Fibonacci as squares rather than a spiral. The squares have sides 1, 1, 2, 3, 5, 8, 13 and so on. The same is true for golden rectangles. You know A0 folds in half to form A1, which folds to form A2 and so on." In the dirt he drew a rectangle and then one on top of the first like an upside-down L.

He said, "The second rectangle here has its length that is twice the width of the first rectangle." Adjacent to the second, he drew a third rectangle. "This is like the A2, if my first rectangle was A4 and then I draw another—A1— that connects us back to the first."

The final series looked like this:

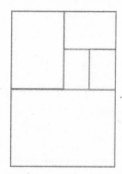

Wael said, "All right, I get the point."

"Well, now draw a diagonal line across one of these and you get a triangle."

"Naturally."

Alex drew a line bisecting the first rectangle. "And the amazing thing is the triangle is approximately three, four, five in dimensions. It's a golden triangle equivalent and the progression is like a Fibonacci sequence—maybe even more special!"

Alex continued to convert his sequence of four rectangles into triangles. "See, a Fibonacci-type spiral appears."

Joachim shook his head, unimpressed.

Wael prompted, "So this means...?"

"Four hoops didn't mean forty. They weren't heel bones. They were deliberately rotated to mean four stages of the sequence. The pillar relates to a circle on the temple layout. It indicates the Isis throne." He added the throne to the diagram and then walked to the bottom right-hand corner of the temple.

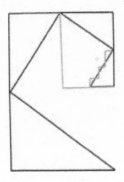

"It's the origin. It's where the first triangle is, the start of the sequence." He indicated a line from the middle of the base to the top end of where the throne would fit. "That would be the hypotenuse. It aligns with the north, yes?"

He didn't wait for a response, but walked the length of the first triangle, counting his paces. When he stopped he indicated a triangle following the line of the temple wall. "The second triangle starts here, goes to the top right corner and finishes top left. The third triangle brings us back." He pointed left, along the line of the base. "It ends at a point the width of the temple on the far side."

Then he started walking again, counting his paces to the top wall of the temple and returned to the bottom corner. "The fourth triangle comes right round and will end over there, the length of the temple away." Pointing south-east, he set off walking in line with the side wall, counting the paces.

When Alex had counted the same number of paces as the length of the temple, he stopped. "The first triangle had sides of three and four. The fourth triangle is eight and twelve. Twelve again. And the eight in the code confirms this is right." He looked back to make sure his line was straight, adjusted slightly then pointed to the ground. "This is where the Map-Stone points to. Whatever it is, is buried here." He looked at Wael, shrugged and half smiled. "I'm afraid there's no access, the dig hasn't covered this area."

In the corner of his eye he saw Joachim advance. Alex turned just in time to see the man lash out, pistol-whipping him into oblivion.

SIXTY-THREE

The mini digger had been brought up the hill and now rumbled and belched diesel fumes. A second Land Rover was parked beside the other outside the hotel. A man Alex hadn't seen before operated the machine, excavating the area known as Temple IV quickly and without care for preserving anything but the now clearly defined walls.

Vanessa cradled Alex's head in her lap, her hands still tied. His hands were also tied, although neither of them had bound legs. Ahmed watched them, a gun pointed casually in their direction. Wael stood close by and Joachim was nearer the hole, directing the dig.

Alex looked at the hasty excavation and then at Wael. "Call yourself an archaeologist? Do you approve of this?"

Wael said nothing, although his eyes held concern.

Vanessa gave Alex a drink from a water bottle as he sat up and looked at the cleared area. There was a central area with steps descending to a door. The final restraining earth was scooped away and Joachim signalled for the digger to move back. He walked into the excavated area, over to the steps and down. It was clearly a tomb entrance.

Wael joined him at the stone door, looked back excitedly and called, "Geese, one in each corner—the four geese!"

Joachim shouldered the other man aside, felt around the stone doorway and then stepped back. The two men spoke animatedly before Wael retreated and Joachim signalled the operator to move the digger. The scoop was positioned in front of the stone door and thrust forward. There was a clap like thunder and they felt it reverberate underground.

Alex said, "If you are expecting treasure, I think you're mistaken."

Wael looked surprised.

"Just so we're clear, the gold on the Map-Stone," Alex started, "I don't think it literally meant there is gold in the tomb. I think it just referred to the geometric progression to identify the temple: the *golden triangles.*"

Wael looked scornful. "Perhaps, but our interest is not really gold."

The scoop jarred against the stone door once more. The door tilted. The digger struck again and a gap, wide enough for a man to clamber through, opened up.

As the digger backed up, Wael darted forward. At the doorway he shone a torch in. After a brief hesitation he disappeared inside. A few moments later he came out and called to the prisoners. "You were right. It looks like a maze in here." He disappeared inside once more.

Alex nodded to Vanessa. She'd been the one to realize the lines on the ceremonial block looked like a maze.

Joachim told Ahmed to keep his gun trained on them and then he darted inside the tomb.

Vanessa whispered something so quietly Alex didn't catch it. He followed her eyes and saw that the digger operator was about to climb out—on the far side.

Just as Alex looked up at Ahmed beside them, the man reeled sideways. Vanessa had swept his legs away. In a smooth movement, she was on her feet and standing on the man's gun hand. Alex realized she must have managed to get her hands untied, because in the next move she had the gun.

She pointed it at the surprised digger operator and beckoned him over. She instructed Ahmed to untie Alex. Then she made Ahmed and the other man walk down the hill to the cars, prodding them in the back, urging them on.

Alex followed. He glanced behind again and again but the others didn't appear from the tomb.

At the car, Vanessa got the car keys and told Alex to tie the prisoners' hands. She made them climb into the rear, locked the doors from the front and threw the keys away. Then she jumped into the driver's seat of the second Land Rover. Alex sat beside her.

After fumbling with the ignition she punched the gears into reverse and shot out of the town. A few faces watched them from the security of their houses and Alex wondered whether their lack of response was because they were used to crazy archaeologists or they recognized trouble.

She came out onto a main road and turned left. At a junction she turned right and then right onto a dual carriageway. "I don't know where I'm going!" she said, and then laughed with relief.

His heart felt like a small bird trapped by the cage of his ribs. He took deep breaths and let himself sink into the seat.

At a service stop, Vanessa pulled around the back and went into the building. They cleaned up in the bathrooms, reunited in the restaurant and ordered coffee. They decided against eating, but after ten minutes recovering and lured by the smell of food, they realized just how hungry they were. They ordered large portions and ate slowly, savouring every mouthful like it was their last meal.

They ate in silence, each locked in their own thoughts. When they had both finished, Alex realized he had been staring out of the window. "We've got to go back," he said.

"No, we need to inform the authorities."

"We experienced the so-called authorities before. We're foreigners, without passports and associated with trouble. The response will be to lock us up—arrest, then question. I don't want to see the inside of a cell again."

"So we go back?"

"Hold on." He disappeared for a few minutes and returned with a book. He opened it up. A map of the region.

He said, "We wait till dark. And find another way around. We make sure they're not there and then we take a look." He pointed to an area just south of Port Said. "We're about here on this road. There're a thousand roads through this delta. We can go around here." He traced a line, zigzagging west and then south. "We can come around to the north and stop at the buildings to the west of the site."

"So, we'll check it out from a distance and won't go near if they're still at the site?"

"You got it."

Vanessa agreed and they decided to drive on to the city of Port Said. By the time they got there she'd managed to persuade him they should get a hotel and wait a day before returning. It would be infuriating for them to drive back only to find the men still there.

Alex realized her logic was good. Wael didn't know everything about the map, but they probably wouldn't give up straight away. Alex knew *he* certainly wouldn't.

Without passports they decided to find a small hotel and were relieved they weren't asked to produce them. They checked into separate rooms and both sunk into relaxing baths. After, they walked to the beach and watched the sun go down from a bar. With a couple of beers inside him, Alex began to feel less tense.

He said, "I still can't get over it."

"What?"

"The golden ratio, *phi*, it's very similar to *pi*. It can't be a coincidence that the Bible refers to the area where the temple is as Pi-Ramesses. Phi is attributed to the Greeks, but they must have got it from the Egyptians. And the pyramids are generally thought to be built based on pi, but it'll be the golden ratio again."

Alex noticed Vanessa didn't seem to share his excitement at the discovery. "Don't you find it amazing?" he asked her.

She forced a smile. "Not really. I'm more interested in whose tomb it is. Who do you think?"

"Must be Nefertiti's. I think Meryra either built the tomb or helped with the design and created the Map-Stone. I don't understand why the block was in Amarna though."

"Are you certain Lord Carnarvon didn't take it from King Tut's tomb? Wouldn't that make more sense since you think Meryra took other things there including documents."

"Two reasons. Firstly, it wasn't Carnarvon's style to lie about where he obtained something. Remember, he was too honest about finding papyri in Tutankhamen's tomb. Secondly, there's the timeline. From the Amarna Letters, Marek—the real one—was sure the trip to the Valley of the Kings was earlier. We think the Map-Stone was taken to Amarna with other records after the queen had died."

"What about Akhenaten? Where's he?"

"If only I knew!" Alex ordered more drinks. He had a twinkle in his eye when he looked back at Vanessa. "You know, there are people who believe Moses was actually Akhenaten."

"Which can't be true. You said yourself Akhenaten died."

Alex held up his hands. "I agree. I agree. But there are many who think the Exodus happened around this time. Remember, Akhenaten's—and by extension Nefertiti's—followers were considered outlaws."

"Yes, I recall you winding me up by saying *Ibiru* meant outlaw and sounds like *Hebrew*."

"You know, one thing that's always bothered me about the Bible is the story of Adam and Eve. They're the first people, right? Eve is made from Adam's rib, but they can't have been the only ones. When Cain kills Abel he is branded so that *others* would know. Later, Cain marries and has a son."

"Called Henoch," Vanessa said quietly.

Alex nodded. "If there weren't other people, then Cain must have married a sister—which he didn't."

Vanessa was drinking a tequila sunrise. After a couple of sips, she said, "I don't know if it's the alcohol or that I'm just suddenly very chilled out, but I'm not going to argue with you." Her laugh prompted him to continue.

"I'll tell you something that may surprise you. There's a theory that Akhenaten and Nefertiti were the Adam and Eve of the Bible. Akhetaten was a new beautiful paradise— Eden. Akhenaten upset God and they were expelled from the city."

"And you believe that?"

"Not really. It's a fun thought though. The city must have been incredible, like nothing the people would have experienced before. Obviously you can't see it nowadays, but there would have been irrigation channels with gardens and trees everywhere. The streets would have been paved, some with beautiful paintings—there's one in the Cairo Museum. Parts would have been open to the sky for the worship of the sun, but scholars believe there were giant awnings strung between buildings so that people could walk in the shade. The temples would have been beautifully painted with blues and yellows and white and green, bringing the buildings to life. Even the statues would have been painted with lifelike colours. It must have been an incredible time—a time of art and music and peace."

"Until it all came to an end."

"But wonderful while it lasted."

"If it was allowed, I'd give you a kiss." She squeezed his arm affectionately. "For an atheist, you've just painted a very religious experience."

SIXTY-FOUR

Gershom stood on the hill overlooking Tell el-Daba. "So this is the temple."

Wael indicated the complete area of what was thought to be two temples, but they now understood it as one: A1 folded to form two A2 sheets. "The temple of Osiris," he said. "Everything fits. It is as you said. And more logical that it would be in the Delta rather than Amarna. The Delta was the centre of the religion."

"And the map showed the entrance to the tomb?" Gershom looked at the crude excavation and open stone entrance.

"It is the one."

"Where is Joachim?"

"He's inside laying explosive." Wael couldn't mask the disgust in his voice.

"What is the matter?"

"I am an archaeologist first and foremost. You know I do not approve of this destruction."

"First and foremost you are a member of the Brotherhood. I sympathize with your concern and yet this is the only way. We must remove the evidence."

Wael looked imploringly at the old man. "But there is no evidence!"

"What?"

"Come, let me show you."

Wael led the way into the crater, waited for the old man to catch up and then ducked beneath a stone lintel and into a corridor. He pulled out a torch and lit the way, switching first left then right through a maze.

The old man's walking stick click-clacked against the stone, reflecting his uncertain slow pace. After the third turn he said, "The map was clear about the way through the maze?"

"Yes, yes, we had no problem until…"

They rounded a corner and saw the light from Joachim's torch. He was standing in a room and had attached explosive to the walls.

The room was empty except for hieroglyphs on the walls.

Gershom said, "The burial chamber?"

Joachim stopped what he was doing and waved his arms around. "Empty. It looks as though the tomb was robbed in antiquity."

"And there is nothing more?"

Wael said, "There is an identical room on the opposite side to this, but this room is the true burial chamber. See, there is nothing here. The hieroglyphs indicate this was the tomb of an important lady—undoubtedly the right tomb, undoubtedly Eighteenth Dynasty, but there is nothing here that needs to be destroyed."

Gershom thought for a moment then tapped his stick as though a decision had been made. "We go. Remove the explosive, Joachim. Wael is correct, there is nothing here we should be afraid of."

Joachim hesitated as though considering an argument, but then he began to disconnect the explosive. Gershom patted Wael on the arm and directed him out of the chamber. Together they retraced their steps to the surface.

Outside, Wael said, "Thank you."

"You have served the Brotherhood of Levi well." Gershom pointed to the Land Rover parked outside the hotel. The driver raised a hand in acknowledgement. "Go back to Cairo and go back to your life."

"And you?"

"I will pray."

As Wael walked down the hill, Gershom found the sacred place in the temple. He stood still for a time, deep in thought, before removing a book from his pocket. Holding it in front of him he raised his head to the sky and began to chant the old sacred words that had been passed down from leader to leader for over three thousand years.

When he finished, the sun was a liquid golden disc on the horizon. For ten more minutes he watched in silence as it disappeared, feeling the same wonder that ancient Egyptians must have felt as they imagined the sun had been swallowed by the goddess Nut, to pass through her body and be reborn the next day. This was the Aten, the sun disc on the horizon. Gershom nodded at the thought: how much easier it would have been if Judaism had been based on Akhenaten's worship of the sun god. Freud's theory had been a cunning misdirection. It would never be proven because there was no evidence either way.

As Gershom turned to walk back he saw Joachim watching, his eyes cold and without appreciation of the moment. He could never be the leader of the Brotherhood. But then neither could Wael.

The younger man said, "Everything is in place."

"Did you ever think Wael would be able to find the tomb?"

"It was possible. Perhaps he could have found the temple, but I doubt if he would have worked out the relevance of the golden triangles and sequence."

In the rapidly fading light, they began to walk down the hill, Joachim walking at the old man's pace.

Joachim said, "But the chamber we have found is not the final tomb. The maze is impossible to solve without the map. And MacLure must know he didn't tell us everything. Are you certain he will come back?"

"He'll be back, either tonight or tomorrow I think." Gershom stopped and looked back towards the temple. "And the explosives?"

Joachim smiled tightly. "As I said, the explosives are in place."

SIXTY-FIVE

The moon was three days off full and cast a spooky glow over the ancient hill. Vanessa had parked in the shadow by farm buildings, where Alex had indicated, and they followed the path to the foot of the mound. They wore black, having spent the day shopping for appropriate clothes in Port Said, and each had a powerful torch. Alex wore a tool belt, just in case a claw hammer or screwdriver was somehow required. He didn't have Vanessa's karate skills and the truth was he liked the idea that the tools could double as weapons.

He checked his watch: just after 1am. They stood, hidden beside a wall, and stared at the eerie hill. Nothing stirred. After thirty minutes they decided to move forward.

A dog barked dryly from the direction of the main cluster of buildings. Someone shouted. Alex and Vanessa stopped, crouched and listened. Another dog barked far away, then silence.

"We're exposed here," Vanessa whispered. "We should just get inside."

Alex nodded and they moved quickly to where the digger had excavated the entrance. In the moonlight, Alex could see that a metal grill like a section of security fence lay across the doorway. A red and white sign warned of danger.

Taking a side each, they carefully lifted the grill and manoeuvred it aside. Then, leading the way, Alex climbed past the stone door. He switched on his torch. A second beam swept across his as Vanessa joined him. The passage was just wide enough for one person with their head bent. Its walls, floor and ceiling were unadorned stone blocks. They walked forward five paces, small stones and sandy earth grating under their feet.

At a T-junction Alex pictured the Map-Stone and knew he should turn left. Vanessa followed a step behind.

Alex pulled up sharply. A red light blinked in the wall. "What the…?"

Vanessa stood close and peered at the object wedged between blocks. The red light was a digital display.

Alex said, "Jesus! It's a timer. This place is rigged to blow."

"According to the timer, that's just under two hours."

He checked his watch again. "Let's hope it's enough," he said, and swept the torch ahead. Two hours seemed a long time, but his breathing quickened and he began to hurry. Three steps and he turned right and then immediately left. At the next junction there was another timer on a package fixed to the wall. Same time as the first. Alex hurried on, going right and then right again.

Vanessa whispered, "This is much bigger than I expected."

He detected something in her voice, turned to look at her. "You OK?"

In the torchlight her face looked ghostly pale. "I don't like confined spaces."

"Not long," he said, and took four paces forward and stopped. It appeared to be a dead end.

Vanessa shone her torch at the wall. "Wrong way?"

Alex stepped forward, sideways and disappeared. His torch lit a sliver of wall where he'd disappeared.

"Optical illusion," he said.

She followed and squeezed through. They switched back and forth before arriving at a chamber.

Alex said. "No more explosives since the false wall. Looks like the other guys didn't get this far. Probably found the mirror image of this chamber."

They shone their torches around the blank walls.

Vanessa said, "Nothing here."

"Another illusion." Alex went to the far end and shone the torch back. Again the overlapping stones, this time with a gap in the floor.

He sat, manoeuvred into the hole and shone the torch down and right. Steps descended into a well of blackness.

"Oh God," Vanessa said.

"If it's too confined for you, wait here."

"I'm coming."

They dropped almost six feet and began to switch back and forth through this new level. The sides were barely shoulder width apart and the low ceiling made them crouch.

"Alex."

"OK?" He swivelled, shone his torch towards her and saw a piece of limestone in her hand and a mark on the wall.

She smiled wanly. "I'm marking our route. It's helping me stay focused and to not worry about being trapped down here. But we've just come back on ourselves."

"I can't do it," he admitted. "I thought I could make sense of the lines on the Map-Stone but I can't."

"I can get us back to the steps. Shall we go back?"

He reluctantly agreed, and after a couple of turns, they were back at the start of the level.

She sat on the steps and he squatted in front of her, thinking. After a few minutes he raised his torch to check Vanessa's face. She looked at him, half patient, half expectant. And then he saw it. Over her left shoulder was a symbol on the wall. He jumped up and looked closely, felt

400

its indentation. A scarab. He shone the torch on the other walls. Each path was marked with a different symbol. Then one made him let out a splutter.

"The knot of Isis," he exclaimed. "It's one of the four amulets for protection in the afterlife. It was put in the hand of the deceased. Of course! Isis is the key of life. *Isis is key.* Ellen's message had another meaning!" He squeezed past her and shone the torch along the walls and checked out each of the next corners.

"This way—we follow the Isis markings."

At the junction, he pointed the light at another Isis knot on the wall, turned and searched the next alternatives. He was moving quicker now and after three switchbacks turned to Vanessa and said, "Almost there. Next turn should take us to the burial corridor. If I've got my bearings, it'll take us back under the temple."

At the junction, they needed to crawl to get into the corridor. Here the air was cool and tasted of dry dust and earth. There was writing on the walls. Alex picked out a series of hieroglyphs.

"It's Neferneferuaten—Nefertiti," Alex said, the excitement almost choking his voice. The hieroglyphs ran along the gently sloping corridor and appeared to be telling a story.

"Can you read it?" Vanessa wanted to know.

"No." Alex ran his hand along. "But here we have the death of a child and then another. This section seems to be about Akhenaten's death and the Aten turning his back on the people." As he moved down he had to climb around wooden ceiling supports.

He switched to the other wall. "This is more positive. Here Nefertiti seems to have taken on the form of Isis and

401

is with her husband Osiris. Here's reference to the Palace of the Great Barque. And four geese!" He played the torch back and forth. "I don't understand. Maybe it's a double meaning again. I didn't expect any more geese."

"Wael said that the geese could symbolize the rise of a new pharaoh."

"He did." Alex thought for a second. "Would Nefertiti celebrate Ay taking power? It doesn't seem likely."

Vanessa said, "How're we doing for time?"

He checked his watch. "Ninety-three minutes."

"Can we keep going? The sooner we're out of here the better."

"But this could be the find of the century! We need to record it before it's too late." Alex took out his phone and, using the torch, snapped photographs of the mural. When he had finished, Vanessa was waiting for him at the end of the passage—the antechamber, Alex surmised. There had once been a stone door, but the debris was scattered around a partial slab where it had originally sealed the chamber.

The floor dropped down and they could stand again, bending their heads. Wooden supports held up the ceiling but further back they had collapsed. Earth and other debris covered the ground. Alex cast the torch beam around and noted nothing he would class as treasure, but amongst the broken pottery some pieces remained intact and there were five wooden caskets of various sizes—three smashed, two intact. Beyond the room was an opening: the entrance to the burial chamber. From appearances, it had been broken into from above. Most of the room was blocked with dirt and rubble.

"Tomb robbers," Alex said. "Probably in antiquity. Either they deliberately dug through from the temple or the roof collapsed first. Nefertiti's sarcophagus may be under there, but I somehow doubt it." He swung the light back into the antechamber. Beautifully painted murals covered every inch, telling the same story as before plus traditional images of resurrection and the afterlife. There was also a scene of the Opening of the Mouth ceremony. Normally this would have been performed by the high priest but this was a significant departure for here the priest seemed to be Osiris himself. Alex took more photographs before turning his attention to the caskets.

The first was about two feet long and deep, and about a foot wide. He lifted the heavy lid. Inside were dozens of clay shabtis. The second complete chest was the size of a bed linen box. Inside this were a stack of clay tablets and neatly rolled papyri. He pulled one out, barely able to breathe with excitement. Slowly, he unrolled it, afraid its brittle material would crumble. It didn't.

He stared at the image drawn on the paper, unable to comprehend what he was looking at: three columns of coloured circles. Against each was written a single word in hieratic script. He snapped a photo then pulled out another and photographed that one. It was confusing. This wasn't what he'd expected at all. There was no *Book of the Dead*, but rather evidence of something else entirely. Again and again he noted Osiris featuring. Suddenly the religious significance of what he was looking at dawned on him.

He pulled out another and gagged at what he was looking at.

"Vanessa," he blurted, "My God, this is about Akhenaten's tomb!"

He'd been so engrossed in the papyri, he hadn't wondered what Vanessa was doing. Now he heard her footsteps. Where was she going? He looked around and then his blood froze. The footfall was approaching. Vanessa had backed into a corner and was just standing there.

A light came into the chamber. Joachim stepped in and pointed his gun at Alex.

SIXTY-SIX

Joachim glanced at Vanessa. "Is this all there is?"

"It looks that way," she answered.

"But it's enough and we've found it," he said. "This is a great day for the Brotherhood of Levi. This is what we have existed for."

Alex had been squatting and now scuttled backwards, the man's gun remaining fixedly pointed at his chest. Joachim said something else but Alex wasn't listening. He stared at Vanessa in disbelief.

"You're working with them?"

Vanessa's eyes briefly met his and then she moved, stepping between the two men.

She said, "Let him go." Not a question, but a command.

Joachim said nothing and smiled.

"There've been enough deaths over this. I did this on the understanding he would be allowed to live. Gershom guaranteed it."

Alex stood and came up behind her, reducing the opportunity for Joachim to shoot him. Vanessa sensed him there and edged right. Alex edged with her. This gave Joachim the chance to see the papyri in the chest. Still with his gun aimed through Vanessa at Alex, he sidestepped to the chest. He removed a bag from his shoulder, placed it on the floor and then dipped into the papyri-filled chest. Removing a scroll, he used one hand and the edge of the box to partially unroll it.

"Shine your torch," he snapped at Vanessa. When she aimed it close by, he briefly glanced at the document, dropped it and looked at another.

Vanessa said, "Is that more explosive in the bag?"

"Don't worry, there's plenty of time for us to get out safely."

Instinctively he'd glanced at the bag as he spoke. That was when Vanessa kicked out. A shower of debris and a chunk of stone flew from her foot towards Joachim. He dropped into a squat and fired the gun, but the shot was wild.

Vanessa was already pulling Alex to the doorway. As she moved she kicked out at an upright.

Joachim shouted and fired again. This time Vanessa grunted. She lunged at the upright and immediately the ceiling began to cave in.

Alex grabbed her arm. He pulled and they tumbled into the corridor. Dust blasted up the corridor, showering them. The ceiling began to crack. A stanchion creaked and snapped.

Alex pulled Vanessa to her feet and helped her up the corridor as it began to crumble. The torch picked out Vanessa's white chalk marks easily and they hurried through the lower level and then the first level of the maze. When they reached the top they staggered up the final steps and collapsed onto the ground.

Alex lay panting and looking up at the stars. Beside him Vanessa stood and looked in the direction of the temple. A man leaning heavily on a walking stick stood not ten paces away.

Alex made himself stand. In the pale moonlight it took a moment to recognize the old man. "Uncle Seth!"

"Not really," Gershom said, his voice as thick as liquid tar. "Cat, where's Joachim?"

Alex heard Vanessa answer that the other man had been crushed by the collapse of the burial chamber. So this was it. No more lucky escapes. He looked at Vanessa. Her arm was slick with blood.

"Vanessa, you were shot!" Alex tore a sleeve off his shirt and tied a tourniquet above the wound. She put her other arm over his shoulder for support and he put an arm around her. Suddenly nothing else seemed to matter. Together they walked out of the trough.

Alex and Vanessa stopped two paces short of the old man.

Gershom said, "Was the evidence there?"

"Yes. And Joachim laid the explosive." Vanessa looked long and hard at the old man. "He tried to kill us. You promised—"

"What did he see?" the old man said, referring to Alex.

"Nothing. The chamber collapsed."

The old man nodded. "Then I say there will be no more deaths," he said.

"Thank you."

"But nothing incriminating can be allowed to leave this place."

Vanessa kissed Alex on the cheek and hugged him tightly. "I'm sorry," she said quietly into his ear. "I had to do it—but something changed. I really fell for you, please remember that." Then she broke the embrace and handed him the keys to the Land Rover.

Gershom checked his watch. "We need to get going before the explosion. And you, young lady, need a doctor."

Alex walked slowly towards the farm buildings and, like an automaton, got into the car. He covered the first few miles in a daze and couldn't recall the route he'd taken. He had the window down, elbow on the frame, the fresh air blowing hard against his arm. It felt like a bad dream. He leaned out and let the rushing air blast his face, waking him up. He thought he heard a dull explosion, but it came and went so quickly he was left wondering.

He turned onto the dual carriageway, pressed the accelerator and headed for Cairo. He found a radio channel playing rock and settled back for the journey, his mind spinning with everything that had happened. Everything he'd seen. He no longer had the evidence, but Vanessa had helped him. Did she know? Of course she knew. He might not have the evidence, but she knew he had taken photographs.

He knew the secret.

SIXTY-SEVEN

Fifteen months later

Abubakar Habib sucked his teeth. "Show me again the area of your planned excavation."

Alex took a deep breath. This had already been approved by the Ministry of Antiquities, but he had quickly learned how things worked in Egypt. There was no point in arguing, that would only aggravate matters. This minor local official either wanted power and respect or money— or perhaps both.

Alex called to his assistant. "Mahmood, please make the inspector a cup of your best coffee."

A young Nubian man waved from the next room and there were soon sounds of a pot on the small gas cooker they all shared.

Alex pulled out the approved documents and looked at the diagram of the four hundred square metre patch in the northern hills of Amarna. Some tombs of nobles were known to be there, but this location had yielded nothing in the past.

Inspector Habib marked the areas of other excavations and also the area where peasants' graves had been found in the plain. "These are not your areas."

"I agree."

Habib pointed at the area Alex was interested in. "There is nothing here." He sucked on his teeth for a moment as though thinking. "Which team did you say you are with?"

Again, Alex pulled out the relevant papers. "Macquarie University, headed by Professor Steele. The permit is for one year."

Mahmood, the Nubian assistant, scurried in with a small steaming cup of Egyptian coffee. He nodded encouragement to Alex, who returned his smile.

Habib tasted the coffee without comment and set it down. "You will not enter any tomb you find, is that understood?"

"Not without you being present."

"If you find anything at all it must be recorded. I will make visits. If I find any item not recorded, your permit will be revoked. Any items and that is it. No more digging."

"Understood."

"You and your team are staying on the site?"

"We are staying in caravans. We will not leave Tell el-Amarna without notifying you."

"Good. When you and your team come and go, you will tell me first. I must know when you leave. If someone comes or goes and you don't tell me, then that is it also. No more digging."

The inspector went over the details of the permit once again before he finished his coffee. Alex was surprised there was no suggestion of money to be paid, but he knew this was just the beginning.

When he was alone again, he sat back in his chair and closed his eyes. It felt much longer than fifteen months. So much had happened. He had checked into a hotel at Cairo airport and flown back to England the following day. He had returned to his flat in Maida Vale without any media attention and caught up on the news. There had been a couple of students murdered, one of which had caught the public's attention because of the mystery surrounding the girl's final movements. And so the attention moved away from Alex and the Highclere burglary.

He felt a mixture of elation and disappointment. He had made an incredible discovery and yet he knew it wouldn't be believed. The photographs didn't prove it was Nefertiti's tomb at Tell el-Daba. The destruction of part of the hill at the ancient site was reported in the local press as a gas explosion. Alex realized that claiming to have discovered the tomb would create unwanted media attention. Another gas explosion. Ellen's death and now the destruction of an ancient site. He could imagine the headlines and the hounding. No, it wasn't worth it.

Alex had searched for the Brotherhood of Levi on the Internet. There was limited information on the group and a conspiracy theory suggested they had senior roles in all Western governments, controlling and censoring, and actively ensured information about them was destroyed. Alex noted that Levi in the Bible was a son of Jacob whose three sons had responded when Moses felt betrayed by his people. In Exodus, while Moses was on Mount Sinai, the Israelites turned to Aaron, a high priest who created a golden calf for the people to worship. In retribution, the sons of Levi killed three thousand of the followers in punishment for turning to other gods. It followed that a modern group would have the same aims.

The golden calf was undoubtedly a bull which was an incarnation of Ra—the sun god. It made sense. While Moses was away, the Israelites returned to worshipping the sun. Maybe this also confirmed that they had come from Akhenaten's city and the worship of the sun by the name of the Aten. Alex was convinced that Aten and Ra were one and the same.

He also knew now that the god of Moses was definitely not the sun god. It was another god entirely. A rival god. A god whose true identity the Brotherhood was clearly determined to erase from their history.

During the first few days Alex reviewed the photographs and sketched what he had seen. Because of the dim light, the photographs were poor, but he managed to reconstruct most of it to his satisfaction. He also began to write potential academic papers that avoided reference to the missing papyri and Judaism, but focused on what might have become of Akhenaten and his queen.

In the second week he was amazed to receive an email from Vanessa saying her wound was healing well and she had finished the article about him.

The article had changed his life. Its publication in a Sunday paper coincided with him finding the item missing from the exhibition. Now that all the pressure was off, he was able to think clearly, able to revisit Highclere Castle and look at the exhibition through Ellen's eyes. What would he have done if he had feared the Map-Stone would be stolen? She wasn't strong so she couldn't carry it far. She also couldn't take it past a camera.

Alex had found it under the four canopic jars in Tutankhamen's mock burial chamber. No one had noticed the jars were a little higher than they used to be.

He had published his paper on the theory that Akhenaten's tomb had been moved and coincided with where the Amarna Letters had originally lain.

On the back of his paper, he managed to persuade Professor Steele to support a dig at Amarna. Officially he wasn't leading the group, but that didn't matter. He was here.

There was no doubt in his mind that the Map-Stone had been meant for Akhenaten's spirit so that he might know where his beloved wife was interred. Perhaps there had been a similar guide in Nefertiti's tomb ensuring they could be reunited for all eternity. A little like the physical link between Senemut's and Pharaoh Hatshepsut's tombs.

Lord Carnarvon had found the ceremonial stone. If it had come from Akhenaten's burial chamber, then the tomb had already been disturbed. Perhaps the Amarna Letters had also originated in the hidden tomb of the heretic pharaoh.

After the initial exchange of emails with Vanessa, he heard nothing more. Now and again he would read an article by her and he guessed she was travelling the world. Her association with Alex and Egyptology gave her credibility that seemed to extend to other ancient civilisations—but always from the human angle. Her latest piece had been on a temple hidden in the jungles of Cambodia. Alex didn't doubt for a moment that she was physically there.

He went into the kitchen and made himself a cup of Earl Grey tea, black. He returned to his desk and relaxed, the scent of the tea wafting away the stressful meeting with the local antiquities official. Was this how Carter and Carnarvon used to feel about them? He suspected it was worse in the mid-1920s because of the political tensions between Britain and Egypt, and in the Middle East generally. The changing rules of discovery and reward must have been infuriating to the two men who spent so long and so much trying to find the boy king's tomb. Their expedition had started because Carter had found evidence suggesting Tutankhamen's tomb was in the Valley of the Kings. The many similarities made Alex smile.

He opened a drawer and looked at the papers he had compiled since returning from Nefertiti's tomb. He understood the sensitivity of what he'd seen, but it didn't make total sense. Was it really enough to kill over?

He picked up the most intriguing. It was a series of colourful circles with names in them. At the time it meant nothing, but a little investigation proved intriguing. The diagram was known as the Tree of Life, part of the Jewish Kabbalah. The very name was a clue since both the ancient Egyptians and the Jews had a Tree of Life. The ancient Egyptian tree was from the story of Osiris, whose coffin was saved from the river by catching in the tree's roots. Effectively, the tree was the doorway to the afterlife.

Alex had learned that, in Judaism, the Tree of Life was used to explain many things from religion to psychology. The relevance to Sigmund Freud was not lost on him. The circles represented characteristics and also archangels. It was the latter that Alex found most interesting, because the papyrus had names written beside them. For Alex it was conclusive evidence that Judaism was based on the ancient Egyptian religion. There were ten interconnected circles on the paper in three columns. Three circles were on each outside column and four in the middle one. There was an eleventh black circle midway between the first triangle of circles and its mirror image below.

Alex couldn't reproduce the writing well enough to be absolutely sure, but it was close. The nine main gods of Egypt, the Ennead were: Shu, Tefnut, Geb, Nut, Osiris, Isis, Seth, Nephthys and of course Ra, known by many names, probably including Aten. Alex had written each of these names on the paper. Each god equated with a Jewish archangel. That left the one at the bottom, which represented *Kingdom*. And the black one, which represented *Da'at*—the void. The first was easy. Alex had written *Pharaoh/Horus* because the association was clear and Horus was the representation of the living god. Finally, against the black circle he had written Amun. Amun was the *hidden one*, and it seemed to tally, although Amun was not of the Ennead. He was the god Akhenaten had disapproved of but had been reinstated after his death and later merged with Ra. Amun's role within the Tree of Life seemed to make sense.

Mahmood disturbed Alex's thoughts, looking sheepishly into the room.

"I'm sorry, Mahmood, what did you say?"

"Mr Alex, there is a phone call."

Mahmood held out the satellite phone shared by the group.

"Hello."

"Alex? It's me."

413

"Vanessa?" Her pen name was Rebecca but her real name was Cat, short for Catherine. Even though he knew this, in his mind she would always be Vanessa. She didn't seem to mind him calling her that.

"Well done on getting the position and licence to dig."

Her voice sounded so great. He felt a thrill run through him. There had been so much left unsaid.

"Vanessa, I—"

"Things have changed, Alex. I've changed. My uncle died a couple of months ago and—"

"Seth? He was really your uncle?"

"Gershom. Yes he was. He was kind of a father to me after my parents died. He left me all of the details about being High Priest. He had planned for Joachim to take over but something must have changed his mind."

"As a woman, could you—?"

"Not officially, but the Brotherhood of Levi was a law unto itself." She sighed. "However I've broken all ties with them. And without a high priest they can't exist anyway."

"Are you saying things will now change about disclosing the links between Egyptian religion and Judaism. That the Jewish God is in fact made up of multiple gods—the archangels?"

Vanessa sounded surprised. "No I am not! Anyway it wasn't that. I thought you'd worked it out. You realized Sigmund Freud had an ulterior motive when he suggested Akhenaten was the founder of monotheism—the worship of the sun."

"Do you mean... are you suggesting it was a distraction from something much worse?"

"In some people's eyes, yes."

And then Alex got it. "It was Osiris not Ra."

"Moses was the high priest of Osiris. You were right about the name. He was known as Osarseph or Osar-moses."

"The god of the afterlife. A revered god. And husband to Isis. It seems appropriate that he would be the one."

"The people fled Amarna when Pharaoh Akhenaten died. I don't know whether Nefertiti was ever Pharaoh, but she led her people to the sanctuary of the Delta. Moses was her high priest and at some point Akhenaten was viewed as Osiris and Nefertiti their Isis."

Alex nodded to himself, remembering the mural on the tunnel to the burial chamber.

Vanessa said, "I don't know how soon after arriving that Nefertiti died, but it seems her death precipitated the persecution of her people, the *Ibiru*. And so Moses led them to Israel."

"Wow!" Alex whistled. "What about the missing papyri. There really were papyri in Tutankhamen's tomb weren't there?"

"Yes."

Alex recalled the story from the clay tablets. Meryra had wanted the truth told. "So the papyri were too sensitive. Lord Carnarvon had them?"

"Yes."

"Was he murdered?"

"Apparently, he refused to give them up. You were right. The Brotherhood had him poisoned. So they got the documents and destroyed them."

"What about Howard Carter?"

"He had nothing. Carnarvon had the evidence. Carter feared for his life most of the time and his threat to the House of Rothschild was just bluster. They knew it, but it was an insignificant price for them to pay for his silence."

"It makes sense."

There was dead air.

He checked to see if the signal had gone. "Vanessa?"

"Still here. I was thinking... Could you do with a writer? Someone to report on your discoveries in Armana?"

"It's very early days. I've found more clay tablets. There were definitely two stories: Meryra's secrets and Yanhamu's life. I believe his story was written down by his wife after his death. I think they loved each other very much."

"So could you?"

"Could I have a writer? I guess so... although..." And then he realized something, "Have you got a recommendation, is that it?"

"Me, dummy."

His heart raced. "When can you get here?"

"I'm in Cairo." She laughed and he imagined her cute crooked smile. "I'll be there by tomorrow morning."

SIXTY-EIGHT

1321 BCE, Thebes

Yanhamu squatted by the pool at the rear of the temple of Amun. He recalled standing in the same spot eight years ago with Nefer-bithia, the magistrate's daughter. She had dared him to throw a stone into the tranquil water. So he had done it and a priest had chased them. The memory made him smile, and he flicked a stone over the edge. The way the ripples spread made him think of events and consequences: something small, spreading outward and wider, becoming something else, becoming something bigger.

He was no longer dressed as an officer in Pharaoh's army, but wore a simple white tunic of indeterminable status. In his own life, he reflected, the stone had been Captain Ani, scarred by Laret. Because of the scar, Ani had become Serq—the Scorpion. Instead of revenge, Yanhamu had discovered friendship, trust and truth. Revenge had become incidental because he knew that his sister wanted him to have a pure heart and that Serq was doomed to be eaten by the Devourer. Life in this world, like the ripples in the pool, lasted only a short time, whereas the afterlife was like the Great River: a flow that had been since the beginning and would be until the end of time.

He dropped another stone into the water and watched the light play across the surface. He thought then about the events that had brought him back here.

Although Meryra's coded notes did not explain Smenkhkare, Yanhamu was pretty sure who it must have been. Yanhamu had delivered the truth to Tutankhamen and, through him, to the gods. Having completed his mission, he bade Thayjem farewell and caught a boat sailing north.

Meryra's final entries had been about fulfilling his destiny. When Horemheb persuaded Ay to take the old way out, Meryra knew it was time to leave and join the woman he recognized as true leader. He had found her in an ancient fortress town in the Delta with thousands of people who believed in Akhenaten, who believed in Nefertiti. She had known it would be impossible to move her husband's body from Akhetaten. In the open, his enemies would destroy it. And so between them they had hatched a plan: Meryra would construct secret tombs for them and give them both a map so that each *ka*—their vital spirits—would find one another on Earth as well as in the afterlife.

As Horemheb persecuted the people of the Two Lands without true Egyptian blood, more and more of the Ibiru united under Nefertiti's leadership. They no longer prayed to Ra or the Aten, but rather their god who had passed to the afterlife—and become one with Osiris, god of the underworld.

Before Yanhamu reached the ancient fortress town, he heard tell that the army had swept through and chased the Ibiru from the land. Nefertiti had died and become one with Isis. Her high priest, Osarseph, the priest of Osiris, led them to the mountains. They said he had taken the blue crown of leadership and the people called him Osar-moses.

Shocked, Yanhamu found the fortress town and its temples burning and dismantled. He stood on the hill surrounded by the scattered stones of the temple and prayed to Osiris, telling him that Meryra had fulfilled his mission and could be found in the Field of Reeds. Afterwards, he prayed for a long time to Nefertiti—who was Isis—asking her to look after his sister until he got there. When he finished he knew it was time for his life to change. He walked back until he hailed a small sailing boat to take him to a port. There he changed out of his officer's uniform and enrolled on a cargo boat heading for Elephantine.

At the house of Lord Khety he discovered a new magistrate had moved in. All they could say was that Lord Khety and his family were no longer in the town. And so Yanhamu had returned to Thebes hoping a sign would tell him where to go, but he had found none and the water by the temple only seemed to reflect memories.

He wandered around the city, along the Avenue of Sphinxes and through the pylons at the great temple of Karnak. Nefertiti had built a pylon here, but it was said to have mysteriously collapsed, as though the gods themselves were passing judgement on the hated regime. Yanhamu no longer believed such propaganda. He passed priests playing senet in the shade of temple walls and decided he too should find protection from the intense heat of the day. He knew where he would go to consider his future: a grove of sycamore fig trees on the edge of the city, a quiet place disturbed only by the sparrows and occasional goat.

He sat for a long time, fingers of sunlight breaking through the canopy. Another memory came to him then. When he was learning to write hieroglyphs, he had tried to impress Khety's daughter by writing her name in the wood of one of these trees. The thought made him smile. He got up and searched for the engraving. When he found it, he blinked in surprise. Beneath his poor attempt at Nefer-bithia was the inscription: Akhmin. After a second's realization he began to run to the merchants' quay.

If he could get passage on a fast boat, Akhmin was only two days away.

As the capital of the ninth nome, Akhmin had a lively merchants' quay. When Yanhamu asked whether Magistrate Kehty worked here, a cargo handler pointed him in the direction of the lower nobles section.

He found the house easily and the sign on the door said City Magistrate. The plaster on the stones was cracked and the paint faded; it was a far cry from the houses Lord Khety had lived in in Thebes and Elephantine. He took a deep breath and quietly opened the door to a small courtyard.

A good-looking woman sat under a pomegranate tree, reading.

He said, "I'm looking for Lord Khety."

She looked up, startled at first and then smiled. "Yani!"

"Bith." He ran to her and they embraced.

She pushed him away gently. "I'm afraid Father died. I'm the judge here now."

"I am sorry to hear about your father but I didn't come back for Lord Khety, Nefer-bithia. I've come back for you."

"Good." She grinned and punched his arm like she had when they were kids. "You can start by proving yourself worthy as my assistant. Then"—she kissed him—"we will see what happens next."

Author's Note

The Amarna letters exist and do include hidden meaning but the historical stories of Yanhamu and Meryra are pure fiction.

Pharaoh Akhenaten was originally entombed in his great city of Amarna. Where his mummy was moved to is a mystery but is likely to have coincided with events similar to those described in the book. There was significant turmoil and political manoeuvrings after his death. Nefertiti wanted to take power and continue the revolution of her husband. There is plenty of evidence, such as the destroyed pylons at Karnak, to suggest she did rule for a while. Whether or not she took the alternate identity of Smenkhare or whether 'he' was some other, unrecorded, relative of Akhenaten, we do not know. We also don't know what happened to Nefertiti. She appears to have been immensely popular with her followers and she may well have led them into hiding. If they were outlaws then her people would have been known as the Ibiru which is likely to have been the origin of the word Hebrew. The Berlin bust certainly appears to be that of an older Nefertiti suggesting she lived on for many years. Her tomb has never been found. Her connection with Moses is conjecture. However there is evidence that he was indeed a priest of Osiris and his full name would have been Osarseph or Osar-moses. There is no evidence to suggest that Moses believed God was Osiris or Ra or the Aten for that matter, however it does make for an interesting story.

Acknowledgments

For two years I became obsessed with Egyptology as I researched and wrote this book. Rewritten four years later, I'm grateful to my wife for making me cut a great deal of detail that bogged down the early drafts. When immersed it's often hard to see what will be interesting to the general reader. Hopefully you haven't felt I've provided too little detail of ancient Egyptian religion, Tutankhamen and the strange events surrounding the discovery of his tomb, Lord Carnarvon's death and Carter's subsequent behaviour. Hello to the Scott-Rimington family who joined me on a trip to Egypt. Thanks for your friendship and accepting me as your pseudo-guide. Also to Jules Round and Andy Bellingham for your company. I must also thank Mohamed Albasha as the genuine Egyptologist and guide. Also to the Egyptologist Dr Aidan Dodson for advice. The Isis puzzle is real and it was discussions with the brilliant inventor, Andrew Reeves, that gave me the initial idea for the story. Thanks also to John Christiansen for additional research and to Pete Tonkin and David Bailey for their editorial comments. Once again, a big thank you to Richard Sheehan, my line editor for the diligent work you do. As always, any mistakes are my own. Finally, concerned that this story should not be seen as anti-Semitic, I'm grateful to my friend, Jonathan Abratt who I used as my sounding board for all things Jewish.

ONE

With the sea air in his nostrils and the sunrise turning the ocean to liquid gold, he considered it one of those good-to-be-alive days. Which he found ironic considering his old job.

The humidity was always a problem. Except for this morning. An unusual cool breeze aided his daily run along the coast. He vaulted the wall into his garden and began his routine of press-ups and burpees. Three sets of a hundred. He stretched and dived into the pool.

When he emerged, his careworn housekeeper was waving at him. He'd learned a while back that it was too dangerous to have an attractive maid. There were plenty of pretty young women in the city. Easy to pick up. Easy to leave.

"Señor que es urgente!"

He snatched up a towel and followed the housekeeper into the air-conditioned villa. She pointed at the study.

He could already hear the beep, and the signal was confirmed by a blinking red light on the console.

"Gracias, Cristina." He flicked the response switch that meant he was ready to take a call and asked Cristina for an espresso.

Five minutes later, dressed and espresso consumed, the phone rang. There were no introductions but he

1

knew the voice. Codename Mustang. He would never use that name even though they both knew the line was scrambled and untraceable.

"I may need you for a cleaning job."

"May?"

"Depends how the dice fall," Mustang said, trying to draw him in no doubt.

"I'm retired."

"Or in exile?"

Cristina bustled past the patio window and he realized he was looking out at the palms, the beach and blue ocean beyond. Yes, Panama had its downsides, which was mainly the humidity. But better hot than the cold. He didn't like cold weather. Nightly electrical storms provided an amazing light show which he figured was down to the humidity. And since the canal had been widened, Panama City had become Central America's version of Dubai. Maybe it wasn't nirvana, but as an escape it was pretty damn good.

Mustang continued: "Just this one and you'll have enough money to retire properly. I presume you have the same account?"

"Yes."

"Check it while I send you the details." The line abruptly ended.

The advance in his bank account was more than he was usually paid in total. The reference code was relevant. Intrigued, he connected to a secure site and used the code to download a file.

Cristina showed no surprise at his request for a pack of gum. He popped a stick in his mouth and unconsciously played with the paper, folding and refolding. It helped him think and at other times it filled long hours of waiting.

He read the file. Remove the guy now; that would seem the easiest option. Mustang didn't explain. There was no *why*, just the *who*. The guy was part of Mustang's plan, and once over, the best case was it'd clean itself up. No need for his services. But plan for the worst. That was why Mustang needed someone. Someone he could trust to do it thoroughly.

The file had scenarios. The job: to get people to make the best case happen. And if it didn't then any witnesses had to be dealt with.

The final payment didn't depend on the scenario. He could buy a small island plus change for that. No more living in Panama. Maybe he'd have a host of pretty girls around the place.

He would never speak directly to Mustang again. Unless something went wrong. But nothing would.

He sat by the pool and re-read the file. Swallows darted across the water and their dips for flies caused a myriad of small ripples. He looked at the papers he'd been unconsciously folding and saw that he'd made a horse.

Why was Mustang so concerned? What had triggered the actions? The main guy was already in play, but which scenario would occur?

A young bird misjudged and hit the water. It flapped and paddled frantically before taking to the air again. He kept his eye on it, watched it swoop around, dipping perfectly the next time. There would be no second shot for him. It had to be right first time, whichever scenario played out. That meant being in control. He needed someone in the States and, he realized, someone else. In that moment his plan began to form. Watch, track and, if necessary, take control. He knew who to use: an ex-lover. She'd be attracted by the money and intrigue and maybe the promise. He needed her in England. In Windsor. That wouldn't be a problem.

Getting her close to the girl may prove more of a challenge.

Time for the Janitor to come out of retirement.

TWO

There are days when a moment, an action, a decision, can determine the course of the rest of our lives. Sometimes we have a premonition or we can look back and recognize a warning sign. For Kate, the change was heralded by a thought, a random thought, as she stood at the rear bedroom window: how much of another person can we really know? Do we only see what they want us to see?

After six months, she was pretty certain the guy who had just left her Windsor apartment was the one for her. *Mr Right*, as her sister would tease. Sure, Kate didn't know everything, but didn't she know enough? A lifetime together would provide plenty of time for all the little facts and details.

Joe appeared at the corner and walked past the garages to his old silver Audi parked along by the fence. Even though he called himself *just a salesman* for a mobile phone company, anyone could see he was much more than that: the way he held himself, the way he walked with strong, confident strides.

He glanced up as he opened the car door and flashed his perfect Hollywood smile.

"Get a new car," she mouthed, and he laughed.

Joe was generous with many things, although never to himself. He would happily treat her, but when it came to something for himself, he would make do. "Need versus want," he would say. "The auto works fine and I don't need a new one."

"What about wanting something?"

"How about: I want you—and you are all I need?"

She smiled at the memory of the conversation. It was a good line, a little corny perhaps, but it worked, just like the line he used when they first met. She checked her watch as the Audi pulled away: 8:05. Whenever she was working part-time as a physio at the private tennis and health club, she used the late start to prepare breakfast for them both. But Joe's schedule always seemed so precise, and there he was again driving off at the same time. That side of him confused her slightly. On the one hand he was relaxed and fun but on the other he liked his routine. A mild case of OCD, perhaps? She could live with his tidiness—so long as the tins in the cupboard weren't lined up with their labels facing the same way.

The thought of tidiness prompted Kate into action. It was her morning to clean the bathroom and she also needed to pop into town.

She was crouching by the bath when the home phone rang. Turning quickly made her heel knock into the bath panel. The panel popped out along part of the top edge. She tried to push it back but it immediately sprang away, only wider this time. Now she could see the dusty floor beneath the bath. In her opinion, no one should ever see the fragility of their home. Builders should make houses into secure cocoons, where bricks and dirt and spiders were on the outside. The thought of a giant house spider lurking under the bath made her neck prickle.

The phone stopped ringing.

Kate knelt beside the bath and, trying not to look into the dark space, gave the panel a solid push. It didn't go back. There was no escaping it: she had to look at what she was doing. After a moment's consideration, she decided the top and bottom would have to be manoeuvred into place. It would have to start with the whole panel coming away. Carefully, as though slow movement would be less likely to result in spiders running out, Kate pulled the panel free from the bath.

She took a breath and looked at the strip along the floor where the bottom edge slotted in. Something caught her eye. A blue bag, the size of a small handbag, nestled under the tub. Gritting her teeth she reached for the bag, pinched a corner between finger and thumb, and pulled it free. She stood, took a step backwards and stared at it.

The shrill ring of the phone snapped her attention away. The only people who rang the home number were cold callers and Kate's mother. A second attempt was sure to be her mother. Perhaps something was wrong. Kate scuttled to the nearest phone.

"Hello?"

"Kate, it's your mother." She always started like that although there was an edge of stress to her voice this morning.

"What's wrong, Mumsie?"

"I can't connect to the internet this morning."

Great! Kate the PC support person. "Check the lights on the router—you know, the black box that connects to the phone line?"

There was a scuffling sound and then: "The lights are all green."

"Yes, but look at the symbol that's like the world. Is that light on?"

"No. Oh God, what do I do?"

"It's all right. Nothing's wrong. Remember, you've had this problem before. All you need to do is reboot—switch the black box off at the wall. Wait a minute and then switch it on again." While Kate listened to silence she stared in the direction of the bathroom. What was in the bag? Had it been left there by mistake? Possibly plumber's tools?

"Are you there, love?"

"I'm still here, Mumsie."

"The internet light blinked for a while and is now lit."

"Great, that should have fixed it."

Kate's mother said she was on the PC, and after a few seconds she reported that her web page had opened. Immediately, she started to chat about other things.

"Mumsie, I'm sorry. I haven't time right now. I'll call you tonight or maybe tomorrow evening. I've things to do."

Kate ended the call abruptly, with her mother still talking, and returned to the bathroom. She stared at the bag. Navy blue, two leather-looking handles, a clasp on top. The material was thick, maybe canvass. There was no dust.

This hadn't been left by a plumber. The apartment was over ten years old and, as far as Kate knew, no plumbing work had been done since construction. No, this bag had been put there deliberately. It had been hidden and only one person could have done it.

The bag dominated the centre of the table. Kate sat, her hands together, her fingers pressed against her lips as though she were praying but preventing the words from coming out.

Her long-haired, chocolate-coloured Siamese cat jumped onto her lap. She pushed him away. "Not now, Tolkien."

Tolkien wound himself around the chair and her legs until she placed a hand out. He stopped and pushed his head against her fingers.

"OK, let's do it." She stood, reached for the clasp, flicked it apart and withdrew her hands. The bag didn't open. She reached forward again, gritted her teeth and pulled at the clasps. It opened like a doctor's bag with a hinged metal frame. Inside was something wrapped in black plastic.

Tip it out or take it out? She opted for tipping. The plastic-wrapped item clunked onto the table, followed by a bundle of money, a British passport and a mobile phone.

Kate sat down again, her hands trembling. Through the plastic it looked like a gun.

THREE

Joe came into the lounge and said, "You're home earlier than I expected." He bent down to kiss her as she lay sprawled on the sofa.

Kate held up a hand to stop him. "Better not—I'm not feeling well." She couldn't bring herself to make eye contact.

"Anything I can get you?"

Kate pulled Tolkien closer to her chest, felt her heartbeat against him. "Nothing at the moment."

"Let me get changed and I'll attend to your every wish, your every whim."

She listened to his footsteps on the stairs. This was the final scene she'd played over and over in her head after calling in sick for work. Her first thought was to leave the house and stay with her sister until he moved out. Then she had decided to stuff all his clothes in a bag and leave them outside. She had started by pulling his clothes from the wardrobe and then stopped. His favourite shirt—the one he had worn on the day they met—had brought the memories flooding back.

I DARE YOU

At Sarah and Peter's engagement party, she found herself watching from the sidelines. Sarah had once been Kate's best friend but she hardly knew anyone else there.

And then the man with the enigmatic eyes and perfect white smile leaned close and whispered, "I dare you."

"Excuse me?"

"I dare you to cut in and ask that guy for a dance."

Kate realized she'd been watching a mismatched couple—the guy tall and thin, the girl's head only coming up to his sternum. Both were dressed in browns and black—dowdy and almost severe—out of place at the party.

Joe said, "I reckon they're from opposing Mafia families and their union was supposed to bring the two together."

Oddly, she'd had a similar thought. "That would explain it," she said with a smile.

"So, I dare you to break it up—and see what happens."

She rose to the challenge, and when she returned, Joe introduced himself.

As they shook hands, he said, "So, what do you think?"

"That while I was watching them, Joe, you were watching me."

"Guilty as charged." His lovely teeth flashed in a smile. "But I meant, what do you think about the odd couple now?"

She stole a glance at the skinny man who was again dancing with his short partner. "He's a Russian spy," she said, "keeping an eye on American expats." Then, before he could respond: "OK, now it's my turn: I dare you to eat one of those disgusting pickled herrings—with a dollop of chocolate sauce."

The childish game of dare continued for over an hour. Between horror and stitches from laughter she learned that Joe was an Italian-American working with Peter at Oskar, a mobile phone company.

"How do you know Sarah?" he asked.

"My best friend from school." While Kate had gone on to study physiotherapy, Sarah had read Business Studies at university then travelled the world before finding she had a penchant for selling foreign houses and settled in the Czech Republic. However, Kate knew that Peter was largely the reason for choosing Prague.

Before the party was over, Joe called for a taxi. They slipped away and were driven out to the countryside to join a Witches' Night celebration. Bonfires pushed flames into the dark sky and the crackle of wood accompanied the cackle of people dressed as witches. Effigies burned on the fires to great cheers and howls of glee and, if not for the food and beer stalls, Kate would have believed they'd been transported back to the Middle Ages.

In the early hours, they drove back to the town square and, after a stroll, found a café where they watched the sun rise over the river.

Kate thought falling in love was for others—if it existed at all—but spending the last few hours with Joe was making her reconsider. Her flight home was booked for the afternoon and, just when she wondered about catching some shut-eye before she'd get ready, Joe asked if she could rollerblade.

"Not since I was a kid."

She laughed nervously and found herself agreeing when he said, "Then I dare you."

With the sun warming a broad azure sky, they hired skates and joined crowds of young people on the streets.

Although Kate's balance was better than she'd feared, she accepted Joe's offered hand. She lost sense of how many miles they'd travelled and, when they reached Prague Zoo, they put their skates in a locker and went in. Kate had been to London Zoo in Regent's Park but had never imagined a zoo as large as Prague's.

"It's over 100 acres with 4,800 animals," Joe said and then grinned. "I'm not the font of all knowledge—I just read it at the gate."

They spent a couple of hours jumping on and off the tram to travel around and see the enclosures. Joe's favourite was the Indonesian Jungle with its exotic animal cries and the humidity of a steam room. For Kate, the giraffe enclosure with its cute baby on long wobbly legs was the best, although Joe likened it to her on skates. A silverback gorilla reminded Kate of Andrew, a close friend and masseuse at the Royal Berkshire club.

Checking the time on her phone, she said, "I'd better get going, if I'm to catch my plane." When she saw what he was thinking, she quickly added, "And don't dare me to miss it. I have work to get to on Monday."

Joe accompanied her back to her hotel to get her things and then saw her off at the airport. She hoped for a farewell kiss and was not disappointed. He seemed to read her mind, leaned in and lightly brushed her lips with his. Then, instead of pulling back, he kissed her more strongly and, as she responded, he pulled her close.

"Where did you learn to kiss like that?" she asked with a Cheshire cat grin once it ended.

"It's the Italian in me." He hesitated, holding her gaze. "I'd like to see you again. How about next weekend? I'll come to you."

Of course, she accepted and could think of nothing else until he turned up at her apartment the following

Friday. They toured Windsor Castle, visited her favourite cafés and took a boat out on the river. She discovered then that they not only shared friends and an interest in exercise but they had both lost someone close in the past few years. Her father had died and he'd lost his twin brother. And that was another connection, because Kate's sister had twins.

A week later she returned to Prague and began a romance that alternated between countries each weekend. In between, he sent her silly poems and messages of love every day and, when they were together, the world became both exciting and interesting and her laughter came easily.

Then after three months he said, "I've been offered a job at O2 in the UK."

"You'll live near me?"

He grinned. "Not only that, but I dare you to let me live with you."

Six months she had known him. Six amazing months.

And now this.

"Kate." Joe had come back into the lounge and stood in the corner. "Where's my bag?" His tone was calm and flat.

She looked at him.

"You've been crying." Now there was concern in his voice.

She said, "What's going on?" Tolkien squirmed in her grasp and managed to escape.

Joe said nothing, took a step towards her.

"Stop!"

He froze and held out his arms like he wanted to hug her.

Kate sat up and glared. Her chest was tight as she forced the words out. "How dare you use me! How dare you lie to me! And how dare you have a bloody gun in my house!"

"I can explain."

There was a long silence and Kate blinked tears from her eyes.

Eventually she said, "I'm waiting."

"It's difficult."

"Difficult to explain why you told me you were American when you have a British passport? I bet it is. And difficult to explain why there's a picture of you in the passport but it's not Joe Rossini. No, it's Joe Ranieri." She shook her head, wiped the tears from her cheeks and stood. She pointed to the stairs. "Get out!"

Joe didn't move. "I'm kind of in protection—witness protection."

"What?"

He sighed, pointed to a chair and sat in it. "You know I said I was in the army? I was. Something happened and… and I had to leave. You see, I know things…"

She waited, held her breath.

He shook his head, sadness in his eyes. "I'm not allowed to talk about it. I shouldn't even tell you this much."

"But… so what? You didn't just quit, you said protection."

"I had to get out and take an identity. For all intents and purposes I'm now Joe Rossini. The job with Oskar Mobile was a cover, part of my new life."

Kate sat down and held her head for a moment. "Are you telling me our relationship has been part of your cover, Joe?"

He moved over to the sofa, knelt and cupped her chin gently. "No! I love you, Kate. I'm telling you this precisely because I love you." He kissed her. After hesitating, she accepted and returned the affection.

When she pulled away, she said, "Why the British passport in the name of Ranieri?"

"That was in case I needed it. I should have changed my ID but you already knew me as Rossini. I shouldn't have gotten involved with anyone but I fell for you. I want to be with you but at the same time don't want you involved."

"And you can't tell me anything else?"

"Not yet. Not until I can."

"And how do I deal with it—knowing, but not really knowing?"

That's when he said, "Trust me. Please just trust me."

And within a month he was gone.